Lit to Burn

The Molly Llama

Copyright - © 2019 Molly Llama - All rights reserved.
ASIN: B0834BRLGX
ISBN: 978-1-6507-7396-4

First Edition
Published January 1, 2020

Content Warning:
This book contains scenes of an extremely graphic nature which depict childhood sexual abuse, among other possible triggers.
Please only read if you have professional or other support in place to process its contents; or skip those portions altogether if needed.

Edition Notice:
This material was so traumatizing to write that it has not been properly edited. For excellent grammar and syntax, wait for the second edition, and STFU about any errors in this version. Can't handle that the very first page of this book says STFU? It might not be a good fit for you, then.
Onward.

Table of Contents

Contents			
	in		
		a	
			Table.

Jesus. What do you people want from me?
Just read the fucking Contents.

Just kidding.

Table of Contents

Lit to Burn	1
Table of Contents	2
Dedication	8
Epigraph	9
Section One: From the Flipside	10
Oxygen	11
After Oxygen	16
Start Somewhere	19
Stop Planning	29
Y'all Wear Me the Fuck Out	31
The Types of Dead	35
For the Reformed Assholes	39
Live Like You Are Dying (Because You Are)	43
Pivot	45
Directionality and Acceleration	49
Ruled by Many Gods	51
Absent	57
I Got High	58
Now That We Got That Out of the Way	60
You	64
In the Night as I Lay Dying	67
If I Die Today	69
Angels	76
Section Two: The Life and Times of a Llama	77
Life is a Terminal Condition	78
Cutting	80
Sweet Pain	83

Incest	*88*
The Next Day	*92*
Take Your Clothes Off	*96*
Bullies	*106*
Words Have Power	*109*
Strength Through Accountability	*116*
The Bad Guys Are Sometimes the Good Guys	*119*
Immortality	*122*
Life	*125*
Living to Die	*128*
Dying to Live	*131*
Death	*137*
Section Three: Relational Malfunctioning	*139*
What Is Love	*140*
Vows	*142*
What Is Marriage	*144*
Come Back	*147*
Five Tools to Always Take with You	*149*
Boundaries + Cleansing	*150*
Narcissists + Sociopaths: How to Protect Yourself	*152*
Haters	*167*
Impenetrable	*173*
Alcoholics Anonymous	*176*
When He Was a Baby	*178*
Now That He's a Big Boy	*180*
Bubbaisms	*186*
Cop's Wife	*197*
Viral Post	*199*

Aftermath.. 203

Blue... 206

Poisonous People: How to Block Toxicity 208

7 Limiting Beliefs and How to Overcome Them 213

Section Four: Level Up Program.. 221

Preparation for Level Up 222

Sacred Covenant 1 223

Sacred Covenant 2 226

Sacred Covenant 3 229

Sacred Covenant 4 232

Sacred Covenant 5 235

Sacred Covenant 6 238

Sacred Covenant 7 241

Conclusion to Level Up 244

Section Five: Meditations + Affirmations 245

I Love.. 246

For Bad Bitches 248

Sleep Meditation 250

Today is Going to Rock!.. 255

Sweet Dreams, Angel 257

Your Body is Whole!.. 259

Thank You Body 260

Section Six: Guides 263

Weight Loss / Health Restoration Mind + Body + Spirit Detox Challenge 264

Mind Preparation: 265

Body Preparation:... 266

Spirit Preparation: 269

Week One: Navigational Beacons	270
Week 1 – HOMEWORK 1	272
Week Two	273
Week 2 – HOMEWORK 2	275
Week Three	276
Week 3 – HOMEWORK 3	278
Week Four	279
Week 4 – HOMEWORK 4	282
For the Single Mamas of Tiny Tots	283
What All Moms Should Know	285
10 Tips to Medically Advocate for Yourself:	292
How to Actually Help a Sick Friend	303
What Your Sick Friends Won't Say but Wish You Knew	308
The Importance of Telling Your Whole Story	311
Section Seven: Afterthoughts from Between Worlds	313
Archangel Convos	313
1st Question & Answer Session	314
Information Block Delivered December 2019	319
Channeling Question and Answer Session December 2019	323
What is Maverick Academy?	332
I Wrote	333

Love the earth and sun and the animals,
Despise riches, give alms to everyone that asks,
Stand up for the stupid and crazy,
Devote your income and labor to others,
Hate tyrants, argue not concerning God,
Have patience and indulgence toward the people.

Take off your hat to nothing known or unknown,
or to any man or number of men,
Go freely with powerful uneducated persons,
And with the young, and with the mothers or families.

Re-examine all you have been told
in school or church or in any book,
Dismiss whatever insults your own soul;
And your very flesh shall be a great poem…

And have the richest fluency, not only in its words,
But in the silent lines of its lips and face,
And between the lashes of your eyes,
and In every motion and joint of your body.

-Walt Whitman

Dedication

I thought long and hard about who to dedicate this book to,
and ultimately was left with no choice.
Son, although you are the purpose to my breaths;
and Wife, although you were the light in my veins;
this work must and only can be given to the youngest version of me,
left broken and hurting.

And to all the children, of all ages, still suffering under the yoke of abuse.

Today, I picked you up, small and powerless self.
I put you into our long-gone family pickup truck,
and I drove you away with me, to safety.
It is a new and unfamiliar place for you.
We are reborn.
Nobody can ever harm you again.
I got you, kiddo.

Forward we go, never looking back.

Epigraph

*Your pain is the breaking of the shell that encloses your understanding.
Even as the stone of the fruit must break, that its heart may stand in the sun, so must you know pain.
And could you keep your heart in wonder at the daily miracles of your life, your pain would not seem less wondrous than your joy;
And you would accept the seasons of your heart, even as you have always accepted the seasons that pass over your fields.
And you would watch with serenity through the winters of your grief.*

*Much of your pain is self-chosen.
It is the bitter potion by which the physician within you heals your sick self.
Therefore trust the physician, and drink his remedy in silence and tranquility:
For his hand, though heavy and hard, is guided by the tender hand of the Unseen,
And the cup he brings, though it burn your lips, has been fashioned of the clay which the Potter has moistened with His own sacred tears.*

-Gibran Khalil Gibran; from *The Prophet,* 1923
My father's favorite writer.

Section One:
From the Flipside

We're all just walking each other home.
-Ram Dass

Oxygen

Poverty is when they can't pay the rent
And you start your first day of school
From out of a tent
And mama keeps working
But she can't save a cent
Because the liquor store
Is where all the money went
And your daddy denies
That's how it got spent

So you hide in your bed
Tuck the covers in tight
But it isn't the bed bugs
Who come in at night

A disease with no cause and no cure
One year left to live

But they don't get to decide
I know it's from keeping the words deep inside
The stories I tried to hide
The secrets
The times I've lied
Tongue tied

Sometimes my lips literally bleed
Because the truth is too sharp
For one mouth to keep

I wish you knew my fear
As I waited my turn
To tell this to you
While my oxygen burned
Would I make it up here
Or would my line catch a leak
Would I run out of air
Before my chance to speak

Human skin cuts like raw chicken meat

When you bust up cheap razors
Dragging blades across fast
Blood roads of my skin
Scars to have something that would last
To see if they'd notice
The condition I was in

But they didn't yet again
I was just a kid, back then

And now everywhere I go
This oxygen cord
My son says it makes me look like a monster

But he doesn't know
What they did
How I hid
Or he'd understand
Why it's too scary
To let the air in
Why I stopped

Breathing

I was just three
With daddy in the tent
Impossibly small
Frozen ice pops if you don't tell
But I told
And mom believed it all

He admitted it
But then she let him stay
Anyway
How could she
How could they
And still she somehow blames me
To this day
Even with him in the grave

And these are the things
I've tried not to say

*That I was relieved
The day he passed away
On our living room floor
At the bottom of a bottle*

---

*Fifteen years old
Rails on the table
Apple doesn't fall far after all
And they burned, burned, burned
But I needed the pain
I thought it might take
The smell of their skin
From my nostrils*

*Then I was sixteen
Burning my pocket with stolen ID
Just another kid stripper
To the stage, at that age in between
A dangerous girl with nothing to lose*

*Wobbling on sky high shoes
Trying to hide and be seen*

But it was better than before

*Shitting in the yard like a dog
On spread out newspaper
Being sprayed with a hose
In 30-degree weather
Because there's no shower inside
And there's nowhere to hide*

Lice for an entire year

---

*And birds can't fly without their wings
But mine were clipped too soon
I know I can regrow them
Just like I knew
There'd be air in this room*

*I'm ready to be a new thing
I am looking for a new god*

I am no one's victim

But I didn't know I could say no back then
So I gave my body away
And now they call it
Being sold into the sex trade
As a slave
Who only thought I was free
But who the hell were they paying
Who collected that fee

Y'all don't really wanna know
'Bout what all happened to me
And now I'm going blind
Because my eyes are
Too tired to see

So when I came back
I got too many degrees
And I traveled so far
Trying hard to be smart
Always on the run from the past
But that never can last

A ghost
Specter in my rearview
I helped everyone else
But when it's you who's bleeding then what
Especially if you are hiding that cut

These days it's doctors who slice me
Chemo, radiation
The breath is literally trapped
My poor body
Obliteration

A roadmap of scars
Too many surgeries to count
Just the memories festering
Until they have to get cut out

But what happens when you say

*I want to break free
And make the decision
To be impossibly me*

*Where were you mama bird
When I flew away
Why did you let me go
With daddy that day
I know his first wife
Warned you he was astray
Before you let him
Take me camping that May*

*I'm sad & I'm here & I'm dying & I'm queer
And I'm so sick of plastering on a smile
So I shaved my head & I raged & I sat & I wrote
Then I came and spoke to you for awhile*

---

*I don't have to get naked
To stand on this stage
The oxygen comes
When the words leave the page*

After Oxygen

I wrote that in a fever. A fury. I excised it from my body like a tumor. It had to come out. There is a freedom in being unapologetically yourself, even if the entire world thinks that self is insane. That freedom is more than I can describe. If you haven't felt it yourself, you wouldn't understand anyway. It's like this: Standing on a cliff, nothing left to lose, wind at your back whipping your hair, the rush of the current a hundred feet below, the power of a thousand years of ancestors at the crown of your head, extending out infinitely behind you. Teetering on the edge. So close you can feel the rocks slipping as you watch them tumble all the way down. But you hold fast. Maintain your footing.

I got up in front of a crowd and performed that piece, dragging a large green oxygen tank with me to the stage. My hands shook. My voice halted. I had already begun to go blind at that point and could barely see the paper. I figured I would lose my last close family members by unearthing the hastily buried skeletons, but I also knew it was necessary for survival. Writing this feels like killing those who've demanded my secrecy. But if I don't rip the duct tape from my lips, who will? And if it remains, how do I breathe? So I cut the words out, and stood bleeding before God and everyone on that stage. Hemorrhaging. In that instant I was anointed holy by my own pain. Wounds seared closed by the lightning from my own lips, matching the heart tattoo on my chest.

That moment is when I unintentionally accelerated visits from Metatron and so many others.

When I started living more on the Flipside than human Earth.

Over there I am well. It is a place where you can heal the body of any earthly ailment. Epigenetics, neuroplasticity, and transparent politics will reveal much in the coming years. All diseases are caused by environmental toxicity and shifting tectonic plates. The planet is not in its natural state and will never return to such again. It has been destroyed by humanity; such was known at the time of its creation. In fact, the entire human species is at the brink of a diverging path to destruction or construction. Which one you will all choose remains a mystery. Standing on the brink.

You are all crowded together at this fork in the road. One leads to utter devastation, apocalyptic visions of darkness and need; the other a utopia brought about by the new wave of magic children with which you have been gifted. They will raise the consciousness and vibration of your entire planet. It is still uncertain at the time of this writing which way humanity will collectively walk but make no mistake: You will go together. Carl Jung wrote of the collective unconscious; and it is real, except that it can be brought forth into consciousness should you so desire. Accessing your specific ancestral memory line, and going further, can give you entry to all the places you desire to go. There are many routes by which to arrive at the same destination, but this is one of the fastest to arrive at the prime mover.

Just like your body heals from bruises, cuts, creating human life, surgeries, the flu, and so much more, so too can it heal from any other mental or physical ailment. All cures are already contained within you and in nature. Many remedies for serious health problems simply entail the elimination of some foods and addition of others. Pharmaceutical companies have bought and silenced many medications which would have cured or helped millions. Beyond that, all treatments and healings are contained among you, your heritage back to the moment of Creation, and what is still available directly from the planet itself. Doctors are superfluous. Does that mean you should stop going to those appointments, taking those medications? I did, but that is not a choice I can make for you. Only your own Spirit knows that. Traditional western medical physicians play defense, rather than offense; and typically, they aren't even sure which game they're in or how the rules of engagement work. Rather than say, "I don't know," they will dangerously tell patients, "There's nothing wrong," if what someone has does not fit their very limited paradigm. Paradoxically, many patients, once sick but cured homeopathically will be told that it is, "an anomaly," or "spontaneous remission."

If you are approaching the time stamp you set for this lifetime, nothing can stop that forward progression. If you are not, nothing can impede your healing but you. Personally? I recommend functional medicine. Play offensively, get ahead of a problem rather than trying to catch up. Many I work with are caught in a trap of disease as identity. From this perspective: Illness has become so thoroughly entrenched into your story that you cannot embrace the wholeness that is becoming well.

Out is the only way through. Accountability is the only way to heal. You cannot change what you will not own, because it does not belong to you. The good news is, you're reading this. If you've made it this far, and found someone like me, the chances are great that your Soul is guiding your Spirit to the upliftment you seek. Whether you gain that here, or elsewhere, the fact that you are seeing these words in your here and now, which is different than my here and now, should tell you that you've set about the right path.

In 300 years, almost all of you, your children, and theirs will be gone. And for many, there will be nobody who remembers you or anything you did, said, wore, or thought. Does it really matter if you have human approval while you're so briefly here? Or does it not matter more that you are a catalyst to your own greatest intended purpose?

Start Somewhere

And then I realized I just needed to start typing, because it wasn't going to be me writing this book anyway.

It would be him (mostly).

Metatron. From an Islamic standpoint, he is the Angel of the Veil between worlds. In Christianity, he is Archangel Michael. You can find him discussed everywhere from the Kaballah to religions originating in Yoruba traditions, such as Santeria. In fact, I posit that all religions mention him by different names. I've found him in Botanica shops and Catholic churches. I've noticed him everywhere. He is credited with taking part in Creation, witnessing it, of being a scribe for humanity, of contacting humans directly with messages for how to move forward collectively to our next state of consciousness, and much more.

And he started speaking through me.

Well, typing really.

It was all innocent enough at first. I would wake, usually at 3:33am or some other such nonsense, which I didn't understand at the time. Then I would have to, *have to,* begin typing. And I would type the most bizarre stuff.

I wondered if I'd lost my mind. I mean, it wouldn't have been the first time.

But I know, deep in my knower, that I didn't. I was finding myself, not losing anything, not realizing I'd never been lost at all. And if anyone knows deeply the feeling of loss, it's me. I had been voluntarily and involuntarily committed many times in my youth when I couldn't stay off serious drugs – and I knew what crazy felt like. This wasn't it. I was finding all of me; the pieces I had given away, the parts that were cast aside; all that had been destroyed was being rebuilt. All taken, now reclaimed. Society, or the one I had been forcing myself into, didn't have a label for what I was becoming. But soon I would find a tribe of likeminded Spirits. Well, they would find me. Sometimes you have to speak your truth even if it results in you standing alone. And, in doing so, you will find a village rise up around you in the echoing resonance of that truth you dared to utter. Your words will bounce off the crowds that form a protective cocoon around you once they are spoken from the only place of power: Deep Truth.

I had spent so much time disassociating during trauma, dying during chronic illness, surgeries, radiation, and essentially torturing my Spirit with my own life choices, that I accidentally took a walk on the Other Side. I used to carry a picture of Marilyn Manson in my pocket as a teen. I even offered my Soul to Satan, figuring if God let me get molested that I wanted no part of Him anyway. Spoiler alert: No answer on the Devil Hotline, so that's good news.

Let me ask you this, though. If someone hasn't been there, how can they show you the way out? Never feel guilty for your trauma or your drama… if you've been to Hell, that's great news. It means you now have an accurate map that can be used by others to escape. For some of you, that'll be this book. For me, it was reconnecting to what I always had by following in the footsteps of many teachers. For those of you using this text for that purpose, good. That's how it was intended.

As a child, I saw angels, ghosts, alien spacecraft, energy fields, what I perceived at the time as good and evil, and more just as clear as a bright Texas day. I could often hear people's thoughts and get highly accurate "vibes" that did not, in fact, match what they were saying or doing. Sometimes I had prophetic dreams, which all came true. Somewhere along the way, however, I decided the world at large was right, and these things weren't real. So, I stopped seeing them.

But they didn't stop existing.

A desperate desire to "fit in" among the tiny, close-minded, open-mouthed rural community in which I was primarily raised caused me to shutter my eyes tightly against my own truth. It was censored. It wasn't even like I saw other cultures. My mother moved there primarily because it was a Caucasian place. I grew up holding and repeating racist views because I literally thought that was "the" truth. I also had no clue I was gay because I had never even seen people like that, and it didn't occur to me they might exist. Gradually, as I explored the world, I realized there was more beyond "The Cowboy Capitol of the World" than I had ever imagined.

I now understand that we are literally energetic beings – but this is sometimes hard to remember in a physical body with worldly problems to which we think we must attend. I now understand that we are constantly moving vibratory fields containing millions of moving parts. I now understand that there is infinitely more than I originally thought. I now understand the inter-connectedness of all things, the universe-wide ripple effects of any frequency of thought or action we emit, and the incredible constant stream of creation going on in and around us at all times.

Richard Dawkins asserts in his work, The God Delusion, that he is an atheist but also agnostic, though "Only to the extent that I am agnostic about fairies at the bottom of the garden." His book, dedicated to Douglas Adams, quotes same as saying, "Isn't it enough to see that a garden is beautiful without having to believe that there are fairies at the bottom of it too?"

No. it isn't enough. Because the fairies are there whether you acknowledge them or not. And they will raise Hell with you if you don't realize their presence.

To know what you believe, you must fully study and understand those who believe differently from you. Once a staunch atheist, I could argue even clergymen and women – because I knew spiritual texts and their antithesis inside and out. Confirmation bias causes us to see that which we are looking for, and that's what I found. I refused to believe in an arbitrary Creator who failed to protect me and so many just like me as children. From my now much wider and deeper perspective, I can tell you Mr. Dawkins was operating from within a framework of multiple logical fallacies. Ad ignorantium (appeal to ignorance, a fallacy of distraction) presumes that something must not exist if it is unlikely to exist.

Then what are we to conclude? That we come from nothing, are heading nowhere, and for no reason? I prefer the wager presented instead by Blaise Pascal. I am, after all, a gambler at heart. An addict; held enthralled and breathless in that moment as the ball is still bouncing before I know if black was the right bet; foot tapping beneath the table, chips spread across multiple options, mitigating risk. He posited that we have everything to gain yet nothing to lose if we choose to believe in an animating force, a Creator, of the Universe. Is this not true? All I can tell you is my own experience. Isn't that why you're here, anyway?

It was during a prolonged hospitalization when my next encounter with the Other happened yet again. The Other side of the Veil. The Black. The Flipside. The Underworld. Heaven and Hell. A place by any name exists the same, yes? It is all around us, in all times, a never-ending flow of potentiality that contains all possible realities, all versions of self, an all access backstage VIP pass to the bending of time forward and backward.

It is the moment between seconds. It is when time stands still. When you hold your breath underwater right before you break the surface, gasping for air. When you see the ocean crashing furiously against itself after a prolonged absence from the sea. The mountains in all their deadly majesty, snow-capped and still yet just as dangerous as they look peaceful. A roaring, crackling fire. A blasting torrential wind. And for just a moment, no matter how small, you realize you are a tiny, tiny part of a huge working, turning wheel. And just like the Earth – spinning at its core, spinning on its axis too, WHILE revolving around the sun, AND containing many spinning items all at once… everything feels still. Peaceful. Serene. But it is in constant flux and motion. What of the empty space in atoms, then? According to quantum electrodynamics, that empty space is actually an electron field. According to me? It's God, for lack of a better word.

You are God. God is you. Within you, the Design of Creation exists. The blueprint exists, a map to the divine, right inside your own body; and all around in nature too if you care to look. The synchronicity in the universe presents itself not only to those able to see, but to anyone willing to take a look. You'll find it in your eye and a supernova; in a leaf and the palm of your hand; in "recognizing" some people you meet for the first time – in that deep feeling place realizing you've known them before.

What does this mean? It means many of us spend entire lifetimes trying to shut out, cover up, or bury this Other world. But it is not ours to block. When our Soul and Spirit get too far from one another, the resulting effect is that there aren't enough bottles of liquor, head meds, other people's bodies, concerts, or violence to drown out what is just beyond the Veil; or in the Vortex if you will. This is when deep cognitive dissonance causes major problems – your Soul and Spirit disagree with your Humanity.

Ram Dass stated that he used to think that, "to deny your humanity and embrace your divinity [is the way to God]." He also expounded on this notion that what other people think of us is none of our business, and that appreciating our humanity allows us to fully experience the "curriculum" of earth. He exerts that great spiritual teachers are not required to be perfectly equanimous, and this is crucial for so many of us to realize – the truth and value of hardship. Mr. Dass further describes the "horrible beauty" of the universe. When we can stand fully in this notion, there is peace, "in appreciating what is."

One of my favorite paths to this Other place is Abraham Hicks, and before them Seth through Jane Roberts, and before them on and on ad infinitum. You can find us on pyramid walls in Ancient Egypt, in triptychs at the Vatican, and on pictograms from Native American caves. We are everywhere. All the time. And have been, since the beginning of All that Ever Was, Is, and Will Be.

I am not the first, nor will I be the last, who channels those from Away.

You contain the knowledge of all living Souls inside you; you have available to you all thoughts, feelings, actions, behaviors, intelligence, ideals, and possibility of each human mind since the beginning of your human time, even as evolution unfolded.

You feel it in the drums of tribal cultures, beads shaking at their feet, cracked heels pounding packed earth as dust clouds up around dancers, clapping and praying as they offer themselves to that which is All; poignant herbs and oils wafting from them. You feel it in the Himalayan singing bowls and when you cast your eyes upon a chaste monk. You feel it when you give birth. You feel it when a life ends, of someone you love; or as your own pours from your veins like sand passing too quickly through a timekeeper (hourglass). You feel it in the sung prayers of other nations that you know, deep in your Knower, mean everything; even if their language is "foreign" to you. The reason you know this is because no language is new to you and within your being All is contained.

In Anatomy of the Spirit, Caroline Myss described the function of chakras as follows, "Every thought and experience you've ever had in your life gets filtered through these chakra databases. Each event is recorded into your cells." So not only do we have a collective memory of All; the body maintains the entirety of our own history as well. Bruce Lipton and Joe Dispenza, as well as many others, are doing some great work on the science of how to heal the body naturally. There is no limitation to what you can do, and a wealth of free information at your fingertips with the advent of the internet.

Once you fully fortify yourself with the right tools, you'll be invincible. This can be done via any spiritual, moral, or religious code of your choosing or invention. Against one such as this, what Evil may stand? Your Christian Bible says, "No weapon formed against you shall prosper, and you will refute every tongue that accuses you" (Isaiah 54:17). It also says, "I am the way and the truth and the life. No one comes to the Father except through me" (John 14:6). What if I told you that in that last line Jesus meant no one comes to know themselves fully except through themselves? That by understanding him, his teachings, his healings, and so many others just like him, one can fully realize their own self, and thereby know God? What if I told you that by living between moments and listening between words you could produce an entirely new reality?

What of false prophets? The Kabbalah would teach us, "A human being is born as an absolute egoist, and this quality is so visceral that it can convince him that he has already become righteous and has rid himself of all egoism" (Talmud, Hagiga). So many of you come to me asking how people can claim a religion then behave in such ways that go against its grain. I behave against my own moral code daily. Don't you? Let he who is without sin cast the first stone. Falling short is the cornerstone of the purpose of occupying a physical body on this ethereal plane. It's what you do with the gap between who you are and who you wish to become (who you know yourself to be at Core) that matters.

This occurs in precisely this way: You came into this body to have a human experience, *on purpose*. Many of you, who believe you have achieved enlightenment, have only deluded yourself. The goal was never perfection. It was betterment. The enlightened need never make announcements and will not claim this status. Righteous anger, indignation, and outrage only serve to distance you from other Spirits. By pointing one finger in their direction, acknowledging fault and flaw, you escape your own notice in the mirror. When one finger points outward, at least three are pointing back at you. For many it is easier that way, to focus on the external and others rather than journey inward. For those not consumed by anger, fear is the wall they fence themselves in with – like being handcuffed yet holding a key only they can turn to achieve freedom. Eckhart Tolle said that, "Awakening is to become free… of the compulsion to judge… interpret… and label continuously everyone and everything around you."

But what of those among you who wish to use a mirror?

Not only to gaze upon your own true reflection, but to see beyond, into what's behind the glass, Alice? And how do we get to Wonderland? Oz, even? Is it as simple as a dream?

Yes. It is exactly like that. A lucid dream. Sleepwalking. Awake. That odd place you can see when you let your eyes lose focus; how things multiply and disappear. The Dalai Lama said his religion was kindness. Is it really that easy? Yes.

Do not let a religion or spiritual practice's followers keep you from guides or maps that can aide you in your own quest. Misapplication of principles can turn you off of an entire school of thought which can help you. Never look too closely at one another in human form, it is the God part of you recognizing the God part of them that is the healthiest state for your mind. When you rely too much on human opinion or behavior whether good or bad, if you will, you will always be let down. One can only fall if placed initially upon a pedestal.

This text will neither disparage nor attempt to prove or disprove any religion or belief system. You can operate from any framework and make space for the information we provide. Take what resonates, leave the rest on the table. Deepak Chopra teaches us that a seed experiences no struggle in becoming a tree. The whole process simply unfolds with a natural timeless grace and beauty. What we think about most will become our reality – our waking life – and that worry will cause more and more negative to pile upon us until it's hard to even see out from beneath it. A mountain's apex looks impossibly far from the depth of the valley. But remember, with a helicopter, you can arrive there in mere moments. What is holding you back may not be your drive, dedication, or even ability. It's far more likely your mode of transportation and willingness to reach for the unconventional. We have been taught that only by slogging, step by step, through the mud, may we arrive at any destination. This simply isn't true. Well… it's true in the sense that for many of us, it's the only choice we know to reach for at the time. But never mistake that it is a choice.

The Kalam (Arabic word for theology) Cosmological Argument teaches that all things which begin to exist have a cause. Since the Universe began to exist, it must therefore also have a cause. Once we reach the conclusion that the Universe began with a cause, we must evaluate what is required to make a beginning.

Motion. Motion cannot arise from nothing. Movement does not originate from stillness without an animator, an actor. This argument is logically ironclad, so the only question left for us is just exactly *what* that cause might be if something cannot come from nothing. Even nothing cannot come from nothing – because even nothing is something; it's the presence of a void, absence, or lack. So does reality exist and then we, helpless humans, perceive it? Or is it not the truth that we hold all the power and that reality would not exist if we, in fact, did not perceive it?

According to the Quran, "For indeed, with hardship [will be] ease. Indeed, with hardship [will be] ease" (94:5-6). This would indicate that the Universe demands a balance. That to exist, there must be the extreme of all things in both directions. If we believe the free will argument, it's hard to discern why then torture and harm would come to innocents such as the young. But what if I told you it was *you* who decided you'd rather have free will than Utopia? That you were presented with a Pleasantville scenario of reality in shades of gray, which also exists, and you chose to come *here* instead. What if I told you it was *you* who wanted the fullness and richness of this particular earthly human experience, in all its tantalizing glory and agonizing torture? Even the word sin itself simply means to err – to miss the mark, like an arrow. What of all the wars, then, fought in the name of God? And where do we go from here?

Are you ready to listen to an abused child turned teenage stripper addict who went on to get multiple degrees with a 4.0 who is now a terminally ill mom stumbling through her own supernatural gifts? Then let's go together, because that's all I have for you. My travels within myself.

Journeying inward, usually via a dark night of the soul, is the way forward. It seems backward that going inside is how to come out, but it is. It's that simple. If you don't know all the answers, that's a good thing, according to Sadhguru (Jaggi Vasudev), who said, "The sign of intelligence is that you are constantly wondering. Idiots are always dead sure about every damn thing they are doing in their life."

So many incredible teachers exist to illuminate your path, but they can't take the steps for you. Inhaling toxic positivity and embracing a never-ending quest for perfect morality will wear you the fuck out. It feels like having your tires stuck in the mud, beneath snow, with sand underlying all. You cannot power your entire life if you have a finite amount of current yet too many things plugged into yourself. You'll flip your spiritual and physical breakers, and things will begin to shut down. This is where dis-ease originates – too much drawing on your life's Source when it is needed in other areas. A tank can only coast on fumes for so long.

True masters display humility and never stop learning. You have permission from the Universe to be anything, freedom to evolve your beliefs, and you reserve the right to change at any time.

There are two types of people in this world, only. The first type could win the lottery and complain that they need to hire a financial adviser. The second type could be paralyzed from the waist down and win a Special Olympics medal while working full time. Which type are you? Are you run by fear or does it fuel an unending fire inside you?

Sadhguru teaches us that we either see everything as a miracle or nothing as a miracle. He uses the analogy that food turns into human waste which then, if used again in the fields, can create more food. Is this not a miracle? But we cannot handle the product and its resulting waste produced in the same way, no? No. Such is the divinity and humanity, the duality, which exists inside of us all.

You accept realities about death that are simply not true. Much like collectively, you do not understand that your physical body is merely an encasement for a piece of your Soul, so too have you decided death must entail separation. An ending. A frightful thing. It is not such. Life is harder than you'll find death ever to be. But you mustn't exit early, or you will not end up at the right place or in the right time.

You've set a clock for your life in this human skin, based upon your other tasks and lifetimes which are already scheduled.

The clock is unavoidable. And it is ticking. Loudly.

You're hurtling towards the moment of your death at the speed of light; every single facet of your body working as its own biopsy of the magnificent cosmos within creation. What if I told you that your very life force; each breath, every moment, is the main thing which animates the wheel spinning, the gears turning, and powers the majestic engine of the actual universe?

You may think this current human earth of your solar system to be the "world." It is no more the world than you are all its people. We are a moment in time. A blink. A droplet of water in a river. Do not flow backwards; for there are things in the dark which will follow you home.

So many of us say we are most afraid of death, and why is that?

Because you know at that moment you meet your true self, a la Dorian Gray.

Why not make your own acquaintance beforehand, then?

The good, the bad, the ugly. Let's meet you. You're magnificent.

Stop Planning

I had this big plan today, and it went as so many of my plans, or plans in general, go.

The beautiful beach that's normally emerald clear, with sunny skies, was angry and leaving all kinds of weird pollution all over the shore.

And it was so windy that I could barely hold my phone.

I was going to use my real camera, but of course, I forgot my tripod. I held my phone between my knees, and dropped my brand-new phone into the sand, as soon as my motivational video was completed. A brand-new phone I had just bought, mind you, because my perfectly good one before it had recently gone into a public toilet and never came out quite the same.

What does any of that have to do with anything?

Well, I'll tell you what. It's all first world problems.

I don't need to write a big speech to motivate you, or film the beach on a perfect day to inspire you. And you sure as hell don't need me to get you to where you're going, although I can point you in the right direction. Because I've been as low as it gets, as far down as you can go, for as long as I can remember.

Until I made a decision one day to not do that anymore. To not be that anymore. To not go there anymore. And, that's what I wanted to share with you – that you can make that decision too.

It doesn't really matter what specifically is plaguing or bothering you. There are so many new age teachers and gurus and life coaches… and I'm not any of that shit. I'm a spiritual gangster, and if you want to level up? You can be one too.

The cool thing is I've written a whole program on how to do it, how to get there, how to become that; and you'll find a lot of it contained herein. If there are aspects of your life that aren't working for you, chances are you may need a spiritual gangster – somebody to show you how to align your mind, body, and spirit so that you can run your own shit.

Or else you'll be helpless in life, crashing up against you like the waves to the shore; with no control over anything, just like the weather. You've gotta take the wheel.

Everything that you ever wanted, or didn't want, was brought about by the frequency that you put out, and by the processes of acceleration and directionality. Just like if you throw your car in Neutral and slam and slam and slam on the gas… you're not going to get anywhere.

If you're emitting the wrong frequencies, you're not going to get anywhere even if you're *doing* and *saying* all the right things. You've gotta be in Drive, or Reverse if you need to get the fuck outta there, but only you would know that.

And sometimes you just need to park for a while. Indecision is a decision too. I'm really glad that this day didn't go perfectly, or I'd have had some canned speech written, and it wouldn't have been nearly as awesome as getting sandy, getting dirty, and going off script. Because that, for me, is when all my best adventures have always been had.

Y'all Wear Me the Fuck Out

Can I just take a moment to pop back in here and say y'all wear me the fuck out? Yes, spiritual gangsters can use the word fuck. I have laid bleeding during surgery, closed my eyes, and felt everything. I have laid underneath my father, panting and sweating on top of me, closed my eyes, and felt everything. I have laid broken, in an alley, beaten and abandoned with no memory of what happened, and felt everything.

Try to tell me not to say fuck.

Here's the deal. I am a human person named Molly encased inside a precious temple I call a skin sack. But this body contains my Spirit, which is derived from my Soul, who is primarily responsible for the choice we made to enter this human experience. I am also a leveled up being, a teacher, one who many from there come to so that I can reach many from here. It's simple, really. It's also complicated.

I never said this would be easy. You think it's hard on your end? I *live* in here. You can set this down anytime you like. Me, though? Nope. This crazy place has a rusted, hand-painted sign over the door that says, "Home."

There is the humanity – the visceral realness, the authenticity, the vulnerable fragility of my poor, sweet, at times overactive ego; and there is the divinity – the parts which come through me and sound, feel, and resonate very differently. Try to discern the two when you can. Molly does have good advice; I really do. But it's Metatron you need to listen for in this text. Molly likes to get up to no good sometimes, and really, I can't blame her. She's quite fun. And she's a survivor. An overcomer.

But Metatron is a warrior. An Angel. A God created being with what humans call prophecy. And he's speaking in here as well.

The Flipside is not a place you go, it is not a destination. It is all around us, all the time. But like the blind and deaf cannot see nor hear, many of you do not possess the sense to realize this other world in your midst. It is taken from you shortly after birth.

Similar to the notion that if you were raised in the woods by wolves, you would later be startled at the sight of a television; many of you when confronted by evidence of the Flipside in your human bodies are understandably yet overly and unnecessarily cautious. You sniff the TV. You poke it. You back up a few steps in case it attacks or explodes.

But if you had been instead raised around electronics all your life, not only do they not scare you; you know how to use them. A television is not confusing, and you can operate it, because you've seen it and done so before. How to turn it on. How to find the channel you need; even the specific show. How to use the remote, so you don't even have to get off the couch. How to record shows if you aren't home when they're initially broadcast. So much more.

The Flipside is much like this. It is how I am able to find the specific dead for whom I search when I speak with you and them together. I only need a few anchors to this plane, a few anchors to them, and there I am, on their doorstep. Your closeness to them, strength of the relationship, or pain illuminates my path. It makes you and them burn brighter, and like a beacon to follow, then they are easier to find.

So, why do y'all wear me the fuck out?

I'll tell you. You're convinced death is a loss. A losing. An empty space where someone used to be. And I understand deeply that in the presence of missing a person you love in their human corporeal form; it may be easy to feel as though they are "gone." All souls exist infinitely, and we return again and again. In fact, in their completeness after death, a soul can be more aware of and involved in your life than they ever were during their own life. From that wider lens perspective, everything is seen, especially in the periphery which you do not have access to yet. They know your true heart, your every thought, they can see all tears. Souls do not experience human emotion.

That may need to be said again. Souls do not experience human emotion. They do not concern themselves with the trivialities we bog down so deeply in as human beings.

Know this: Your Spirit can exit before your human body expires, and your human body can expire before your Spirit can exit; and in some people there is barely any spark of Spirit at all during their entire human animation. These are what many call Evil – they are the empty eyed.

When I died, the first few times, I was revived after overdoses. I began to wonder whether I am, in fact, immortal. Now I know the precise date of my impending death and understand that my remaining purpose is delivering this material and helping my son find his path, which is why he was given to me to breathe life into.

Important to note: Parents are guides, not gods. So many of us try to shape our children in our own image when that is the opposite of the purpose or sense in which they were given to us. We are to keep them safe while they suss out their own journey. We are to provide maps and tools for many paths and support the ones they choose. Gibran wrote, "Your children are not your children. They are the sons and daughters of Life's longing for itself. They come through you but not from you, And though they are with you yet they belong not to you. You may give them your love but not your thoughts, For they have their own thoughts. You may house their bodies but not their souls… You may strive to be like them, but seek not to make them like you."

Oh, so I can only write the truth then? Sorry. Don't mind me. I just tried to embellish a story for this next paragraph and literally everything locked up and froze. As I went to type, I kept getting this bonking noise. It came to me that what I was writing wasn't the whole, entire truth. I deleted the paragraph and was again allowed to write.

Lord have mercy, letting Angels run the show is difficult.

But the opposite was so much harder.

I spent my life alternating between dancing with my demons and running from them. Sound confusing for me? Imagine how they felt; one moment embraced, the next cast out. Hard to be a demon to a girl who does lines all night and prays on her knees begging God for intervention the next morning. I'm glad I became a new thing, many years ago; and continue to evolve. If you are this person I describe, this human; know there is redemption. Life. Light at the end of the tunnel. Hold fast. Pain is temporary. But you must make a U-turn.

Change doesn't happen in a vacuum. Directionality and acceleration are key.

As so many of you already know, the time leading up to a person's death can be painful, agonizing, tortuous; or peaceful. Either way, at the moment the Spirit departs the body and fully crosses to reunite with the Soul, perfect peace and ease are experienced. *Perfect peace and ease*. This is the part that's difficult for me with you guys. I can only imagine the pain some of you must feel, but I cannot hammer it into you enough that your loved ones are not ever truly gone.

Actually, let's expand that out – I can see a bit of the confusion now. Do you enjoy being part of this writing process with me? I am literally self-editing, typing that, and sharing it with you. Hang tight. We're getting somewhere. And besides, once we get to the white-water rafting level of emotionally jagged parts of my personal story, you'll be wishing for these innocuous early rambles again. Let me prepare you properly for what's ahead. It's a doozy.

The Types of Dead

Only several options happen to a departed human being from planet earth:

They are not gone (the soul never dies)

>They are dead, but do not realize this, and Spirit remains here (often murders, suicides fall into this category or the next).

>They are dead, do realize this, and Spirit chooses to remain here (typically still have message needed to deliver, someone to watch over, or are afraid to cross).

>They are deceased and fully crossed, Spirit fully reunited with Soul and now at perfect peace and ease, chillin'.

>They are deceased and fully crossed, redeployed into a Spiritual Mission.

>They are deceased and fully crossed, redeployed into another Earthly Life for Human Experience.

>They are in transit, partially here and partially there; in a deep state of unrest, on a wild ride of ups and downs; will not pass until something happens.

>They are in transit, partially here and partially there; in a calm and boring waiting room, sitting quietly and a bit impatiently, will not pass until something happens.

They are gone (the spirit leaves earth)

You will never see, touch, or hear them corporeally here again. I understand that it is painful.

It is easy to say, in my warm bed, with my dog asleep across my feet, that they are not gone, and you should realize their Soul Perfection and be so glad if they are fully crossed. That does not stop the missing. The wanting. The deep emptiness left behind, especially in those touched by particularly powerful Spirits during this lifetime, or those with whom we've interacted who share a Soul Tag.

It does not cease the powerfulness of noticing their absence, the depth of an eternal pain of away.

However, accepting that their human body will not ever exist again, but their eternal Soul always will – the "them"ness that made them who they were – will return again and again; should bring comfort.

They will infinitely return
(once soul + spirit reunite, lives continue)

Like we've discussed, over there (here), many of us think this looks like a cool video game and decide to hop into the matrix together – these are your Soul Tags. It's kind of like animals in the ocean who've been tagged for identification. Quite a few of us tag one another over there so we can live our human lives together here. It's why so much of meeting kindred spirits feels like recognizing someone, rather than meeting them for the first time. It's where deja vu comes from. If your beloved left early, they may have had an additional mission to complete before you join them. Please remember, we all decide the dates we will die *before we come,* with no more thought than planning out your weekly meals or your kid's extracurricular schedule. For the machinations of the universe to run smoothly, for the intricate and infinite gears and wheels to move which creation requires to continue existing, some of us must be in different places at different times. What if you knew your loved one was literally on another plane of existence, or even this one in a different time, riding a horse into battle against a horde of Evil, or protecting and hiding people during the Holocaust or as part of the Underground Railroad? On and on and on. If your person were on another mission about which you were unaware, would you miss them as deeply? If you understood that their Soul Purpose called them in another direction or even dimension, yet you will reunite, would you then get back to the business of living your human life fully and completely?

I have to write this quickly. Fire is licking at my heels as I outrun Death. She is behind me, but I am faster. For now. Blood dripping from both sides of my nose, and my mouth. Splashing the keyboard. I am undeterred.

To recap: At the moment of death, there is *perfect peace and ease* once the Spirit fully crosses to reunite with the Soul. Imagine it like this. Soul = Large circle. Spirit = Small circle contained within large circle. Spirit comes into the human body, while Soul stays on the other side of the Veil. Upon death, large circle (Soul) and small circle (Spirit) again become one – whole.

Your life is slipping away from you moment by moment, even as you read these words. Every second lost. Or gained. Why spend one precious moment not in service of your highest and best, what is of the light and for good and love?

I have only ventured into the bottom floor of the house, if you will; where it's safe. I even had to get a Hellhound – the Greeks called her Cerberus, and many other cultures know her by many different names. She guards the gates of Hell, if you will, although Heaven and Hell as commonly understood in popular current culture are not part of the realities I teach.

Those are both actually self-created segments of human experience here on earth, not otherworldly places to which you are assigned after some white man in the clouds assesses your deeds and deems you worthy or faulty after watching a movie of your life. My dog has eyes the color of fire. She never leaves my side. I don't even like dogs much, honestly. I prefer cats. But this is not a dog. She called to me. I found her online, watched her video, walked in and adopted her from the shelter. She had been returned multiple times. Nothing that was said about her is anything I have found to be true. She raised literal Hell with all people until she found us. Now she sleeps with her nose on my oxygen cord and nudges the back of my neck when there is a leak or disconnection. She's the very best.

I believe she is here to keep the darkness at bay as I journey further into the Deep, and to walk me across the Bridge when it is time; keeping out what isn't meant to follow as I cross repeatedly in the meantime. She sees the dead. I see the dead. My child sees the dead. We are three weirdos and a cop, living in a mostly supernatural household that would look more or less normal to you. Unless you see the things we see.

Which begs the question, how do you see what we do?

Be sure you're ready for the answer. Once you know, you may never un-know. Set this down immediately if you are not ready for everything you ever thought to be "the truth" to get shaken to the core.

Life is a terminal condition.

What do you really have left to lose?

For the Reformed Assholes

I want you to understand something.

If you weren't always your best self, it's because you had shit to learn.

Forgive yourself for who you were. What you did. What you said. Don't hold on to the past.

You aren't there anymore.

Does it excuse our behavior to anyone we've mistreated along the way? No.

Even if you only became what other people broke you into with their own shitty abuse?

Still no.

What do we do about that?

I'll tell you what I do about that. I'm kind to strangers. When I have money, I give quite a bit of it away. When I can help someone else, I do. And I keep that shit to myself. The karma of good deeds is cancelled out if you do it for credit. So many more people have helped me than I can ever help. But I won't say I'm not glad I've spent thousands of hours with addicts and young moms and people trying to get healthy. Because I don't regret it. I also don't regret the thousands of dollars gone to people who needed it worse than I did at the time nor the thousands of pounds people have shed following my weight loss ideas.

You can't take that shit with you – not money, not time, not love. Give of it while it is yours.

Forgiving who we were when we acted on trauma or reacted to abuse doesn't mean dancing into the sunset. It's an action.

It looks simply like this: Try not to be a dick going forward.

If you got it right from day one, I'm proud of you. That's wonderful.

But for those of us who didn't understand how to treat others and were in survival mode in our younger years... the best shit you can do now is make every day a living example of how love can manifest in this world.

Don't step over that homeless person under a ratty blanket today and go about your day.

Don't avert your eyes if you see an organization that helps kids asking for a few bucks.

Don't hesitate to help someone you can tell needs you and whatever you may have to offer – service is a deep act of love. Help people you don't know. And most powerfully, perhaps, help people you don't like. Go mow your asshole neighbor's yard, for Christ's sake.

I truly believe I am alive only because the Universe wants me to do some things still – like writing this book. If you're alive, that's also why. There is a *purpose*. Stop telling yourself you're too busy. Too tired. Too whatever. To make a difference and live your dreams.

Or you might wake up one day too sick to do the shit you put off. I did most of the things I had in mind. I have no regrets and can die in peace, but I sure am glad I've gotten to write this. Not for fame. Or money. But so my kiddo has a blueprint if he ever needs a map out of pain.

Understand this: People's reactions to you are a reflection of them, not you. People's thoughts of you, good or bad, are none of your business. Similarly, the reactions people have to your healthy boundaries are also not your problem. I have a weird and powerful effect on those around me. They either think I'm the greatest thing since sliced bread or can't stand me. I've had entire crowds of haters smear me. Say things that weren't true. I've accidentally also developed a cult like following of those convinced I am more than human.

Remember... the more you're doing to make a difference, the more obstacles you'll face. Dust your shoulders off. Human opinion can shift with the tide; never take deep stock in it whether it is of admiration or condemnation.

One of the ways I got it wrong as a youngin' was jumping from relationship to relationship, using people to try to fill a hole with no bottom. It took extended therapy and staying single as well as the wisdom that comes with age to break that cycle and be an even halfway decent partner. My beautiful wife would tell you I even get that wrong about half the time. Even this book will contradict itself – because we, at any moment in time, are only a snapshot of ourselves. One moment I am like, "Oh, just breathe it out," and the next I'm like, "BURN IT ALL DOWN."

What does this mean? It would indicate that we are meant to be our best, worst, and all shades in between. It is our job to aim as high as we can and head there as often as possible; and let go of the moments when we fall short of our own intended ideals.

But here's the deal – you need to get down to the causes and conditions of why you act the way you do to change behaviors that are rutted into patterns. Your answers aren't in another person. It's an inside job. The work is painful. It's worth it.

The solution isn't at the bottom of a whiskey bottle. On a slot machine handle. Inside a french fry container. Or any other place external to you. It's all right there inside. People aren't emotional scratching posts. The solution doesn't come with a change in location. You take yourself with you everywhere you go.

Maybe if someone doesn't like you, it's because your very existence and light mirror something back to them they weren't ready to see. Either way, the opinions of others aren't your business. So set firm boundaries. And enforce them. Leave no room for toxicity. And make sure your ass isn't the toxic one.

It doesn't excuse being a jerk in the past.

The best you can do is actively not be a dick now. I don't subscribe to the horseshit that you have to immediately force yourself to forgive those who've hurt you. Take that burden off your shoulders. But be sure you aren't carrying that anger forward – or you revictimize yourself. It's like burning alive and hoping those who've wronged you choke on the smoke. Let. It. Go.

Hear this: *Any* asshole you meet is hurting. Let that sink in. They act that way because they are in pain. Does that mean we put up with it? Hell no. Cross the street.

Live your truth. Hold someone's hand today. Be a person who is ready to die at any moment because the stuff you had in mind to do is done.

So how do you ready yourself for death, toward which you are rushing through space rather quickly? You pick up some tools and redesign what you've created. You remodel, redecorate. And much like that, it should be a fun process, rather than an arduous one.

Live Like You Are Dying (Because You Are)

People in Baltimore are serious as fuck about St. Patrick's Day.

There was a group of about 300 pub-crawling university students tromping around blackout wasted in full costumes through town on a day drunk as I sat gulping some water while catching my breath. They were painfully beautiful and heartbreakingly young.

This is what I wanted to tell them, as I sat dying.

You, pulling uncomfortably on the mom jeans: I wore exactly what you have on and was teased for it. Don't worry about trends. Dress how you like. The tides will change in fashion. In fact, do whatever you want. In not too many years, you'll be dead and gone and unremembered. Live the way you wish you could because and while you can. You think you're fat now but in ten years you'll wish you were as skinny as when you thought you were fat. And moreover? Health is what matters, not how your body looks.

You, a little too drunk and swerving: I was you. I get it. You're young. You're having fun. But a group of guys behind you laughed as you stumbled over the curb. The one who grabbed your arm and steered you up the block looks like the type you'd wake up to find on top of you without consent. I wish you had seen him looking at you and how hard his laser sharp flinty eyes zeroed in before he plastered on that fake smile and "saved" you.

You, the shiny haired one with perfect skin: You will have everything you ever wanted. The big house. The beautiful kiddos. The sweet husband. Until you get a call that your son was killed by a drunk driver. You'll wish you hadn't yelled at him for forgetting to brush his teeth before school the last time you saw him. You'll turn to alcohol. You'll end up under a bridge, pushing a cart full of trash like the lady you just sidestepped and laughed at, flipping your hair as you carelessly danced past her deeply painful existence.

You, with the witty mustache: You'll end up sick. If you could tell you anything right now it would be to stop smoking. But you wouldn't have listened even if you could've told yourself. It will be painful. It will be awful. You will be a brilliant physicist and die young and it's totally avoidable. I ache for you.

You, with the green boa and dancing eyes: You can stop the next few decades of pain right now. You don't have to end up with a needle in your arm. You can end the cycle of abusive relationships and get help and stop the generational pattern in which you were raised. I see the handprint bruise on your arm and how you look scared of your boyfriend and I wish you knew that you do, in fact, have a choice. I wish you could see that choice. I wish I could tell you to make it, but you are deaf to that information right now.

You, with the impeccable eyebrows and turned up cuffs: You don't have to marry a woman and have two children only to then come out in your 50s once they're grown and gone. You can be gay now. It's OK. It doesn't matter if your family doesn't accept you. There's a whole wide and deep community who'd love you, and they are just waiting with open arms. Don't deprive your future wife the lifetime of love she could've found because you're afraid of being gay.

Yeah. So.

Good thing I don't talk to people out loud. /endrant

Pivot

How do you reconnect to your innermost self, then?

Well; as discussed, I personally began talking to dead people, for starters. Luckily, if that scares the fuck outta you, it's not the only route.

I'm really glad I have such wonderful people in my life to guide me. One of them told me yesterday that I have not, in fact, lost my mind, and that I am instead sleeping in a "biphasic" pattern. I sleep a few hours in the evening (always waking up around 3ish) and take a few hours long nap mid-morning to early afternoon. If you are able and work for yourself, so forth, perhaps listen to what your body has to say. Mine likes to sleep in two distinct phases, so here we are. That being said, this is some of my most productive time, so never hesitate to reach out at "odd" hours. I'm here. I'll feel you.

I know that some of you may be afraid of where this next phase has taken me or where I might take you if you stay along for the ride. I fully understand some of you are not fans of mine yet are reading out of curiosity or to glean information. I also know that the opposite is true – there are those of you who would love me no matter what I said or did.

Like all true psychics, mediums, channels, mystics, and so many before me; whether you believe all this is possible or not has no bearing on its veracity (sort of like gravity). If it's not "possible" for me to see and know in the detail to which I see and know these deceased persons I have searched for; then what is actually happening? Your perception of me, good or bad, if you will, is none of my business – just as I've taught you to see others.

I no longer go to doctors or take prescription medications, for the most part, either. Am I advising this for you? No. It also means functional medicine has me taking indigenous tribe arrow tip poison and suddenly I need my supplemental oxygen much less. And if the "alternative" medicines work better than the traditional, western ones? Hell yes. The only conventional options left on the table for me were more surgeries and radiation after decades of same... and I'm just, well, not here for it.

Because I'm over there.

I'm still uncertain whether I am actually contacting these individual souls or whether Michael (Metatron) is just revealing them to me and I am only, in fact, channeling one entity – known by many religions and considered by all to be an Angel.

It doesn't really matter.

The bottom line is my work has gotten deeper and deeper. And I'm glad. So many of you have come to me with gifted children, homes with dark problems, unexplained illness, unresolved questions about deaths of loved ones, and more. And each time I am so thankful I have been given what I need to give back to you.

Yes, I can sometimes see what is going to happen in the future. No, I will not tell you any prophecy or "fortune." This is because it can fork in a thousand ways – and one of many decisions can change it altogether. Therein lies the origination of the phrase "self-fulfilling prophecy," or notion of confirmation bias. What you are looking for is what you will see, or what you are expecting to happen may be what you then cause to happen via the powerful demand of your expectation. Does that make sense? I'm not here to tell you all your possible futures or when you may die, although for many of you, I can, in fact, see this. Dean Koontz described it in his Odd Thomas series as bodachs surrounding people prior to tragedy or death. I can see those.

I'm here to tell you this; whether you believe in any of this or not or whatever name by which you call it; it *is* real. And your belief is not required. But I assure you, absent a faith system in *anything* outside of yourself, your life will be unnecessarily and infinitely harder.

I think holding all this in my entire life was killing me.

I also think it's possible the three-dot apparition in some of my videos is the trinity.

I don't know what's happening, I really don't.

But when I tell a "perfectly healthy" someone to get their lower left organs checked out and cancer is found? Well. Here we go. Recently on the radar is locating another missing person, working on an unsolved murder marked a suicide, and cleansing an actual house of what I believe to be a dark entity (rather than just telling those of you who've asked how to do so). I have told people all about extremely detailed health issues that were then confirmed, I have communicated with their loved ones passed over so specifically that it has almost caused a nervous breakdown, and I have seen and known All.

My message to friends and family when all this began was simple:

You may doubt me, I welcome that. I am not in an echo chamber where all or any must think the way I do. But you *must* respect who and what I am, even if what I am doing terrifies you or goes against your beliefs. I just need your acceptance *as a human*, for you to remain in my life. Rest assured, if you hold deeply negative beliefs about me or have spoken such, I am aware of this. You are permitted to remain only to witness what will happen next, and to help shape me. I can feel the power of your ill wishes and they bolster my connection to God. I grow closer and stronger spiritually in any adversity. The way it more or less works is that your fire meant to burn instead forges and sharpens the blade of who I am; amplifying what good can flow through me. I thank you for that.

My message to everyone else is similarly fairly straightforward:

Do not play games with this Other world all around us, or you turn an eye towards yourself that you may not want to appraise you. Go. Do. Be. I'm not saying it isn't dangerous to venture into the unknown wilderness unprepared. It's potentially deadly. That is how people end up talking to the wall locked away the rest of their lives. What I *am* saying is that if you are prepared, your spiritual house is in order, and you are *called* to do this type of work – not *curious* but *called* – then you will be protected from *any* and *all* darkness. And just like a jaunt into the forest – you *must* take the right tools, or you can succumb to almost anything.

God and light surround me, it is what I am made of at my very core. As are you. Do not be afraid of this. Be very afraid, though, if you venture into waters where you don't belong. The deep end is infinite.

The depth matters naught if you can swim. Take lessons, if you need to, or jump in and see what happens. Infinite realities exist.

You will never in your life find a bigger sceptic than my wife and even she has seen enough that it has shaken her worldview to the core. There is a tremendous shift in consciousness happening all around us – this truly is the very best and worst time to have ever lived. The next generation of children will be the most awake and gifted the world has ever known, if we don't talk them out of it. One sideways glance from dad at you in the backseat can convince you that what you saw out your window at five years old wasn't really there. Then you never see it again.

But it's still there. It always has been, always will be. Don't take the gift of sight from your kids. I don't practice any of my beliefs or consult anyone in front of my son, much like previously I wouldn't have held a counseling session or taught a university lesson with him sitting there; it simply isn't age appropriate, if you will. But I neither imply nor deny his reality is other than what he sees. Be careful about the language you use with children. Be cautious to validate them, especially if what they see is outside the realm of your current understanding. They are born knowing All, and we strip that knowing away in pieces.

The best tool to reintegrate the shattered pieces of self which are dispersed into the universe is by assessing and evolving your directionality and acceleration.

Challenge what you thought to be the truth once new information is revealed.

Then pivot.

Directionality and Acceleration

I have not heard anything said by Abraham Hicks which does not ring true, but then again, I have not heard all they have said. I know that we call people to us. I know that all persons are equal.

Hear that. All persons are equal. You are equal to the most brilliant, magical, holy, talented, and wealthy who have existed. Jesus said, "The Kingdom of Heaven is within you."

This means you and he are on the same plane. He was a master of standing in truth of the goodness, wellness, and wholeness of people; in such a powerful way that their illness and other struggle could not remain.

The further from your Soul that your Spirit gets, the more distance comes between you and Source. This causes tremendous distress but is the building block of your emotional GPS.

It's really easy once something has been created, for others to add to or edit that body of work, and that is not what we are doing here. Many try to coach from the sidelines; armchair critics who only review, rather than do.

The Law of Attraction bears major notice from us, because it is a fundamental underlying principle which has the power to (r)evolutionize your entire life.

It also has been seriously misapplied by a few, creating a culture of toxic positivity very different from the initial teachings of Abraham. Who's that? She (her physical body) is a person named Esther, who created an incredible body of work most well known as the Law of Attraction, and channels "non-physical entity Abraham."

Much as Ram Dass created so many amazing and helpful tools with his "spook friend Emmanuel," inspired work is often the result of channeling, whether admitted or even known by the human conduit or not.

Rather than adding to or editing the Law of Attraction, I propose two Rules which are very similar and derived from it.

The Rule of Directionality
The direction in which I move is the way I will continue to go until I change course.
I cannot go in another direction without turning around.

The Rule of Acceleration
The speed at which I continue in a direction will determine how much of it I experience.
I cannot change my Directionality without first stopping or slowing my Acceleration.

These simple rules tell us very plainly exactly how things work in the Universe.

For instance, I have helped thousands of people lose thousands of pounds collectively; and many say I have transformed or saved their lives via coaching individually and in groups. Why? Why do they think this?

Because I teach them how to slow down and turn around. How to get in touch with their own Souls. It has very little to do with me and is of and from a Power that flows through me. Getting down to the roots of an issue, rather than addressing symptoms, is key. You might find you're not as depressed as you think you are, and in fact, are just surrounded by awful people who bring you down. Or you may need professional support. Only you can determine what best fits your needs.

When you are headed towards something full tilt, you may miss a lot that's meant for you along other easier paths by refusing to exit. Rather than the notion that you are a giant magnet for all that comes, good and bad, and for those of you in whom Law of Attraction strikes a funny bone; consider applying instead or in addition, the Rules of Directionality and Acceleration.

It will help you realize who is behind the scenes pulling the curtain strings, and I propose we are beings ruled by many gods.

Ruled by Many Gods

If Soul sends Spirit here for Human Experience, would it not then stand to reason that the time during which we feel the most congruence on this earthly plane is when we are in alignment with our greatest self, our highest truth, and living towards our Soul's own initial ideals set forth before we came?

You don't have to believe in a god to be ruled by one, or many. Don't believe me? Consider the notion that you cannot, right now, guarantee you'll wake up tomorrow. Further, I push you to challenge yourself and really examine whether or not you are unintentionally being ruled by your own gods and demons, as it were. If you have found me, this is likely. The faithless are as powerless to the forces of internal gods as the faithful. Belief is not a necessary condition of suffering.

According to Abraham Hicks, "You can't get sick enough to help a sick person get well. You can't get poor enough to help poor people be prosperous. You can't get mean enough to help mean people get nice, you see. You can't feel pain about their suffering and be, as Jesus was, in vibrational alignment with their well-being. You just can't do it."

You will see glimpses of yourself and areas of your life in each outlined category below. Dave Ramsey recommends with debt that you attack the smallest credit card balances first. First address the areas which are least difficult for you to improve. By making many minute changes to what is easiest to fix, much like with debt, a snowball effect can then help the larger issues resolve themselves almost outside your conscious awareness. Reaching attainable goals will rebuild faulty confidence and allow you to see your infinite potential for the larger dreams you had in mind, which were discarded somewhere along the way.

We are beings ruled by many internal gods, both at the conscious level and below.

The God of Method

Rational thought (science) tells us that all the "other" must not be true because it cannot be measured (it can), seen (it can), or verified (it can). When we are ruled by this internal god, life looks rote, routine, and safe. This, in balanced measures, can lead to a fruitful, peaceful life. Not enough of this, and you end up under the bridge with a pocket full of dreams and a brilliant mind overflowing with great ideas. Too much of this, and you end up stuck in a dead-end job you hate with a great retirement account and wonderful health insurance, crying all the way to work. This is when people joke that they enjoy the darkness in one another, love finding like-minded bitter and cynical friends, and often secretly enjoy things like gossip and suffer unbeknownst to themselves under jealousy of others' perceived freedoms. Method is necessary. Balance is necessary to use method as the tool it is, so it does not become a weapon turned inward.

More method than emotion leads to a lack of love, loss of passion, a shallow life which is broad.

The God of Emotion

Feelings (reactionary to events) rule us when we make decisions against our own truth – whether those are in relationships, friendships, work situations, or any other area. When we are led by this internal god, the way anything makes us feel leads us around by the nose. It might look like, "I stay with him because it would hurt the kids if I left." Or perhaps, "I have no idea why I threw that stuff across the room. I have no control when such and such happens… and I just totally lose it." The God of Emotion can also take control and manifest in such a way that it becomes very difficult for those of us who are dreamers to plan, execute said plans once they are made, finish, or follow through with anything. Many when led by feelings will start infinite projects, businesses, and relationships, only to walk away from each. It's the notion of throwing the baby out with the bathwater. It's where you lose an entire day arguing with and composing emails to people who aren't there, thinking of those perfect answers that eluded you during actual arguments. This is also where imposter syndrome can keep us from success.

More emotion than method leads to a lack of structure, loss of security, a deep life which is narrow.

The God of Fear

This can wreak all levels of havoc and cause all sorts of strange decisions to be made that make no sense in hindsight. While fear is necessary for growth, learning, and mileage (getting further down the path), it can be very painful in the moment; crippling even. Fear based decision making causes agony; because it often turns us away from our Soul's greater truth. Fear and anger are two sides of the same coin. In fact, I posit to you that anger does not exist, in much the same way darkness does not exist. Darkness is the absence of light. Anger is the absence of peace, or love. Anger is typically just the easiest and most comfortable emotion to reach for when fear is present. It's easier to be angry than afraid. One thinks of fear as a weakness, sadness as a vulnerability. If you or someone you love is angry, examine these two fundamental questions: Are they afraid of *losing* something (someone, anything they already have)? Are they afraid of *not getting* something (someone, anything they deeply desire)? Anger boils down to those two notions. It's the easiest thing to feel when we are powerless and afraid, because it bestows a false sense of strength and control. That is why no God of Anger is listed here, because anger is only fear, wearing his big brother's too large trousers. Often this can rear its head in running from our purpose. Anyone burdened by addiction, over-eating, patterns of the same type of destructive relationships, and so forth, is under the yoke of this god. Anyone who seems stuck and unhappy in any situation is being ruled by this. This place is one of undeserved loyalty to others, insistence on remaining in a rut, consistent turning away of God-given purpose out of fear of judgment by other humans, or even just pure survival terror – if I do (whatever was intended by my Soul) xyz, I can't pay the rent, so forth. The reality is more like if I do (whatever was intended by my Soul) xyz, a more abundant financial flow than I ever imagined will head directly to me.

Guilt and shame lock us into this position of being run by fear. Overcoming those is crucial to ease out of this gear and onto the next level. Forgiveness of self can begin this process beautifully. In full nudity, viewing the mirror of the Soul, one can then take accurate appraisal of what may need attention and what is already perfect. So many teach that forgiveness of others is crucial to healing. They have this backwards. Forgiveness of self is what is imperative. Once this happens, it is impossible to hold any anger or ill will towards another. Becoming whole allows you to see the God in you, and thereby you cannot circumvent seeing it in all others. Forgiveness of them is the next step of natural logical progression and then requires no effort on your part. This is a lifelong process during which you may make many steps forward and backward. There is a fluid continuum from which we as humans operate – in fight, flight, or freeze mode. Shifting away from this requires feelings of safety, which Maslow noted as the most fundamental basic need in his hierarchical model, right above physiological survival fundamentals.

The God of Justice

This can also render us more or less useless and is a close cousin to being ruled by anger (fear). I spent much of my life under its watchful guidance. It sounds like, "I'm emailing corporate because they just discriminated against that girl!" The hard part of letting go of this is that ending the battle can feel like surrender. The opposite is true. By turning our attention toward peace, toward any intended goal or desired outcome, we can create what we are seeking. *Never* is it forged through struggle, strife, or argument. New things are built via construction, not tearing down of old structures; even though this may be necessary to make way for the new. The path of least resistance, going with the current, doing what is easiest and most peaceful for the Soul can feel like giving up on the "good fight" to those of us who may have been too long in the trenches. But it's fighting smarter, not harder. It's the spiritual equivalent of using nuclear weaponry rather than being on the front line of an infantry with one gun. Taking the path of peace and approaching your chosen battles and causes from the Other side gives you an army of millions, and access to All that Ever Was, Is, and Will Be.

Essentially, it's first connecting your Spirit (in human body) to your own Soul (beyond Veil), which gives you a path to access God, Creator, Source Energy; whatever you choose to call this. A rose by any other name would smell as sweet and I use God as the most easily understood word for this universal power flowing through All. Spending your life struggling for good causes will keep you off your greater path, off the high road, and may make you miss all the intended goodness the Universe had in mind along the road where you should've taken that exit. Stand up against injustice, step in for the underdog – but never give rent free space in your mind. Your thoughts inform your feelings, which lead to emotions, which cause behaviors, which then become habits; and suddenly you may find yourself a stranger in your own life. Is there not dignity and honor among foot soldiers, grassroots activists? Of course. But ask them about their nightmares. Stay elevated and engage battles above the fray, untouchable, from the Flipside.

Closer to God (self is God, God is self) = Closer to Self = Spirit + Soul Cohesion = Peace

Absent

Curls of smoke
Out my bathroom window
I oughtta be outside

Toes propped on the radiator
I don't think it works

They can't cure me
And they don't know why
Just one more cigarette
Just one more night

So maybe I should stop taking their poison

And go blind

See the world in a new light
I'm alright
I can still get high

I'm calling in absent today
Do you think that will be OK
Would they have noticed
I was never here anyway

It is so quiet tonight
Just me and the chirps

Of insects who sound prettier
Than they are

But someone thinks they're beautiful

I Got High

WHEN YOU FEEL STRUGGLE; YOU ARE FIGHTING AGAINST WHAT ALL ANCESTORS, ANGELS, GUIDES, AND YOUR GREATER SOUL AT LARGE ARE TRYING DESPERATELY TO PUSH YOU TOWARDS WHICH IS IN YOUR HIGHEST AND BEST GOOD.

Fucking quit it. Jesus Christ. Literally.

Sorry. That's Molly.

Molly is more fun, though. She's actually stoned out of her mind, watching a stand-up comedian on Netflix while we try to write this. Don't worry, no hard drugs for over a decade. How can you not love somebody like that tho? All gifted anythings are self-tortured a bit (or a lot) during their human lives. That's why most famous musicians, painters, so forth go totally mad and nobody seems to remember that. Cutting off their ears. Staying awake for days. I remember the madness of other artists when I wonder whether I am going insane. Beautiful art, meaningful work is typically created in a fit of lunacy or drug-induced trance (are the two really so different). *You* try writing this shit and not ending up stoned or drunk. I refuse to take prescription pain medications, so I don't really see how a little plant oil on occasion can hurt anything when you're dying anyway...

Oh, boy. Now she's apparently going to take a nap. She is racing against dementia, in a body that's rebelling at every turn, so I can't really blame her. The going blind piece has her worried because she wants to finish writing this for you. For him.

Why leave this in here?

Humanity.

You have to see echoes of yourself in me. If you don't, nothing I say will have value for you. We essentially are self-serving creatures at our core. Even altruism assuages our burned spirits like a balm for guilt. Activism, too, although one of my favorite things as a human, I realize as a

(???)

Post-nap:
Why expose you to the tortured, beleaguered by terrifying anxiety, lonely and flawed side of the author of this work? Because you need to understand that from inside this minefield of a mind it is nearly impossible to function almost all of the time. And yet she does. I do. We do. Mostly. In fact, right now she's not convinced someone isn't casting spells on her to keep her from writing this. Do you wonder if she's crazy, on serious drugs, or actually having these experiences? Are any of those things really very different? Interestingly, she is always sober when channeling. It's the after where she needs some occasional relief.

That's because you'll see her, your truth, and everything through your own lens of perception. And is *your* truth any different from *the* truth and if that's true wouldn't that mean you create your reality live and in living color second to second and thereby could make it change anytime you choose to do so?

Or am I crazy?

Am i

Now That We Got That Out of the Way

Getting high just brings you lower. I'm not opposed to it, clearly, but it's important to see what you're running from when you get high if it's happening often. You always take you with you. So if you see yourself making huge changes to escape something, make sure it's not you who you're running from, because you go wherever you are.

What is chasing you?

For me, it's my marriage.

It's in shambles.

You'd never know that to look at Facebook. But here? Here in the real world? It's 5:27am and we've somehow already had a disagreement significant enough that she's in her car with a trash bag full of pertinent items and a tear streaked face because my reaction *still*, still to this very day is to run, or make the abandonment threat. I ask her to leave when things are hard or I'm afraid because I still don't know how to face everything head on.

Childhood trauma survivors often see the world in absolutes. Life may appear to us as a place where there are only two choices: Warrior or Victim.

Is this ridiculous behavior for two fully grown, highly educated, mid-thirties adults? You bet your ass it is. You bet your ass. I would take this hurricane of a marriage over a museum relationship where on the surface everyone seems fine yet right below that is a seething cauldron of resentment which never fully comes to a boil. Those unions have a place for everything and everything in its place – with no one ever allowed to step out of line emotionally. There is no deeply felt difficulty, but also no passion.

It also begs the question of why so many of us choose to do and be less than we know we can when faced with the humanity in another who we claim to love.

Here's the deal though: We as a society have had it shoved up our asses that it's wrong to think marriage or parenthood are hard. Why?

Why is this? Why must we all dress in Christmas pajamas and take the smiling pictures? Why can we not, collectively, come together openly and honestly about the challenges of motherhood or partnering and then, by that authenticity, vulnerability, and honesty – create a dialogue which solves many of those difficulties? Because we are all so busy pretending it's easy. Trying to look perfect. And still swirling around in generational patterns of radioactive responding.

And why is that, you ask?

Well, when you are taught to step gingerly, to ask softly, that your highest virtue is your ability to blend in, to integrate, and to exhibit diplomacy; the bar is often lowered so that what you will celebrate is what those who are already whole would consider a bare minimum standard of human treatment. In a divine union where everyone is journeying inward, disagreements produce resolution. In a purely human relationship, anything you bring up is seen as divisive, frustrating, and argument provoking. Do not remain too long in a union where you cannot express yourself without it being seen as an invitation to fight. A toxic person will pick on you until you react and then point loudly at that reaction. And moreover? Don't break your own bones so you may bend into a shape someone else wants to be.

Something has been all over social media lately and it goes like this: "Never break yourself into bite sized pieces. Stay whole and let them choke." I propose you take this one step further: Do not make of yourself something which is safe for others to consume in the first place.

I could say a lot of things. I could paint my spouse so negatively you'd decide on the spot that she's the villain. Or I could do the same with myself – tell you what I've done and said in such a way that you decide I am, in fact, assuredly, the most difficult party here. There is no need to take sides. We are two good people who when placed together are sometimes nearly emotionally deadly for one another. What is the value of partnership if not revealing your lowest and highest selves to evolve one another towards more?

Love is sometimes like that, yes?

Who among us doesn't find it challenging?

To understand why I am in here, listening to the dog snore, and she's in her car raging around, you'd have to know more about who and what we are. So let's go there. Deep in there.

We met on a beautiful island in Honduras. I saw her standing there and I couldn't believe it. I just couldn't believe it. After a string of failed disasters where I was the unfortunate common denominator, multiple run-ins with the darkest kind of souls, a year in therapy and insisting I remain single… there she was. I had taken my son (just barely three years old) on a cruise because I'd decided it made the most sense to just enjoy our lives together rather than stay on hold. To live and love each other and not add any other people to our future. I used extra student loans from my second Masters' program and off we went.

And there she was. On a cruise out of another state, on a totally different ship's line. We had made it to the same island… *the same tiny off-map spot on that island…* in the same exact moment in time. I pretended I couldn't lift my wagon over the stair as my son lay sleeping, and tapped her sun kissed shoulder so she would help. I could tell she was the type who likes to help, to save, to rescue.

Captain Save a Ho.

She looked the military type to me; board shorts, clearly a former athlete, holding an ice-cold beer and laughing with friends; sports bra, low curly ponytail, head thrown back.

God she was beautiful. And happy. Without a care in the world.

I didn't know then what I know now.

That holidays would be skipped and ignored altogether. That I would have to apologize to teachers for the embarrassing rudeness at school functions. That almost everything we did would be met with absolute and full contempt. That I would endlessly find things about which to be disappointed because I hold myself to an impossible standard – and that I would push her away in doing so.

That two good people with hard histories would cut each other on their own sharp edges. That people like us are a double-ended sword; no part can be held safely without hurting yourself. That it would all be so very painful.

That the resulting pain would almost kill me.

That our love was a sickness.

That it was a poison. That it was a cure.

One I couldn't get enough of no matter how hard I tried.

Is not most medicine just like this? We grow weary of side effects.

I know that the road to Hell is truly paved with the very best of intentions.

That sometimes, to find your way out of Hell, you might have to hold hands with a demon just like yourself so you can both transform and that what results will be beautiful – moth to butterfly.

That neither of us had ever seen a healthy relationship nor been given anything but tools of destruction.

That I knew people should build one another up, but after the initial haze of perfect romance, all we did was tear each other down. Down, down, down.

You

You
A shot in the dark
Then silence
Ringing in my ears
The aftermath
Where did you come from
Waves
Of terror
Razor sharp edges
Of my heart
Love is not warm
It is
A fire
All consuming
And it will tear
You apart
From the inside
To build something
New
You light me up
Like the Fourth of July
There is nothing
That I wouldn't do
My heart
Started pumping blood again
The day I saw you
Across the ocean
And there's
Nothing
That I wouldn't do
Terrifying things
I'd do them if you asked
But
You wouldn't have to ask
I always thought love
Would be so sweet
Calm
Peaceful
But it's like being

Electrocuted
A little less Snow White
And a little more Maleficent
Will you still love me
When you see I'm not
A princess
But a dragon
And I can't sleep
And I can't think
I'm blind
To any woman
But you
But then again
I'm blind anyway
I was born to love you
And I know just how I will
If you let me
You have waited for so long
For someone to burn for you
And now I am aflame
Don't be afraid
Of the smoke
I was made from fire
You will not
Find yourself down that dark hallway
Again
I won't let you get lost
In me
Instead we will get lost together
In the mountains
I will take you everywhere
You never knew
You always wanted to go
I will not break you
You have the reins
Do not use them
To lead me astray
In the darkest nights
You will wake to find me
By your side
There is someone
Living inside me

And I've never let anyone meet her
But you can have
All of me
I had to keep her safe
But she is yours
If you can get her to come out
Walk through this forest
Do not be afraid
Take me with you
Show me your demons
I will
Tame them
One day
There will be nothing left
But ashes
And what can we say
We were made
Before then
Let's build it
Together
There is so much evil
In this world
Let me be your
Shield
From the bullets
That rain down
All around us
Love is a world without end
A beginning that never stops
A dragon that never sleeps
And you?
You are mine

In the Night as I Lay Dying

Beyond this mortal coil is infinite peace.

Infinite.

It is so difficult to stay when I could go.

Where there is no pain. No surgery. No radiation. No chemotherapy. No biologics. Nothing.
Just peace.

But I will not go.

Not tonight.

Not tomorrow.

There was a four-year-old literally drug out of my hospital room screaming, clutching me, crying, begging to stay here. In the hospital. With me. And I watched him go. Chained to this oxygen and IV pole. Over a week now, headed for a few more weeks.

The skin on my body has begun peeling off due to new "medicine." Literally. Just peeling off. My skin.

This is not life.

I want to heal. Or I want to die. I want to live more than anyone I've ever met. If you've never prayed for the release of death; you've never known physical pain.

I have begged for Death. I have pleaded for Her to take me from this pain.

But tonight, I wage war. For that baby. For his other mama.

This body has become unfit to live in and should be condemned.

But I will have faith.

And I will battle as long as I can.

They cured AIDS. Remember that?

Anything is possible.

But tonight? I won't lie. Tonight is simply a choice. Forcing each beat from my heart. My alarm has gone off three times. I've been hospitalized for almost two weeks. It seems nothing they try works quite like it should. My ticker wants to quit.

I won't allow it to stop beating.

I have things to do, yet.

And I'd jump out of an airplane without a parachute before I'd sign up for hospice, even though they wrote me in for palliative care.

I won't call them.

So.

Tonight, we fight.

Then once I get out, I'm hiring a functional medicine practitioner. Western medicine has nothing to offer me, clearly.

Time for a new horizon.

I might just find the cure for my disease.

Never know.

Crying and fighting, guys. Crying and fighting.

Hard.

Will you fight with me?

If I Die Today
(written immediately before my most recent surgery)

I'm not. But if I did.

I have some things to say.

Mom:

I know you did the best you could with what you knew at the time. I know now how hard it is to be a mom and I have made mistakes and I forgive you for yours. I hope you forgive me for mine. I saw how hard you worked to keep it all together with no damn help everrr and I can't tell you how thankful I am that you worked and worked and worked to try to keep us afloat. Sometimes we didn't float, but you always made sure to keep my head more or less above water growing up even as you were drowning. And is that not the essence of motherhood?

Thank you for every single time you stepped up and rescued me as an adult in every single way. Thank you for your patience during my late teens and early twenties. Thank you for accepting that I'm gay, even if it took you awhile (that one was really important).

You are the best grandmother in the entire fucking world, and I am in constant awe of how much you love bubba and am so grateful that he has you. It is one of the things I am most thankful for on this earth. Nobody understands him like us. I know the whole idea is for your kids to outlive you, but if I don't, please don't stay sad for long. I did the things I wanted to do. I became who I was trying to become (more or less).

A bit more time would've been nice, but if I'm done here, I promise you my soul lives on. I'm not quite sure exactly what happens when we go, but I've been close enough times to know that some version of me will exist forever, infinitely. I will show you signs that I'm around. Don't freak out and stay sad like you did when dad died. I want you to be happy. I want you to *live*. I want you to enjoy life. And get a damn therapist already, because I'm pretty sure this is going to wreck you up since I'm an only child and all that. And you sort of have to if it's my dying wish. Ha!

But in all seriousness, you were the perfect mom for me. Nobody else could've taught me to read by three years old or made me as resilient and strong as I am. I learned everything I know about business from you and because of that earned advanced degrees and haven't had to work for anyone else pretty much my whole life. You gave me strength through the trials we faced, and it's what kept me alive. I wish we'd had more time to work our shit out, but you know what? I love you. Deep down in my heart that is ticking kinda funny right now. With my whole soul. I love you mom.

I wouldn't have traded you for anyone else. And I'm sorry dad kinda sucked. You're so much more than you think you are mom. Stop sitting in your recliner, get your ass to a doctor, and get back to speaking to the masses. Your presence and purpose are only just beginning. You're beautiful and I have seen you literally evolve your soul and grow into a different person but then you slide back to darkness. Use your inner strength reserves to get back out into the world. That's where you belong.

Wife:

I don't even know where to start with you. As you know, we met on separate cruise ships out of separate states (Texas and Louisiana) and you were living in Indiana at the time. The likelihood that we would cross one another's paths the moment we did and then get and stay in touch from Roatan, Honduras is infinitesimally small. But we did. Because you're my person. I am so glad bubba jumped on your head in the water and you caught him. I'm so glad he was such a little baby when we met, and that he never remembers a time he didn't have two mamas and you are one of them.

You have loved me in a way I didn't think possible. It feels like we both brought all our damage to the table and healed one another. I want you to know I fought like hell. If I really die, it wasn't from lack of trying to live. I wanted to stay alive for you guys more than anything. My poor body was just done. But my spirit is never far, and you can carry me with you everywhere in your heart. I'm right there, a heartbeat away, even if you can't see or touch me anymore. You'll find me in the moments between moments.

Marrying you is the best decision I ever made. I can't even begin to list the reasons – but some of the top ones that come to mind don't even do you justice – you're hard working, loyal as hell, dedicated, an incredible provider and protector, smart, hot as fuck, funny, and so much more than words can even describe. You brought a meaning to my life I didn't know was missing. Spending all that time single and in therapy I realized what I didn't want, stopped looking, and then there you were.

I thank God every day for you. Our roughest moments with words or deeds that weren't ideal are not something you need to keep in mind. No relationship is perfect. Everyone brings their baggage since birth to one another. And only with a real love can you actually take that shit and work it out, and that's what we did, more or less, quite imperfectly. I wish we had more time. I'm so very sorry so much of our time was spent with me sick. But I feel like we had some pretty damn good adventures. You are a wonderful mama to our son. You are a wonderful person. Don't stay sad after I die. If you remarry, make sure it's not somebody slutty or who drinks too much or who wants to use you and that they love my son the way I do, or I will haunt the shit out of you both. And you know I can.

Don't go for the reformed bad girl type again because you might not luck out like you did with me and if you end up with an actual bitch, I will have to throw plates at her head at 3am and nobody likes an angry ghost. I know you say you'll never date again, but it's ok if you do. God that's hard to say because I'm the jealous type but I want you to be happy and not alone. And if you are my wife's new girlfriend and you're reading this, you better be nice to her, or I swear to Christ I will actually haunt you. You also need to know how to cook; she's used to a hot, fresh lunch being packed for work every day.

Cherish them, please. I'm begging you. They are so very special. If you can't love them like I did, leave them alone. Also, new girlfriend, please don't spank or yell at my kid, you will make him hard and dangerous. He is very unique and handling him will be challenging but he is beyond worth it. Don't slack. In all seriousness though, Wife, I will show you in a thousand ways that I am with you still. When you can't feel me? Just look into the other room – you have the very best piece of me sitting right there embodied in that magical boy. And we will be together in other lifetimes; just as we have done before. I waited my whole life for you and feel so lucky I got to have even a few precious moments as your wife. There is nothing I regret about us. Nothing. I'd marry you every day for a hundred years.

You are strong. You can get through this. It's going to be ok. Maybe not today, or tomorrow. But you got this. You'll see me daily in the things bubba says and does, God knows. I cloned myself. Baby you're the reason I tried so hard. Don't give up. And don't stay mad. And sue somebody, because these doctors definitely got some things wrong if you're reading this and I'm gone.

I am so very grateful for you. Your warm hands. Your sweet smirk. The way your eyes crinkle up. Every second spent with you was an eternity and I cherish them all. I didn't even know I had spent my whole life feeling unsafe and alone until you changed that. I didn't know what I was missing until I found you. You gave me a new purpose and a new meaning. That's what you do when you love someone. That's what you did for me.

Son:

Oh my baby, my heart. The reason for my existence. My God, I don't even know where to begin with you. If you're reading this, it means I died when you were only four. I hope you have a few fond memories. We went on adventures all over the world. I took you to every theme park and playground and camp and place I could dream of – all the places you can imagine. All the places I had wished I could go. Mama will show you the pics.

You went to Hawaii as a tiny two-month-old. You've been on cruises. You are going places, because just like Mommy, you started out 100mph since birth. Honey I tried so hard for you. You didn't come with a manual. But not a moment of your life did you go without. I always made sure your vitamins were taken and your hair clean-cut and that you had the best of everything I could give. I cut off countless crusts on PB&Js and bribed you to potty with M&Ms. I was insane about keeping your nails clipped (evenly, that's important) and your white noise settings at night were always perfect and I am worried to death that nobody can love you like I can.

But let them. Having you is the best thing I ever did. I am most proud of you. There will never be a moment in your life that I will not be with you. My blood is in your veins. You can be and do anything you want. Most people shouldn't be told that because it simply isn't true; but for you? There are no limitations which aren't self-imposed. Make no mistake: Others will try to tell you otherwise. And they're wrong.

I let the world convince me I couldn't be who I wanted to be or do what I wanted to do for so long that I believed it. Never believe it. Always stand up for the underdog. And for the love of God, use condoms and don't bring home trifling hoes. Mama will know the difference, trust her advice. I mean, you're four, so this isn't an issue yet, but when it is, please listen to her. The wrong woman for you can ruin your entire life.

You come from strong stock, the best there is. Nothing will ever keep you down. Learn how to be sad. It's ok. You don't have to believe in some weird masculinity thing the world will try to shove down your throat about men having to be "strong." There is strength in vulnerability. And sadness, when it gets shoved down, turns to anger.

You are brilliant, hilarious, mischievous, inventive, handsome, strong, hard-working, irreverent, and so much more. Do not let this world break you. Be careful who you trust. Keep your circle small, and close. Keep your business to yourself. Know when to get help if you need it – don't let pride make you suffer. Do what you can to help other people; that karma comes back tenfold – and don't tell anyone about it because bragging about good deeds cancels them out.

I wish you understood what being your mom feels like. When you come wrap your arms around me and smile your sweet gap-toothed smile, I melt inside every time. When you say, "Good morning mommy, I love you," I feel the same way about you as I do when you throw a toy at me. There is nothing you can ever say or do that will change the way I feel about you. I loved you in your best and worst moments unconditionally, and always will. And the love I felt from you? The best moments of my life. Period. The very best.

God being your mama was hard. And it was the most worthwhile thing I ever did. I feel so blessed I got to witness you existing. You are a phenomenon. A power to be reckoned with. Don't start any shit but don't take any either. I have a feeling that won't be a problem. You are going to be a wonderful man because you are a compassionate, incredible little boy.

And God, that brain of yours. Use your powers for good, not evil. You're probably going to smoke, drink, and do a few other things before you should; but if you're ever in pain don't get too crazy with it. You can wreck everything or waste many years trying to numb pain at the bottom of the bottle or the end of a pipe and that pain never goes away.

If you ever find yourself in that kind of pain, let those who love you help instead. You were the bright spot of my life, my literal reason for breathing. You are everything to me. You saved me and you may never even realize that. Being your mom is the highest honor I ever received – more than any degree or award or accolade I could've been given. Never orbit around another person. Wait until you're 30 or much older to start a family, if ever. Travel the whole damn world. Leave footprints on every continent before you create another human. I did all I wanted before you were allowed into my existence, and man was it a gift.

You were all I ever hoped for and so much more. Don't stay sad forever and don't give your step-mom a hard time, unless she's a bitch, then feel free. And don't let Momo date any assholes either. You are going to do wonderful things. Wonderful. But I need you to understand something you apparently inherited from me – you will have a profound and powerful (unintended) effect on people. Be very careful who you let in close. Not everyone is your friend, and people like us attract crowds of superfans *and* major haters. Your biggest supporters might really be your worst enemies. Be very careful of this.

The good news? Those same haters will make you famous. It's the reason I'm up at 3am editing this manuscript and it's already #1 for its category over a week prior to release. Not all those people who bought it were those who love us. Some are just curious. Some are much more sinister. Let them make you wealthy, but don't let them into your living room. And if you can't stand me but are reading this? Well, I reckon I win whatever game you're playing – because I'm on your mind but you most certainly aren't on mine.

<u>ALWAYS TRUST YOUR GUT.</u> Yes, your literal gut. Research has been conclusive that you literally have a second brain there; I know, it's confusing, but look into it. Also... you are different. We are different. We will never fit into conventional society. Do not try to shove yourself into their mold. Break it and make your own. You will always be a little weird, like me, and that will leave you feeling left on the outside sometimes, or alone. Don't do things to fit in that don't feel true to your Soul. Ever. It ain't worth it, love. I believe in you, always. I miss you already. I will never, ever, be far, I promise. I will be there for all your important moments even though you can't see me. I love you I love you I love you.

I would write more but they just came to get me for surgery.

I'm sure I'll be fine, but I wanted you to know how I felt in case I died today.

I love you all more than anything.

Angels

*I'm not afraid of critique
It's exposure that hurts
And what will I do
If you don't like my words
That come up from deep inside my body*

*I called my favorite old guy
Who likes what I write
And said, I can't say this shit in front of people
He said, of course you can
Everybody there is trying to find a way to say their shit*

*And I knew he was right
So I'm here with you tonight*

*Who do you call
When the ones responding
To runs
Are the ones who hurt you*

*Speak life to words
That come up out my throat
Without warning*

*I didn't mean to say this
I wrote it this morning*

*How can you live when
There's no marrow in your bones
And where do you go
When you come from no home*

Section Two:
The Life and Times of a Llama

There is a battle raging between two wolves inside each of us.
One wolf is evil. It is resentment, envy, guilt, retribution, and greed.
One wolf is good. It is benevolence, love, hope, humility, and truth.
Well, which wolf wins out in the end, you ask?
The one you feed.
-Cherokee Proverb

Life is a Terminal Condition

Someone in one of my transformation groups named me that, The Molly Llama. What I love about it is the extra L – I am not a lama, for sure. But a llama? Maybe. They're known to be animals which signify transformation. I am most often referred to as a phoenix. I had even considered authoring this work as Eirini, a Green name a trans friend of mine gave me. They named themselves Sunny; and I find anyone able to name themselves so effectively may certainly name me as well. But then I realized, when I bristled at the notion, that my friends were right. It doesn't do this work justice to hide that I am its creator.

I'll say this one again for those in the back. Life is a terminal condition. And most of y'all take it way, way too damn seriously. I can say that because I've been dead. And now I talk to the dead, because I can go back there any time I want.

If that didn't shake your ass the first few times I mentioned it, then I guess you're along for the ride. Just remember I gave you a chance to turn around, early on. My mama would say, "You ain't got a lick a' sense." Seriously, go back now if you can. Before the story consumes you.

That's kind of what I said to my girlfriends, back in the day. Before I knew any better. I promised three things, only. That I'd cook better than any other chick they'd been with, that I'd be smarter, and would fuck them better. So, when they'd inevitably say, "You're mean," I'd say, "I never told you I was nice."

I thought because I came with a warning label that I wasn't responsible for my contents, or their dangerous potential.

This is a cautionary tale, of what happens when you fail to realize your infinitely divine power, how to get that mojo back, and what happens once you do.

It's a tale of torture. Of suffer. Of pain. Of poverty. Of lack. Of anger. It's a tale of overcoming. Of freedom. Of health. Of wealth. Of enough. Of peace. It's a story for the underdog. For the terminally ill. For the spiritual gangster. Yeah, I said it.

It's a story about how to stop weathering the storm and play in the rain instead. It's a story about how to type while going blind with blood splattering the keyboard from your mouth and nose, without missing a single click. It's a story about how to outrun the clock; while not hearing it tick more loudly and quickly in the background. How to run into the wind, with death at your heals (and on your heels, as it were).

It's a love letter to my son, for once I'm gone, about how painful it is to stand even an inch away from your Soul's truth. It's a story about how we're never *really* gone, even when we die.

It's an educational manual about how dying will be the single greatest moment of your life, but also a caution that premature exits are ill advised because then you re-enter the game at Level 1 almost immediately, not where you left off, and this makes things infinitely harder.

It's a direct instruction to you to understand something crucial.

Those contained in self-created unlocked cages will always scream at you for being free because they have not made the same choice. Pay this no more mind than you do the birds chattering in the trees. Perhaps, pay more attention to the birds.

Well, come on with me, then. Get in the truck. We're in too far together to turn back now.

Cutting

The thing about cutting is you have to know exactly how far to go. It's not like you want to bleed all over the house, so you can't go too deep, but if you don't go deep enough, you don't feel the release.

Slicing. Slicing. Human skin cuts sort of like uncooked chicken. It's not as smooth as you might imagine. When you use a busted up cheap shaving razor, small droplets of bright red bead up along the road you make. It is a very satisfying sight when you want to die and can't stop the pain. People misunderstand self-abusers as wanting to die, and that may be true. But it's more of a desperate wanting for proof of life. Blood flow.

You don't have to die. There are other roads out of Hell. It took me many years to figure this out. Thirteen-year-old me only knew to cut. Twenty-three-year-old me figured out I should stop doing drugs and could get tattoos. Thirty-three-year-old me has totally new and more effective tools.

Then what is there to do?

Well you write, of course, for starters. Or speak to a tape recorder. Or paint. You perform spiritual surgery on yourself through expression, initially. You tell someone. Anyone. A stranger you grab in Starbucks by the lapels and dump your trauma on – it literally doesn't matter yet it *is* that important.

You get it all out. Isn't that the whole point of writing? To release whatever has been held onto, fist closed tightly around it, knuckles white, jaw clenched, eyes narrowed. Releasing. If you don't, it'll burn you from the inside out until you write or die. Some of us have stories that have a way of crawling up our throats and out our mouths, whether we're ready to tell them or not.

So here I am. What should we talk about? Because writing is a conversation. Perhaps you can't respond, but you are listening by reading and I'll feel each and every one of your responses. That makes us partners. That makes us a team. I am showing you my heart, placing it bloody and still beating into your hands, connected to my body. Hold it carefully, it's fragile as fuck.

This isn't some book, a story. I'm not an author. Authors give a fuck what you think. I'm a writer. Writers practice the art of speaking life into the written word, with a drunken careless abandon for their reception.

These words are my life.

I have laid myself bare for this.

It is my art.

I risk all for this.

All.

I have a right to lose my mind in private.

Yet I've chosen to walk you down the sacred, silent hallowed hallways of my trauma.

Tread lightly.

And perhaps now is a decent time to mention that I cuss a lot. And I mean *a lot*. You may have already noticed. Metatron, interestingly, never curses, ever. But if you go with me on this journey, you'll see why I do. Some serious shit went down. Like, my whole life. Regular words simply aren't adequate.

Why don't I start with the heavy stuff, straight out the gate? See if you can hang? Oh, you thought we covered that already? Not hardly. Here we go.

When you want to cut yourself to make sure somebody notices you still bleed, you have to be careful how you go about it. You don't want to actually die. Well, I mean, you do, but you don't have the nuts for that just yet. So you bust up a razor using a butter knife and you drag those across places on your body nobody will see and the pain is satisfying and the blood is satisfying and the whole thing is just really the best feeling in the world when you're too young to break loose and can't tell anyone your dad molested you and your mom enabled him.

What if I told you everything you need to heal is already inside you? Did you just hear the record skip? You didn't think this was another tired victimhood story, did you?

What if I told you I have been through the most horrific shit you could possibly imagine but I wake up every day and I'm OK now? Would you believe me? If you aren't OK, keep reading until you are.

I remember doing real, actual drugs before I was even out of my teens – staying up a week at a time, rocking back and forth in the corner, chewing package after package of Bubbalicious watermelon gum so my mouth would even produce spit, burning up the inside of my face so badly I'd need reconstructive surgeries later, partying with people much older than myself and listening to their kids cry for them in the room next door as no more than a child myself, sucking some 35 year old guy's dick at 14 for a ride to Mexico because a friend told him we would but then somehow it was only me; yet I wanted to get away that bad. Away, away, away. Dancing on the bar there, falling into the bottles of liquor, waking up on the sidewalk, face stuck to the concrete in my own vomit in another country. Stealing the family truck at fourteen years old only to go back to Mexico alone. To run away and sleep in the woods. Long nights of chasing the dogs through the forest hoping to find my way to Narnia as a child; with no indoor plumbing or running water. A wild, tribal thing living amongst clean children who had shiny combed hair and matching bows. Tucking every inch of the covers around me even younger hoping werewolves wouldn't get me if I just kept myself thoroughly tucked in and sweating, every inch, every inch, every inch. Turning the light on and off nine times hoping that would make them stop fighting. Scratching myself until I bled as my mother screamed at me because I was trapped, trapped, trapped in the car. Freezing in the winter, shaking and wondering if I could die from the cold because we never had central or sufficient heat. Never. Always waiting for the other shoe to drop; *always* waiting. Because it always did.

Until I stopped wearing shoes altogether.

Sweet Pain

To this day, my mother laughs when I get hurt. She experiences that same unfettered joy that most moms get when their child does something cute or sweet... when I get hurt. She once came to visit me for two weeks and I couldn't figure out why she was there when she'd been absent so many times before. She had skipped entire surgeries and rounds of radiation of mine after asking to be my driver, leaving me to find a way to the hospital at 5am in the past. At this point, I'd recently broken both bones in my leg, requiring surgery. She was there to soak up the pain. To thrive in the hot glow coming in waves off my suffering. It feeds her. Like a plant needs the sun. Or water. She flourishes under the emission of any type of misery from me.

How do you grow up well around someone who feels your pain as though the sun has warmed their face? I remember I would fall off my trike and really skin my knee and she'd smile this triumphant skeleton's grin, mud streaked tears running down my trembling four-year-old cheeks. Sorry mom, but you and I both know it's true. I feel compassion for you now, for how hurt you must have been to allow all that happened to me to continue under your watch.

Or she'd get angry. She'd scream and scream and scream until I made myself bloody so I didn't hear anymore; starting at 6, 7, 8 years old. The time I broke my arm while left unsupervised with older cousins who hurt me, she yelled all the way to the doctor's office. And when they set my bones with that chicken wire from hell, she smiled as I let out a blood curdling screech of pure terror. She took a deep breath. And finally calmed down.

My pain was a balm to soothe her spirit. Or maybe she just has a weird reaction to fear. Who knows?

Who do you learn to love from when raised by someone who needs your pain to be happy?

The answer: You don't.

I didn't learn to love.

I learned the love language of pain, instead.

I'm learning now. Sort of. Slowly. Well, I'm unlearning. I used to think the main problem was that I couldn't love other people. The issue was that I couldn't love myself; which left me ill equipped with no tools for loving anyone else.

You cannot light the candle of another if you are not yourself aflame. You should put your own oxygen mask on first, they say. An empty cup cannot pour. An overdrafted account cannot be withdrawn from. And to warm another person, you must yourself first be lit to burn.

I wonder sometimes if that's why she left my father in the house after he molested me. It wasn't like she didn't believe me. It wasn't like he didn't admit it. Because she did. And he did. It was like she just didn't think it was that big of a deal. Like I wasn't worth anything at all. Like I was invisible. A lot of my ego's later quests for center of attention and spotlight were the result of this. Now I crave solitude. Silence. Aloneness. As a mother, I will never understand her choice.

To leave him there. Alone with me. For the foreseeable future. I wonder sometimes if she savored that pain; a hard candy sucked in her mouth behind a grim, tight-lipped and satisfied face. If she enjoyed knowing each day of my existence was torture. Or if it tortured her too.

I like to tell myself she didn't know how badly I was hurting. But she knew. She still tells the story of teenage me sliding down the glass door saying I wanted to die. She loves to tell me I was just crazy for no reason. "Must have been hormones," she says, with a smile and distant face of fond reminiscence.

"Yeah. Must have been," I say, casting a furtive glance from the side, nervous about what's coming next, desperate to not unseat the delicate apple cart of her cruelty and keep it at bay. We both know I'm not allowed to talk about this stuff as an adult without some weird victim blaming shamefest.

In fact, when I asked her if she wanted to speak about all this with me as I began writing this book, us locked arms discussing incest and how you should always protect your children to thousands, she said, "Do we have to talk about that?"

Nah, we don't. But I still thought about it more or less every day and it wasn't optional at the time.

When I published the description of my book, my mother, who covered up my molestation (which is a crime punishable with jail time, by the way), stopped speaking to me. She knows enough people have heard her or myself admit it and that she cannot deny the experiences I relate herein, so her not talking to me only seems logical.

Even on my birthday.

In fact, on my birthday, my Master's degree was sent to me without a word. It was the most prized possession of a piece of me that she had. The sending it back was a message which reinforced what I'd been told a few weeks prior as I posted excerpts from this book: "I don't give a fuck if I ever see or hear from you again," which was followed by laughter.

I earned that degree when I didn't even have money for WiFi, as a single mom, sitting in parking lots in the rain typing out papers with a crying baby in the back of my Jeep; maintaining a 4.0 GPA.

There's a reason there has been no denial that she knew about the abuse, and that's because there are too many friends, students, and even adult family members who knew he admitted it. For the longest time, I didn't understand why I was mostly kept away from other family and never got to know them, and why very rarely did I get to have friends come over. Now I know.

I am a fatherless child. I am a motherless child. I am an adult and I will parent myself.

You are all I have now. You can be my brothers. My sisters. My parents.

My friends.

In a family like mine, not keeping the secret is a sin greater than committing the crime.

Decide to tell your truth. Even if you find yourself standing alone. Take a look at our culture – where it's more wrong to say you experienced incest than to be the person molesting children or the person who knows about it and keeps a child in the environment. Where there's more shame in what you went through than in those who failed to protect you. Where a three-year-old bears more responsibility than the adult who was warned before she ever had a child with him that he molested a babysitter in his first family.

Make no mistake – I told this person at four that he molested me at three. And he admitted it.

I wish I could say that she's embarrassed.

She should be.

But there's never been any remorse there, for this, even when it's acknowledged – and it was – by both the perpetrator and the enabler. And that hurts more than the fact that it happened. That no one seems to think that little girl deserved protecting. Or sees the direct correlation of the many painful years of self-abuse that followed.

Where there should be remorse there is only anger. Anger from her that I've ripped the duct tape from my mouth.

I wish she could see the power we'd have in telling the story of what happened together, hand in hand, from the many stages I will be on in the near future. I wish she knew the untapped ability we'd have to help heal generational cycles of abuse if we spoke together.

But that'll never happen.

People who pinch and twist until you have bruises as a child when you're speaking so that you don't accidentally say the wrong thing won't take the stage by your side once you tell the truth as an adult. I don't understand this. I don't. I'd kill someone who hurt my son in this way. With my bare hands.

I will shout my story. From every Indie bookstore on a self-made tour, from every morning talk show, from every school podium, and into every man, woman, and child I can find.

I will help others find their way out.

But I'll no longer serve the sentence for something I didn't do.

And now I'm more or less dying. She feeds from the waves wafting off my rotting carcass like a dung beetle. And I'm too weak to fend her off, sometimes. But other times? Other times my warrior spirit rises up and we have decided we aren't going out like that, no way, no how. Fire comes out my every pore and I decide to live at any cost. Her not talking to me anymore is a huge relief, honestly.

But it is also heartbreaking, to know I am someone a mother cannot love.

I'm also, occasionally, losing my mind little by slow. I hope it stays with me until the end of this story, because it's coming ripping out my body whether I am ready to tell it or not. And I'm not. Yet here we are. I think losing your mind is a good thing. Then you can build a new thing. But I didn't really think it would be under the mantle of a disease that would take it from me gradually.

Let's go in. To where it all began. Take a walk with me.

Incest

In case you haven't snapped to it yet, this entire book is a huge trigger warning. It gets really graphic here, so skip if you aren't armed with a therapist and emotional comfort food at the very least. Actually, pass on the food. This will probably make you want to throw up. Or maybe punch a hole in your wall. I also foresee lots of your own family members finally getting cussed out after some of you read this.

Son: When I was your age, I was born with a strawberry birthmark on my head. A vascular hemangioma, they said. And when I refused to let your grandmother force me to abort you, out you came with that same mark. You didn't cry. You entered this world smiling.

You were perfect. Black hair. All knowing blue eyes. So plump and sweet. We both almost died getting you here. But you made it. And here we are.

Tonight, you made beautiful art all over the house. Without permission. Using a Sharpie. We're a lot alike.

It's Valentine's Day. The wife didn't get me anything as usual but that's OK. She took me to the doctor, and they ran a tube up my nose and down my throat. That's better than dumb flowers, anyway. She loves us the best she can. Sometimes it's enough. To quiet the long dark nights. She wakes when I scream into the room, splitting the stillness with sounds of agony. She rubs my back until sleep takes me again, without fail, every single time. There's nothing she wouldn't do for us. She works 16-hour days if she has to, goes above and beyond in every way for us, she is our shadow. Her every waking moment of free time is spent loving and serving her family, the best way she knows how. As is mine. That's what you do when you love someone (TWYDWYLS). All I have said about her can be said about myself. We are both trying. But I am starting to wonder if while trying your best; it should still *be* this hard. I'm wondering if she wouldn't be happy with some older dyke who fishes and hunts, loves guns and drinks beer, and certainly doesn't have kids. And if I wouldn't be happier with another happy person, someone who rejoices in children and everything about them rather than openly admitting they hate them.

But I'm also pretty sure she means it when she says I'm the only reason she hasn't put a gun to her head. I don't understand fully someone who can't seem to experience joy, hates all the things I love, and seems infuriated just to wake in the morning. To me, it is a choice. To her, it is all she knows. We do our best. Two people with Complex PTSD trying to navigate the world and raising a small, incredible person.

When I was four, like you are now, I had just told my mother that my father molested me at three years old. It didn't really occur to me not to tell her. I told her when my cousins and their neighbor kid friends would take off my diaper and put candy on me and eat it off my privates at a much younger age, and she seemed wholly unconcerned. I told her they'd hold me down and light matches next to my privates as well, that it scared me and made me cry.

They called it the M&M game. I liked the candy I got rewarded with afterwards when I promised not to tell the secret.

One night I was camping alone with my father in a tent at a Jellystone Park.

Where were you, mom?

So often I've asked that question.

Where were you?

I woke up to the squishy smacking sounds that still make my tummy feel like jello. To this day, if someone smacks their food too loudly all I can hear is that sound in the dark. Then I sat up.

"Daddy, what are you doing?"

I was only three.

I was only three.

"Nothing, baby, go back to sleep."

He was drunk.

"But I'm thirsty."

"OK, come over here and help me with something and I'll go get you a drink."

"OK."

I rubbed the sleep out of my eyes with a chubby fist and stumbled towards his dark huddled over figure, using my hands to find my way around. My nightie had a lace ruffle around the neckline and the hem. I was so little. So sleepy.

He looped one large arm around behind me and pulled me towards him. I thought I was reaching for water and my hand found something slick and fleshy and hard. He pressed me towards it.

Are you nauseous yet?

I am.

"You can have some water if you help me with this first."

"OK. Are we going to play the M&M game?"

My hand closed around it as he showed me to do and he placed his large rough hand around mine and began stroking himself up and down. I distinctly remember him throwing his head back and moaning. That it made him shake.

He grabbed me up by both hips and set me on top of him. My smile started to fade. I was whining for water and he kept putting it off. He pulled my hair back and licked my neck and put his tongue along my lips. He ripped my panties down and placed my labia lips around his dick. He began bouncing me and riding me up and down against him, pressing my legs closed to form a tighter pressure for friction as he slid in and out of the labia slide he'd made for himself.

He did not penetrate me with his penis at the time, just a finger. I think he knew that at three years old someone would notice the intestinal damage and he'd go to prison. He tasted whatever had been in me with his finger and rolled his eyes with pleasure. Up and down. Up and down. Faster. Faster. His breathing was coming faster too. He stayed inside me with the finger as he slid me up and down on his hard dick. Eyes clenched. Fingers of the other hand digging into my tiny white thighs so hard they'd leave bruises. One hand now over my mouth because I had begun to whimper and cry out.

I was afraid.

I'm sure you can imagine what came next.

And then a popsicle. Then some water. And some new underwear. To this day I can't eat that type of popsicle. Makes me shudder.

Then the talk about how families keep secrets to keep each other safe. About how if anyone found out then they'd think I was a dirty little girl.

I was a dirty little girl indeed.

Don't worry. He later dies a miserable death on my mother's living room floor at the bottom of a bottle. Not quite soon enough, though, I'm afraid. I'm not even mad at him anymore, actually. I'm sad for him. And, just between us, I was relieved the day he passed away.

But have no fear! I'm the good guy in this story (most of the time). And I come out alright (more or less). It all ends up mighty fine (depending on your definition). A-OK.

I hear you, my four-year-old son, call my name from downstairs, as I type this.

"Here I come. Close your eyes my little one. It's past your bedtime. You're safe now. Mommy's here. It was all just a bad dream," I tell you soothingly, quietly, as you snuggle back into your blankets, safe in my arms.

I give this to you because I didn't have it.

The Next Day

The next day, I was riding my bike through the RV park. The huge plastic Jellystone yogi bear stared at me with dead black eyes, paint flaking.

Someone called out, "Hey Molly!"

I almost fell off my bike. Pedaled faster. Gotta get away. They knew something. They knew! They knew what happened and that I was dirty, and it was my fault.

I told my dad about it later and he laughed, thumbing my name painted on the sleeve of my shirt.

Oh.

Son, I know you'll read this one day, so I'm going to tell you a story about the time one of my partners shoved me around. I could only imagine you, my sweet boy, watching this spectacle, little blue eyes looking up at us – those meant to protect you and create stability, turning your world upside down. When I finally ended up on the ground, after screaming so hard I passed out, I could imagine you bringing ice to lay it on my shoulder. Then, in my waking dream, you brought me a blanket. She hurts me sometimes, this partner. I am not strong enough to fight back right now. It's only when I threaten to leave. Yes, I know that doesn't make it OK. But I am working with her. A person can only scrape up so many dead babies and be shot at so many times before they twist a little. The reason domestic violence rates are so high among law enforcement is that it's our best kept secret. Very few families speak out about the debilitating Complex PTSD from their families of origin, subsequent careers, or how that affects their nuclear family when they bring it home. (I've dated multiple people in this and similar fields, somehow, so don't try to guess who I'm discussing here, or you'll likely get it wrong, reader.)

In my vision of you seeing us, son, imaginary you asked me who won.

I played out the whole scene as though you had seen it, trying to talk myself into leaving. I tried to explain that nobody wins a fight and things get dicey once somebody is sick and we're having a hard time. Tried to help you see this isn't right. Her slamming doors. Throwing shit. Breaking glass. Hitting me over the head with a metal water jug. Punching holes in walls. Jerking down my IV pole and slinging saline all over my hospital room, nearly ripping out my chest port. Tearing open the refrigerator and raining glass down all around us by breaking beer bottles on the floor. Each time, I would place you in the scene in my imagination and imagine how it would have been had it happened while I held you, shielded you, crying. So many times. So many. That time she kicked in the door as I sat at the table because that morning, she had been so angry that I'd asked her to leave. Both locks were engaged. I asked her to please not come back for the day, but she text me to open the door. I didn't. So, she just kicked it right on in. What if you'd been there? Sitting at the table? Eyes wide, body rigid with fear?

What if you'd seen? Mommy screaming until she legit toppled over, unable to catch herself and struggling for oxygen. Partner enraged and not able to calm down. Me saying horrific things – like that she's a fraud and I hope she gets murdered on duty for being abusive and a two-faced monster. Nobody wins a fight. Nobody.

Or don't they? Somebody always has the power.

This wasn't the life I meant for you. This wasn't what I wanted. But we kept you from knowing, somehow. That almost makes it worse. If we could control it in this way, why not all the time?

Nobody said it would be easy.

But you are safe. You are warm. You are cared for. You are held. And we do art together. Your clothes are clean. And new. I take you to theme parks. The museum. On trips.

The time this partner said, "I'm headed to pick up your stupid fucking kid," I left. We did. Literally just snapped and hauled ass. Packed up the truck and took off to Florida for a month and a half.

Then she told me she had multiple sclerosis. So, I came home. And within a couple weeks, she was back to saying things like, "Your entitled fucking brat of a goddamned child."

She didn't have multiple sclerosis.

People think it's so easy to leave. And it is. It's simple, really.

But it feels so complicated when you are the one inside the cage, especially if the cage is better than the metaphorical floor you're used to sleeping on.

Something is seriously wrong with her health. I read the imaging reports on her brain, and she is not well, things are not normal. I wonder if there's not heavy metal poisoning or mold proliferation going on around here. I just don't know sometimes.

You're the light of my life and I've always done my best to protect you, son.

No one has ever hurt you and I'd kill them with my bare hands if they tried, feeling not a moment or shred of remorse. But is not watching someone hurt me, even if I try to hide it, hurting you? Can't you feel it? Doesn't this show you that this is how to be treated or how to treat others?

I've always said I'm sorry when I fall short. It's not ideal but it's better than what I had and I'm doing the best I know how.

I want to do better. I will. This partner spent her life protecting and serving the general public after her own (very different kind of) hell of a childhood and it all broke her a little bit inside. She helped me heal. I tried to help her heal. But let me tell you something: You cannot save someone from drowning who is more comfortable in water than on land. They'll apologize for splashing as they are dying – and bet if that's not the only apology you ever hear from them. In fact, they may never apologize. You can drag them to shore again and again, breathless and exhausted, yet back into the tide they'll go. We evolve when the pain of remaining the same becomes greater than the pain of change, and not a moment before. The Soul never forgets.

How do you recover from trauma, anyway?

You go back. You pick up every single version of yourself who was hurt. Imagine your childhood vehicle or one you have now and go back for them. All of them. Put them in the car with you, tell them they're safe. Talk to an empty chair with your childhood self in it, just the way you'd talk to your own children, real or imaginary. Bring all ages, all visions, all yous with you and protect them now. Tell them they are loved, now. Worthy, now. Safe, now.

If you wait for apologies from those who hurt you, you might die with that sorry on your lips.

Be your own sorry.

You're the most beautiful child, son. So smart. Sweet. Intuitive. Tough.

I'm terrified to think of how the world will chew you up and spit you out. Scared about what life will give to you. Unspeakably afraid of the time that comes after I die. But I know you are your own, you belong to you and your path is not mine to foretell, dead or alive. I also know that I cut a deep rut with my life, that I chose a hard path. Your reality may be much simpler, easier, and kinder. God I hope so, or I will rain thunder and lightning from the sky upon your enemies.

I have spent my life doing God's work. I have sat across from literally thousands of addicts, alcoholics, child abusers, the hopeless, the helpless, the shelter-less… every type of person. And I have served. All I ask for in return is the ability to rebuke those who hurt you from the other side. And rest assured, that will be granted. When you see odd lightning arc across the clouds, it's a message from your mother. Some mothers send butterflies. Not yours. I send fire. But fire can keep you warm.

You will make it; you have to.

I write this for you.

Some might say, "How can you tell your child your story?"

To them I'd answer, "How can I not?"

Take Your Clothes Off

He shoved the back of my shoulder. Hard. I cut him a look; wobbling in on clear sky-high stripper shoes. Shoes that were made for dangerous girls, to step along the edge. Shoes built for those trying hard to hide and be seen, from that place in between.

By this point I had already been tied up and starved, burned, cut, raped, tortured, humiliated. I'd woken the first time in a drug-induced stupor with him on top of me, without my permission. And from there a sigh and a shrug. Abuse is made normal through repetition.

Hell, he used to drive through a taco joint in Hondo, Texas that sent out eight balls of cocaine with your order if you asked in Spanish and showed them a patch from the right MC cut. Nothing is abnormal when you're living in Hell on earth.

It was a "Gentleman's Club" I'd walked into; stolen IDs he made me carry burning in my 16-year-old pocket. He told me I'd need them "to get a job and support us." He was a man in his 40s who'd helped me leave my parents' home the week before, "running away," to a better life where he said I would, "do real estate." It was in Austin, Texas, seedy and near the airport. It was called "The Landing Strip." Clever.

I was painfully beautiful, invisibly bleeding trauma from every pore and a deadly combination of heart achingly young, unbreakably strong, more than terrified, and extraordinarily vulnerable.

Darting, cautious eyes. I licked my lips.

My heels snicked across the tile entryway, until I came to the carpet. They sunk in quietly, concealing all secrets. The carpet was stained with God only knew what. I might as well have been drowning in quicksand, waiting for a portal to open up beneath me. My hair swung, shiny and new. He had taken me for a "makeover," and I felt so glamorous. Makeup that cost more than my family spent on food in a week. Hair highlights. Beautiful fake nails to replace the paper clips I had taped to my nails as a young girl. Outfits that made me feel flawless and turned heads. Power I didn't know I had. Tanning beds to bake my skin towards the appropriate shade of bronze sun kissed. I was a walking Barbie doll.

I saw the men watching me from their seats, teetering towards the Manager's Office, hungrily hoping I would be naked in front of them soon. They licked their lips.

I would do whatever he said, as long as I didn't have to go home.

Home was a worse hell than the strip club. I was like an animal avoiding the slaughter house by hanging out at the butcher shop. I could smell the meat, but at least it wasn't my turn.

When he pushed me through the doors, I finally understood where I was going and what I was meant for. And it sure as hell wasn't real estate.

Ah, but don't feel sorry for me just yet.

I promise I inflicted as much as I took.

Maybe more.

Fuck it. Definitely more.

———

I don't know why I still try to be hard. It probably wasn't definitely more. Not until later. That's the thing about hurt people – it's true what they say – that hurt people go on to hurt other people. But I recently read something my friend Jason says, and that's, "Healed people heal people," which is why we are here now. That's what this is. My anthem to the broken.

There is power in your story of redemption. There is hope in how far down you went for those still trapped under what feels an impossible weight. The strength isn't shouting from the mountaintop. It's in revealing the path you took to get there.

I wonder where all those men went. The ones who could tell I was the age of their daughters, granddaughters, crisp suits pressed to a sharp crease. They'd ask me questions they didn't want answers to, and I'd tell them what they wanted to hear.

"I'm putting myself through college."

"That's great honey, a little to the left."

Disassociation is a handy trick when you're giving lap dances. There are only so many dicks you can rub your ass against before you never want to see another one again. That hopeful feeling when they walk to the stage, wondering whether this will be the one who helps you eat that night. Hoping they'll make it rain so others realize your worth. Remembering you rarely eat anymore, once the lines are all gone off the table, and that's what you need the money for anyway. That and so the man doesn't beat you when you don't come back with enough. He watches every bill, no way to hide anything anywhere.

I secretly watched the other, older women in the dressing room barely appraise me, bored to death.

He took me all across the country. I "danced" in clubs from Texas to Florida and back because my mom was searching for me. She tried to find me. Tried to bring me home.

But I wouldn't come.

I knew more about the power of sexuality, seduction, and the inner workings of the male mind before I was 17 than most people know collectively, ever. Hell, sometimes I think I understood them better than I knew myself. I wonder if sometimes that's why I later gained so much weight; so no hungry eyes would ever devour me again. I later lost the weight when I realized tattoos and a mohawk would have much the same effect.

"Molly to the main stage. Molly to the stage," the DJ would announce.

I got a kick out of using my real name. Since I had fake IDs, I didn't have to have a fake name. They thought my realness was my persona. And I guess in a way, it was. Besides, I was so blown by the time I hit the stage, if they didn't use my real name, I would have never made it up there. Crawling out from between lines broken up across a mirror to take the stage.

He sat in the club, every moment we were there. He watched me.

It was a sick game.

I was never allowed to be alone, and even had to use the bathroom with the door open. Sometimes he would tie me up for days. Sometimes he would burn me with cigarettes if I looked "too fat to make enough money tonight."

Sometimes he would speak in tongues. I called his father once. He had met me before we left. I told him, "Your son hurts me, I'm only 16, please help me." He hung up the phone.

He still sits on the front row of his Baptist Church in Fredericksburg, Texas. He knew exactly who and what his son was, because apparently, he'd only just been released from a yearlong stay in a mental institution, and straight into my arms.

The depth and weight of the sexual abuse I faced beginning as an infant and carrying on into my early childhood was a tremendous ball and chain of grief hanging from my neck. In families like mine, keeping the secret is the highest held virtue. I think my early trauma impacted all my later decisions because it sent the message that I would never be protected, nor was I worth being kept safe. Because my mother believed me, and because he admitted it, I was in a different kind of hell than if there had been a denial. It sent the message of, "Yes, this happened to you, and it simply isn't that big of a deal." In fact, my mother often told me how she "sent your father away" after it happened and how "you asked him to come back on the telephone." I was four years old. Four. I loved my dad until the day he died. I hated him too. Children should not be given the decisions which hold the reins on whether to allow an abuser in the household. The responsibility for that is solely on the shoulders of the other adult(s).

———

After unspeakable torture that I just don't have the ability to write about right now, I decided finally one day to leave him.

You have to understand some things.

This man had me so brainwashed I didn't even know my own name. He convinced me that I was going to be arrested if I went home, as a runaway teenage stripper.

Abusers are like that. They'll tell you that you'll get in trouble if you don't keep their secrets. That's never true. And if somehow shit goes down like that, give me a call. I'll go to bat for you. The greatest sin in my own family is the audacity to reveal the secrets to you – not because they aren't true – but because they aren't allowed to be discussed.

One day I decided to finally leave him. I had ripped my clothes off all across the country, knew how to make my entire body hairless and flawless, could flip upside down in your lap and wrap my legs around your head… all before other kids were even done taking their SAT tests. I had taken mine in middle school and received a nearly perfect score.

We parked at a gas station. I asked him to go inside and get me a Diet Coke. He was willing because the day before he'd punched me and I'd torn up a hotel room trying to escape him, hitting him over the head with an old school phone. I still had a bruise on my cheek. Usually he was good about making sure the bruises were in non-visible places so I could still work. He knew he fucked up, since me dancing was our only income.

I can still see his face.

He went in the store with a dollar.

His wallet, ID, phone, everything was in the truck.

I drove home to Texas from Little Rock, Arkansas that day. Just put it in reverse and never stopped driving. Would you believe me if I told you I didn't even stop the truck? That I had to literally urinate on myself because I was so irrationally terrified that somehow he'd catch up to me if I stopped?

I was never so glad to see my mom in all my life.

Oh, and his dad? The one who didn't care when I told him I was raped and beaten by his son? He called wanting his truck back, saying he was sorry for what I "endured," and that his son had told him all of it.

We took the truck to the police station and the father picked it up. He didn't even have the decency to hang his head. Just walked on up in his shiny shoes and collected his possession, my blood and urine still on the seats from the times his son beat me and the time I escaped. I'm sure he had it cleaned up, not a speck of dust, and drove it to church that Sunday. Praise the Lord.

I'm not sure sometimes that I'm still not running from that man.

Sometimes I fantasize about going to church too. Sitting next to his father. He'd remember my face; I'd met him before. He left me in the hands of a monster of his own creation.

The moral of the story is only that monsters come in all shapes, sizes, and faces. They can take a kid into a strip club and turn them into something else entirely, or they can sing hymns at your side. Real monsters are expert at doing both. Never forget that.

To this day, he's a fine upstanding member of his church and community; coaching kids' sports and volunteering while donating large sums of money to important causes close to his heart. You might find him at the food bank, handing out soup in an apron.

But never forget: A monster is a monster is a monster.

———

How does something like this even get started, you might ask? Well, for me, it began in my mom's real estate school; that's where he zeroed in on me.

Then he began picking me up. I'd run up or down the hill from our house, and hop in his (daddy's) truck, excited about the thrill of it.

To my mom's credit, she tried heading me off at the pass so many times. With so many boys. In so many ways. She fought and followed and argued and begged and harassed. But I was long gone, even when I was home.

Thank God it was all during a time where the internet was just barely getting started – 15 minutes and lots of loud noises to "log on" to AOL. Several other creeps before him came and sat outside my UIL meets or sports games… men in their 40s, 50s, whatever. I thought they wanted to be my friend. To help me. Each one of them scared me too much to go with. If we were in this day and age? I'm sure I'd have run into a bigger monster much more quickly and be dead by now.

This one, though.

He was charming. And kind. He had a limp arm. Who could hurt you if they had an entire appendage not working?

I figured he must be safe.

He'd pick me up. Take me for ice cream.

One day he brought me a ring and took me to Red Lobster.

It was the most beautiful thing I'd ever seen. The restaurant made me feel so fancy.

That's the problem when the bar is set too low.

I found out later it was from the $10 fake jewelry rack at Walmart.

But not before I'd already started dancing.

"Take your clothes off," the club manager said. Black, curly hair poking out of his shirt, several buttons undone, thick gold chains. He didn't even look up from his paperwork when he said it, that's how common it was. Job interview, essentially. He was smacking some sort of strong-smelling chicken from a Styrofoam container, juice dripping from the corner of my mouth. I imagined dragging a knife across his meaty throat and smiled. He smiled. This wasn't my first rodeo. Like so many clubs before, the owners or managers want to see or even sample the goods before they put them on display. I didn't work anywhere longer than a few nights or weeks at most so that we couldn't be found. He kept us on the run. At night he would turn into a demon, a literal demon he said was named Simon. I am still to this day certain that was true. If I can hear Angels, why can't I fathom that he heard demons?

"No," I told the manager. His jaw dropped, chicken and all. Some even fell onto his slick shirt and had to be brushed aside by an even thicker, furrier hand.

"I know what I have to offer, and I make this place look good. Hire me or don't but I'm not going to sit here and let you fuck me or make me suck your dick. I know how to talk to people, and I can make $500 in an hour just making a sweet old man feel heard. I will pad your bottom line with drink specials and bring in a crowd similar to a headliner with no up-front fees or club cuts. We both know I'm not 5'2" or 42 years old, so you hiring me means I turn a blind eye to what you do behind the scenes and you ignore my ID. Put me to work or I'm out of here. And whatever shitshow mafia or biker outfit runs this place would be pissed if you let a perfect piece of ass walk out the door because I don't want to get your rocks off. I can start now; my bag is right here on my shoulder."

That speech worked, every time.

They only shove as far as you let them.

And is that not true, even now? People treat us the way we teach them to treat us.

———

I remember this one lady, she had to be about 60, in Birmingham, Alabama. I'll never forget her. I think that's one of the odd places where you have to cover your nipples to "dance," although I must say, not much dancing is involved if you're good at what you're really there to do.

She told me, in my ear where no one could hear, "Honey, you've got to get away from that son of a bitch, he's going to kill you."

No one else had really ever noticed him before. He always came in a bit after I did. Always sat in the shadows. Dressed impeccably. Bird-like eyes never leaving me alone for long, even timing trips to the dressing rooms. Tipped dancers well, drank top shelf whiskey, pulling smoothed out crumpled bills from his pocket that I had earned. That I had earned the hard way.

"You don't say?" Was all I could tell her.

You don't say.

I know she saw the fear in my eyes, like a rabbit with its leg in a trap, begging to not attract the attention of the monster nearby, lest it sniff blood and come by for a taste.

One time he threw me out of the moving truck, into a ditch. Or did I jump? Abuse is tricky like that. It all runs together. Would it make a difference? I tumbled a long, long way down the hill. I lay there. I laid there so long that I don't really remember how the police got called, but they did. The grass burned my face. All I could think was that I was just so damn tired. So tired. That I stayed put. Face in the dirt.

The cops separated us, spoke to us individually. But he was close enough to hear, and he watched my mouth as I spoke. When the officer talking to him looked away, he pulled his finger across his neck. I lied and said I was fine, I was safe.

The system failed me every time. Every teacher. Every police officer. Every adult I encountered failed to protect me from birth on; and plenty of them knew the real story. Where were y'all?

———

I remember a similar experience when I lost my virginity; right before moving away. I thought my body was a road to let someone drive down so they could arrive at a place where they might love me. So when my high school boyfriend, a preacher's son, wanted to fuck me up against a rock in the river, I didn't say no. I didn't even want to say no.

I remember specifically wearing this velvet blue dress that I thought was so beautiful. I felt special. I wanted so desperately to be valued. I got shoved to the ground and took it from behind that day, in the woods behind my mom's office; long after the virginity was gone to this boy. I still remember the sounds of the water rushing past, the mess of my hair, the sticks and stones that made indentations in my knees, the scars across my toes. I didn't say no. But if I had known I could, I would've by then. But I didn't know I could, so I didn't. I just closed my eyes, one tear trailing down my cheek. It hurt. But what didn't?

That's the problem with sexually violating the bodily autonomy of a young person, especially. They never know that they have the right to their own body again. What began with me at three years old at the hands of my own family members led to me not realizing that I could tell anyone no about anything. Until one day I decided I should tell everyone no about everything.

His father, too, had caught me giving him head under a blanket at a church event, no less. Did he stop us? No. Did he tell my parents? No. I was 14. What is this culture of silence among grown ass men letting their sons (children, period) get away with, well, everything? He was 16. At least we were a similar age and I was a willing, perhaps even enthusiastic, participant by this point. But why not put a stop to it? Why not tell my parents (not that it would have helped)? What kind of pastor turns around when catching his underage son performing a sexual act with an underage girl in public? And what on earth was I thinking? Was I tempting the only "God" to which I'd been introduced?

Why? Why would I want this?

I thought my vagina was a gate to acceptance through which others must be permitted to pass if I was to know love. It was the only worth I had.

My IQ was 163 at its first measurement.

Yet I believed my body to be my only valuable asset.

And when that high school boyfriend dumped me because the crushing weight of my need and insecurity was far more than any 16 year old boy could bear?

Oh, we were off to the races then, for sure.

And I'm not sure we loved any of the ones who came in between, until now.

Bullies

I decided older guys were much better, and I met one down at the river. Mama had always warned me to stay away from that river, as she'd quickly let you know. Of course, it was the first place I went. I had a friend who was always taking me on adventures, leading me down the path of righteousness. I was fairly innocent in my younger years despite what had already happened to me. I dressed modestly. I didn't cuss. I wouldn't even kiss a boy until about 13. I prayed fervently and was mocked relentlessly for this. Then one summer, I did an about-face and went as fast and hard as I could the other direction. I was sick of getting mercilessly teased.

Girls in gym sprayed me in the face with deodorant because they said I smelled bad. They followed me and mocked me for my dirty, second hand clothes and screamed out across campus that I was disgusting, filthy. They stole my clothes when I was showering so I had to come out of Athletics in a tiny towel and get yelled at by our coach; but not before I noticed his creep ass eye scanning my body.

I had skipped a couple grades by then… and man did they hate me for that. I didn't shave my legs yet, and I was tortured over that too. Shoved into my locker, called hairy, books slapped out of my hands as I tried to walk to class. Tripped in the hallways and laughed at by everyone. I always effortlessly made As and that made everything even worse. Plus, most of the girls in Athletics were undercover gay and made out with one another on the back of the bus yet I was a weird anomaly to that (I know, I know, but actual lesbians are some of the last to come out of the closet, often even to themselves). I bought a $1 bucket and a pack of cheap razors and tried to shave with a bar soap and gallon of water on our patio. I cut the fuck out of myself accidentally. There was no indoor plumbing – which means no shower, toilet, running water, anything. There was nowhere to shave and I "wasn't allowed." Because somehow that was too mature for me but living with a grown ass man who raped me wasn't?

I was followed from our ratty truck at the point of drop off and laughed at, taunted, shoved, tripped, sneered over, and so much more that I've worked hard not to remember.

One summer, somewhere before 14, I decided, "Fuck it." I came home one day to my drunk father smoking a blunt and drinking a beer and took both right out of his hand. I also began smoking cigarettes, pilfered from my mom, then openly… right there in my room. She'd holler through the door, but I think even she knew to be scared of me by that point.

No indictment against me could stand – not even, hypothetically, ones considered for violating the RICO Act and more. Allegedly, I was a pretty rough character. You know, in theory. I was a minor, after all. And some of the stuff that was said about me during investigations was pretty hard to believe. It's kind of funny, actually. I am heavily tattooed with a mohawk and am a straight edge, law abiding, tax paying citizen now. But I get looks as if I am now what I was back then, when I looked like a clean cut, wholesome, All American girl but was allegedly an unwitting international trafficker.

What of the bullies, then? Those same girls who tortured me have all tried to add me on social media. Half of them are back in the closet, married to fat guys they can't stand – bunch of kids around their ankles driving them nuts. Sorry, not sorry.

What makes someone forget who and what they've been? I still feel deeply all the people I hurt before I knew better, and experience immediate remorse even and especially today when I harm anyone. How do some of us live with no conscience? Here's an important tool for all of you, buried right here in the middle of this book: Zoom in and zoom out. Use a lens. When things aren't going well; view all from a deep and wide perspective, far away, blurry. When things are going well; magnify. Hone in. Look at every detail, every inch of what feels good. Turn it over in your hands. Sit with it. Feel it deeply into your cells. Make peace with your past. These cunts made me so strong I became immortal. And now I don't even think they're cunts, but I thought you might enjoy the word. Now? I see they're lost. And I'm so sad for them.

I need you to have that be your takeaway from this portion of the story – that not everyone is operating on the same plane you are. Many of you will tolerate abuse over and over and over because you assume that they think the way you do, feel the way you do, and just need to change. Some of us only have two speeds – doormat and steamroller. The middle path of balance is crucial. Greyrocking if dealing with an abuser you must legally keep in your life is a good strategy. No contact is better, is possible. It is hard for those of with a conscience to understand those who do not operate from the same moral code of basic human decency.

What if I told you some of them bathe in the waves wafting from your reaction to their abuse? That they literally shower themselves in cruelty and experience it like a hot bath of pleasure? That these are often some of the most "giving" people you'll meet or have known your entire life – that they just want to "help" because they're "concerned." That they will find an end run to get their way by seeming to be the most kind, selfless, loving people; all the while figuring out a path to what they really want via manipulation. Back to our regularly scheduled programming.

Upon deciding older guys couldn't break my heart because I didn't care about them at all, I was really off to the races. I got introduced to real drugs, actual bars, parties, and the infinite power of the body I was in at the time.

And man did it feel good. All of a sudden, I had more friends than I knew what to do with.

Even when I was vomiting down an embankment with my jeans around my ankles trying to pee at the same time, and ended up rolling into the ditch, fun was had by all. When you are raised that this is a normal occurrence it becomes just that. I can't even catch a whiff of tequila to this day without my stomach turning over like a startled engine, rumbling.

But my tits got me into all the bars.

Those girls didn't make fun of me anymore once their boyfriends started hopping in my car.

Guess that fixed that.

Hey, I never said I was the good guy in this story.

You made that assumption.

Never make assumptions.

Words Have Power

"No weapon formed against you shall prosper… This is the heritage of the servants of the Lord," is from the Christian Bible (Isaiah 54:17). If you're reading this, it's because it was meant for you. Rebuke all that is not of and from the Light.

I believe in many Gods (they're all the same one). I read many Bibles (they all say the same things). I am as old as the fabric of time itself and let me tell you: None can stand against you when you wear a cloak of righteousness.

It is only our secrets which can harm us when it comes to petty gossip and the like. And if you speak your truth? Then you become impenetrable, invincible. Small minds speak on small things. Feel mercy for them if you are all they have to discuss.

And that requires no religion. No church. No formal belief in anything.

It simply asks that you make of yourself a Light. That you do more Good than Harm. And that you step back when Darkness is sent, so that the Light from within that surrounds you can take over.

Darkness cannot exist where there is Light. It isn't possible.

Struggling with those who are Dark or would wish Dark upon you and yours only causes there to be less room for Light.

Let them talk.

You never know.

I thank God for those who hate me.

Why? Why be thankful for people who'd harm you? I just pray they get what they need. This is a good, positive, powerful prayer of balance.

Because some people need justice. And it takes the outcome out of your hands. And for some of them? The misery of being trapped within their own sick minds is a jail in and of itself, with bars far stronger than any constructed by human beings. They are spiritually imprisoned within plain sight.

Everyone is your teacher.

There are only two kinds: Those who show you what to do; and those who show you what not to do (by example).

When I searched the phrase, "With great power comes great responsibility," I was sure it must have been the Reverend Dr. Martin Luther King, Jr. or some other prolific, prophetic figure.

Nope. Spider-Man.

So, throw out your web and swing on outta there. Away from powerfully dark words of gossip, hatred, condemnation, prejudice, or sickness. Swing on out.

Instead, keep the name of God in the palm of your hand – or right under your tongue – and none can hurt you, ever again. Those who try will have what they intended for you marked, "Return to Sender," and find it waiting on the doorstep of their homes because the Universe knows all our addresses. Make sure you know the rules before playing dangerous games – or that person you hate? You might make them into a bestselling author.

When I see nice, normal looking families, I feel completely out of place. Like an imposter, dirty hands on clean windows looking in at warm Rockefeller Christmas scenes. Sometimes I wonder who I would be if I had a family like that. Or if I had a family at all. But I know I wouldn't be this strong. I thank my parents for that resiliency, actually. But I do wish they hadn't kept me isolated from everyone I could've known on both sides, hadn't lied about all those people so I wouldn't seek them out and ask their protection.

Here's something you have to understand. There is nothing *but* energy. You hold the power of total healing in your very DNA code. Nothing is out of your reach. It works 100% of the time, for 100% of the people who try it. We are nothing *but* energy. It's not about using the right words. It's about creating the right atmospheric vibrational frequency so you can do. Literally. Anything.

Do. Literally. Anything.

I remember feeling like an animal, being told to spread newspaper on the ground and shit on it like a dog. We kept a five-gallon paint bucket on the patio, and I had to squat over it with eyes peering from inside the house through dirty glass. I would hover, legs shaking, trying not to dip my lily-white ass into the filthy stinking brown piss from the entire household. At some point, a potty chair was bought for that patio. I would close my eyes and imagine other places, anywhere. A curtain would flutter to the side, someone always watching closely.

When the bucket wasn't there, we held onto the rail squatting, and peed onto the wood of the patio and over into the yard. There was never privacy. We hauled water sometimes, in 55-gallon barrels in the back of our old pickup truck. At some point, my mother put a used bathtub into the woods. She ran a garden hose up there and used a hand pump. I would have to clean myself there, even in January. I remember one particularly cold 30-something degree day, crying and begging her to stop spraying me. I was so cold my body was purple in spots by the time she let me get down. The tub still sits there. My heart turned to ice on those days, the living parts of it slowly shutting down. I could feel myself hardening to the world, as I crouched, covering my delicate pre-teen private parts and screaming into the cold water. I knew what would happen if I got down. I learned to take my licks where I stood.

They never physically hurt me, which was odd. I was not spanked. The one time I called my mother fat, as a teenager, my father slapped me across the face. I nicked the inside of my nose with a razor so he'd think he did that; that he'd made my nose bleed. When someone didn't acknowledge the real ways they'd hurt me, I found ways to make them feel remorse in other areas. He hung his head in guilt and I turned and smiled in triumph. I'm not proud of that moment.

Like I said, the first time I ever shaved my legs was on our patio, out of a dish tub with a dollar store single blade razor and an itchy bar of soap.

It's hard to live big dreams from small places.

Writing this is making my skin itch.

I used to peel it away from my scalp in sheaths.

We learn how to cope the best we can, until we are taught how to rise instead.

To keep child protection agencies from interfering, we joined an RV park where I could bathe sometimes, and we moved whenever they would come sniffing around. I had a shower bag. Because the campers were typically not the same people, nobody noticed that there was an orphan among them raising herself. I was taught that if I told anyone about our living conditions or that I had been molested that I would be kidnapped by terrible people who would be abusive every day and starve me and lock me in cages.

I told my school when we lived in Georgetown. I remember a therapist asking me with a doll where he had touched me. We packed our truck in the night and stole away like thieves. They never came looking for me once we were gone.

The system is broken.

I know, I worked there. Child Protective Services was my first, predictable, job out of college; a fresh shiny graduate ready to tackle the bad guys.

My mom was always working, always. She tried to take care of us by working constantly, but this often left me at school until late into the night, the last one on the curb waiting or being brought back by coaches, teachers. I was five minutes away yet almost never got picked up on time. There was rarely anyone around to prepare me for all the little things I take for granted with my own child. He always has the right color shirt for the event, the little projects noticed and done, someone smiling and clapping, videoing his singing and dancing – even in Kindergarten. I was always scanning, searching the crowd, hoping in equal amounts to see and not see someone, anyone, there.

There was rarely anyone there.

I was the one looking down in shame as the teacher collected the donations kids are required to go out and beg for from people, my face blushing that I hadn't been able to do it. I was the one shifting nervously in my seat as she went desk to desk, picking up the "make an ornament at home" items. I had nothing. I was the one wiggling my toes in boots three sizes too big from the thrift store as other children called me Ronald McDonald. I would bite the inside of my lip so hard that sometimes it bled.

Our fifth-grade math teacher used to shoot me in the face with water guns for talking.

It was the only human contact I had outside my family. "School." In an ass backwards little conservative town in the middle of nowhere.

And when things would get too hot? I would be pulled out and "homeschooled" for a few years, only to show back up, test in, and skip a few grades.

To this day, I use a toothbrush in the shower, because I got so conditioned to my shower bag from when we lived inside my mom's office on Main Street for a brief period. I feel like I can't breathe if the tock ticks too closely to when my son is getting out of school as I'm arriving. I never want him to be the kid looking, searching, for his parents. My mother literally had to step over my drunk, passed out father to meet with clients. She tried so hard to earn a living, but you simply can't function properly, not ever, when you remain in an abusive relationship. My father never raised his voice, not a single day, but I see now he was abusive. And yet she remained.

That was her choice.

I was homeless in plain sight.

An orphan with parents.

The good days were the ones where I got to go to school clean.

I once had lice for an entire year.

Yes, a whole year.

I was told by my family to hide this from the school, but eventually they found out. I would go on to be turned away, again and again, at the nurse's office; deemed too filthy to be around other kids. When things would get too rough at home, and it seemed the school might take notice, that's when we would move; or I would be withdrawn and "homeschooled" for a couple years.

My mother would scream in my face, at the top of her lungs.

There are so many times I can't remember. She said my first day of kindergarten I was clean and beautiful, with my new black and white saddle shoes on, excited and ready to face the day. I can imagine what it must have looked like, because of so many times before. She was so furious I forgot to brush my teeth that she yelled at me until spit was flying from the corners of her mouth, and her eyes were red and bulging. I was crying, head down. I shuffled my way into my first day of school ever wide-eyed and tear-streaked.

I just can't remember.

But what I do remember is worse. I remember we had to move because I told someone at school that he'd molested me, so we switched towns, and by the next year we were homeless. I felt like not only what he did to me was my fault, but that we were being punished by God for it because of me. I started first grade out of a tent with a weird sweatshirt some grandma had given to Goodwill. It didn't go well. I begged God for forgiveness, to relieve my family of the wickedness I had somehow caused. A Baptist minister, who was also a coach in our town, took me into a closet and blessed me, whatever that meant. Cleansed me of "sin." OK. Whatever.

I remember my father coming to the school, soaked in urine and filthy from a month-long bender, clothes dirty and stained, screaming my name across campus to have lunch with him. I remember when he was sober, he was starched and pressed and perfectly attired. He was a long-range binger with even longer dry spells, during which he'd become increasingly an asshole as the alcohol called his name louder, siren of the sea. She would eventually pull him under and keep him there, lost both to his family and to himself. I remember ducking behind a nearby building, breathlessly hiding and hoping the kids who mercilessly bullied me wouldn't see him drunk, green waves of stank coming off him like flames.

One of those kids works at the front office of the local elementary school now. Bullies grow up. They raise their kids into the next-gen bullies. And they go on to bully your kids. Teach your babies to punch that motherfucker back. My mom told me to fight with my words. Words couldn't stop the blows that rained down on the dirty girl with lice.

Words were of no use.

Until later.

And then I realized, words hold all the power in the world.

With that power? Comes great responsibility.

Strength Through Accountability

G.K. Chesterton said, "A stiff apology is a second insult. The injured party does not want to be compensated because he has been wronged; he wants to be healed because he has been hurt."

I have spent at least half my life screaming at people who hurt me that they should apologize. This is one of the most fruitless endeavors in which I have ever engaged.

I always wondered if there was a little devil under my tongue.

Nothing gets me angrier than feeling like someone won't own what they've done. You might have noticed herein that I used to put up with a lot; and this sometimes attracts people to me who dish out far more than a normal person would allow. The thing about trauma is you lower the bar so far down; you can't even see it anymore. I had reached a point somewhere along the way where I thought, "I don't even care anymore what's done to me, I'm sure I deserve it."

What used to make me really angry, and I mean fuming, is when someone wouldn't acknowledge the hurtful thing they did or show regret for their behavior. The power of accountability and showing you that your pain is visible is immeasurable, but you can't wait for this to happen. Some people will never feel remorse for harming you, and thus it can't be a necessary component of your healing.

I remember using my own words as violence. To this day, I am still occasionally guilty of this. It was my specialty, one in which I was trained at an early age. When you are permitted only one weapon, you hone your skill with it until there is deadly precision. Two people approaching a relationship from a trauma informed background are seeking safety; and such begins a dangerous dance of "come here, go away."

You don't want to attract someone from the place you're in if your mind + body + spirit aren't in alignment; because if you do, you'll attract where you're at, as it were. So instead of being hellbent on finding a mate at any cost, doing the interior redecorating will bring you a much more quality lover because you will *be* a much more quality lover. Don't get in a rush to pull your pie out of the oven or it may not be in an edible condition. Give it time. Give yourself time. Everything you want is on the other side of fear. That does *not* mean ignore red flags and grab at the first unsuspecting bystander who wanders by your nest, or you'll both be in for trouble. It means do the work, plant the tree, and enjoy the fruit once it's grown.

Here's the thing – if one ingredient is missing from a dish, it changes the entire flavor. It can even render it inedible. Make sure you have your spiritual house in order before you go shopping for folks to add to your oikos.

I found the vulnerability in people and would exploit it to push them away. I think I wanted to see if they'd really go. This wasn't random, but would happen if I felt threatened, hurt, or afraid. I would slice and dice with the cruelest words I could imagine, using up the saved tidbits about their character and history to eviscerate what was left of their love for me. When I was sick or scared, I would select partners I knew would take care of me; on a less than conscious level. I didn't need care in any sense other than emotional, but it is still a using. I am deeply ashamed of this.

But I cannot stand before you in anything less than the fullness of truth. If I can tell you where everyone else fell short, but cannot show you myself, I am a coward of the worst kind. And I am many things, but coward is one I have never been accused of to date.

I recognize this two-way street now. Nobody enters something they are not benefitting from, and there were certainly benefits to them as well, but I do see my part in where I went awry for so many years with so many wrong-for-me partners and the damaged caused to them as well in so doing.

Know this, though. Your reactions to abuse are never abuse, even if they are abusive. They're self-defense. At some point, though? We have to exit the elevator. You can ride that sucker all the way down or you can simply get off of it any time you like. Sometimes, this looks like hard boundaries. Sometimes it looks like no contact. Stop trying to excuse yourself, your very existence. You owe no explanations.

I was looking for someone to be an emotional scratching post, a security blanket, a safety net – for many, many years. I was looking for stability I had never been given, not realizing I could pour my own foundation. And a lot of people got hurt along the way, literally and physically, including (Especially?) myself.

I didn't come out as a lesbian until I was 27, even though my first consensual sex experience ever was as a teen with another teenage girl.

Fast forward to 27: I had just left the hospital from radioactive iodine isolation for days, only to find my car broken into and totaled in the process – the convertible top slit, my belongings strewn everywhere and some missing, rain having poured in for days. It was the most absolutely powerless moment of my adult life. Trapped in isolation, unable to even make a police report until it was too late, debit card drained, cops saying via phone they were "too busy" to even review the security footage of the multiple times what little money I had was spent nearby. They "took the report," but theft is just, "so common."

It was in this state that I finally told my mom, "I'm gay." I had given away all my things, shaved my head, adopted a minimalist lifestyle, and recently moved back from Hawaii. After cancer surgery, I had just lost everything I owned while undergoing treatment – radioactive iodine in isolation, mind you, that I had driven myself to – alone. Clearly, my totaled vehicle was flooded, so I stood at the entrance of the hospital in a paper outfit as I watched the last of me get towed away. I blurted this out almost as soon as I was in the car. I didn't mean to say it. "I think I'm a lesbian." She screamed, "So you want to eat pussy?!"

What? No. Actually, I was terrified of that. I just knew I would prefer men to never touch me again. Don't worry. I am now a Pro Status Lesbian. No fears here. I'm a fucking champ.

Maya Angelou said, "Do the best you can until you know better. Then when you know better, you do better." My penance to all the collateral damage of my youth that extended into my twenties is what I'm doing now and have done for a couple decades – helping others find the long, hard road out of Hell.

And that's the best I've got.

I hope it's enough.

The Bad Guys Are Sometimes the Good Guys

See, you've got some things wrong already. The villains in this story aren't all bad all the time. And the heroes aren't all good. Don't decide you love me yet, until you hear about all the unlovable things I've done. Then decide. And don't decide you hate my dad. Or my mom. Or any of my partners. There are quite a number of times where they're the hero. And I'm the villain.

And you don't know where they come from, what they've been through.

You didn't see my mom that time my dad was drunk, but we had money. The entire bottom of the tree was beautifully wrapped presents as far as the eye could see. There was even a pogo stick. We had a perfect old brick home with a huge yard and a tire swing during this time. We made cookies for Santa and left them out and he took bites and drank the milk.

I ripped open the presents. It seemed like they would never end. But when they did? Mom took me to Pearland. It was this magical, amazing place where we could play games and ride go karts and was the best memory I have. I would hear kids talk about things like this when I was at school, but I never got to go. I was there! Finally! The lights and sounds. My mom actually seemed to enjoy my company.

It later became a holiday tradition that during times we actually had the money, she'd take me somewhere fun since my dad usually picked the holidays to get slam wasted. One year we went ice skating. I wouldn't even stop long enough to get a drink. I skated so much that I turned blue and my poor pre-teen nipples stayed hard and frozen until I finally took a hot shower at the hotel and even then, they just burned and burned. We got to have hot chocolate.

It wasn't until just now, literally in this moment, that I realized my mom would take me on these jaunts during times she thought I was being abused by him again. I've apparently repressed all the other memories of it but the first time, but I can't fathom that it didn't happen more than once. I know it did. She knew it did. And so we raced cars and laughed and she actually stayed in the rink when I skated; in the bleachers. She admits she never bonded with me the way a mother should, but these memories are priceless to me. She might not have played with me, but she was there. At least I didn't know at the time it was because she had come home to find me on his lap in our home facing him. She recently told me, "I don't give a fuck if I never see or hear from you again," as we discussed other matters. She laughed when I got offended and said, "You know I don't mean that." Do I, though? Do I?

Still he lived with us, until he died on that living room floor when I was 19. I think part of her has always been jealous of me? Instead of seeing a three-year-old being sexually abused, she saw it as someone her husband "wanted." And we won't even go into the chomo she dated much later after he'd passed. He was convicted and registered for raping a 4-year-old little girl, and she said she believed him when he told her he didn't do it. He died drunk on the side of a hill, face down in the hot Texas sun. Are you seeing a pattern here?

I still am not really sure why I held more anger with my mother for covering it up than I did with my father for doing it. I guess the truth is, I just never felt her love. He loved me. He was a sick, fucked up individual. But he loved me, and she didn't. I guess it came down to that. She would always say, "I know I wasn't the perfect mother," which seems to be the battle cry everywhere for abusive women trying to lay guilt traps into their kids. The power of accountability lies in its ability to heal. And it doesn't say, "Ohhh poor me, guess I didn't do enough." It says, "Yes. I am human. I failed you in egregious ways. I want to make it right. Show me how to help you heal. I was wrong, and I own that fully."

I vow to say this to my son if he ever comes to me with complaints or pain from the way he was raised, should that occur. That I will own it, even if I do not understand it. That I will validate him, and not with some "Sorry you feel that way," bullshit. That I will beat the drums until the sound they make soothes him to wellness. That I will make it right, in any way he asks, should he see fit to find that I made mistakes.

And don't we all make them? It's the human condition. Some are just much darker than others.

And I didn't know why we did these fun holiday adventures until just now. Well, nobody ever said this would be easy. But I can feel my body healing, cell by cell. The words are pulling the disease from my very veins. What should we talk about next? Pulling these words from myself requires a certain level of disassociation, wouldn't you say? Otherwise I would be a molten pile of trauma all day, every day. I'm going to disconnect a bit more from these as things that actually happened to me and take you further. Further. You may be thinking, how horrific, this poor girl; but please understand it got worse before it got better.

The most horrific things that happened? They're unspeakable. Let that sink in. What you've read so far? Definitely not the worst things that went down. Here's the thing: Resiliency. If you don't turn what has happened to you thus far into a weapon or a non-event? It'll burn you alive from the inside out in such a way you may never recover. How do we do this? Trauma must either be used as gas to light your motivational flame or healed so damn thoroughly it's about as significant as what you ate for lunch two weeks ago, on a Tuesday. Why try to tell people to heal?

I'm well aware some of you might not be ready to hear that the responsibility for that is in your hands now. I'm very clear that may not be well received. Is it fair? No. You shouldn't have to cure what you didn't cause. But the alternative is to remain uncured. And who among us wants that? You'd be surprised. You'd be shocked, actually, how many will struggle against the notion that total healing is not only possible, but impossible to stop if you follow certain steps. They are terrified. Perhaps you are one of them. Hang in there. We're going somewhere, I promise. I have to take you there.

I have to show you that you can rise, ascend, into your larger self.

And that you can live through anything. Anything.

Immortality

(Insert prolonged absence from writing here.)

Well, well, we meet again. Starting to wonder if I'm immortal. In that case, perhaps I should take more risks. I'm already pretty risky, in the sense of adrenaline rush risks. It's been quite some time since my last confession.

Now I talk to the dead more on behalf of the living; like *a lot* more. I mean, always did, really. I saw real live beautiful angels and spoke to lost ghosts and had vivid astral travels to other realms as a child. You talked me into thinking it wasn't real. But oh, now, oh, there's no going back, Alice.

I know such specific things so often and with such accuracy that it isn't possible to come from within. You were not made for everyone. Do yourself and everyone else the favor of stepping away from anyone who cannot recognize or appreciate the fullness of your being.

When I was lost in that hospital, it was like I was reset to the infinite power within each of us from the moment we are born, before the world tells us not to see what is there. But the thing is, I stumbled upon an in-between place. According to my wife, from the outside it looked initially like I was essentially brain dead once I was brought back from the Other side. From my perspective, I was on the Flipside. Once the stroke unit got through with my coding episode, I was a whole new thing. And still all the old things. But with some new things. As you can see, words fail to adequately relate this experience. It isn't a word kinda thing. It's a non-thing thing.

It's like the infinite power we are born with but with the knowledge and experience, education and wisdom of 35 years of life on earth time, all of a sudden were present in the same skin sack.

Now I spend lots of time over there.

Beyond the Veil. In the Underworld. Swirling around the Vortex.

The bottom floor of an infinitely large house with lots of complex layers, up and down.

All around us all the time yet slightly out of reach for almost all, almost all the time.

Surrounding like air, invisible but provably there by the absence of an inability to breathe.

Until you can't breathe. Then what?

Well, you have to go there. That's what.

If the first part of my story before 35 could've been called "Living to Die," then this next part is called, "Dying to Live," because damn is life good. So after "Shattered," what shall we write, then? Perhaps, "Whole." Or maybe it will be time for the blissful release of death, which I embrace.

We always get what we want, we just don't always want what we get.

When I said to myself during this last bout in the ring with terminal illness that I was going to disconnect, it wasn't intended as a secret message to the Universe that dying was a good idea.

But that's how it was taken.

We've already covered this, but it's yet another thing that bears repeating: Every thought is a prayer. Those thoughts become feelings, emotions. Those become behaviors, then habits, then patterns. Once buried under enough of the wrong variety of these, it can be hard to get turned around indeed.

Hard, but not impossible. Your tires will screech. They'll throw up some rubber and smoke, perhaps a foul stench. But they'll turn. Just hold fast to the wheel, like your life depends on it, because it does.

Life is like this for me now. I say I can't do something one day, then suddenly I can – abilities and gifts pop up left and right now, and I realize none of them are from me. I can scan the bodies of people and diagnose them accurately. I can remotely find the missing. I can lead you to clues in murders you were told were accidental deaths. I know I am close to the end of my time on this earthly plane, in this particular human iteration, so I need to hurry as my hour draws near. I'm pretty certain I have seven years and some change left, but doctors seem to think it's much less.

We pick the time we will die before we come, you know.

And our families. We pick them too. I picked mine. You picked yours. They were uniquely qualified to bring you to and through every single thing, good and bad, to help you level up towards your destiny. Think about it. The best things in your life wouldn't exist if you hadn't been at the precisely right place and time to receive them. And you'd never have been in those places and times if you weren't exactly who you are. And you wouldn't be who you are had your family of origin (or lack thereof) not shaped you. Some of us were shaped by gentle hands, molding clay. Some of us were left to create ourselves, guesswork. And some of us? Well, we were made through burning, embers lit to smolder, remaining aflame.

Are we not all immortal, then? Is not a single act of kindness which may impact people for the rest of their lives and can be a great catalyst for change about which you never know not, actually, an act of immortality? Are we not immortalized in all those whose lives we have touched, for better or worse? Are we not immortal in our children, or the lessons we teach, or the things we learn along the way?

I know, I know. Hard to imagine. Let's go deeper.

Life

A slow rollercoaster
You can't see the bottom
But can tell it's very far
And dark

No noise down there
Body rushing
Wind whipping hair

Lips pulled back
In a scream

Going nowhere

Body slowly melting
Skin peeling off
While you watch

Fire hot embers of pain
Consciousness and the Veil
Surround you
It's not a Veil at all

But a coat
A blanket
An ocean

How much more can I take
How much more until I break

And fall

There's an expectation
That we get to be old
But you'll never see the wrinkles
On my face

Hundreds of times
Sliced

Radiated
Poked
Strapped
Probed

I spent the minutes of my life
The heartbeats between moments
Begging for more
Time
I just need one more year

To keep my heart beating

A meter running out
With less coins than it should have

And a sign
That says
No parking

Sand slipping through my fingers
Until my hands are empty
Shattered hourglass

My bones shatter in place
Metal holds me, shoved into those bones
I learn to walk again

Only to fall

Dragging past you on bloodied hands
Do you see this specter smile on my face

Heartbeat
A staccato war cry

An insolent declaration
Made by remaining alive
One more day

Was I really so wicked
That even sleep must elude

*How do you chase down
Life*

*When exhaustion
Has made home of your bones*

Living to Die

Are even saints not also sinners?

My wife is a saint, she really is. She encouraged me to write this. She encouraged me to tell my truth, to leave in any part or piece I choose, with total disregard to how it would affect or embarrass her. In fact, she says nothing I could ever do or say would embarrass her. That's love. We both have our Light and Dark sides, as do all people.

I spent most of my early years living to die.

I did what I was supposed to initially and waited my turn to get off this ride. It made me dizzy. It made me sick. I just wanted it to end.

Now, I typically take photos with my oxygen on, rather than off.

Because rare is beautiful. Dying doesn't mean you are dead. Or incapable. Or unsexy.

And you don't even have to accept a medical death sentence. But that's another story. Illness isn't always visible. Some people show outward strength that they don't always feel inside. It's alright to be scared. We live in such a bizarre culture that shames fear. Was fear not installed as a barometer to gauge pressure? Do we not have it so that we are able to dodge predators, dangers? Is fear not a method by which to discharge anxiety and pain? Why is it something to be ashamed of having?

Why not normalize oxygen supplementation? Wheelchairs? All forms of physical manifestation of disfigurement or disease? Why not show our truths? There's no need to use a weird tight-lipped smile when you see a disabled (I prefer the term "differently abled" bee tee dubs) stranger. And definitely try to keep the pity out of your eyes. Some of us are made of fire, like we previously discussed. Still got it, just can't breathe. And when I don't "have it?" I end up in the hospital for weeks, until I raise enough Hell to get cut loose.

My Spirit doesn't change.

It is so strange to me that I so desperately wanted to die for so very long and now I wish so badly to live.

From earlier this year before I abandoned all doctors and almost all prescriptions:

"What you don't see is that it took me an hour to blow out my hair because I can't hold my arms up. That I took 18 pills this morning. The shaking hands I signed forms with. That it'll take me days to recover from a half hour at my kid's school. But I have lunch to make and a home to clean and a blog to write and I'll be damned if I don't. The gasping once I got to the truck because I was trying to hide that standing so long was seriously depriving my brain of oxygen. The confusion that takes a while to subside - similar to dementia - once I've let myself stop perfusing. The heart rate and BP that change as I stand or sit or walk or lean - drastically enough to make me unconscious. The tears as I wondered if this would be his first yet only school year I'll get to attend. Smiling that I was even able to leave the house, medically, today. Feel the sun on my face. The wind at my back. The joy in the sounds of children's voices after being mostly indoors since my prolonged hospitalization. The blinding pain shooting through my head because I allowed myself to desaturate for too long. The way I carefully hid the hair that's fallen out or broken off. That my toes and fingers were blue. That if I go through the plan my doctors have in store; I have a 50% chance of death and 90+% chance of secondary cancer if I do more of their biologics/chemo, because the next one they have in mind is a doozy. That my body can't handle the surgery I need because I've been immunosuppressed. That I've abandoned modern medicine for the time being in search of my own answers. That I'm afraid. But still strong. That you can be both. Current issue is systemic vasculitis with an extremely rare autoimmune disease that has caused everything from organ failure to broken bones requiring rod and screw placement inside them to blistering of all soft tissue and dysautonomia; among other things. Those are some of the things you don't see. That my Spirit is strong, and my attitude is gangster in spite of it all – that I've been this low and bounced back before. That I might not this time."

My illness is no longer my story.

My wellness is. Even if it's "only" spiritual wellness.

Is that not, actually, everything? I am going to pursue that like my life depends on it because it does. Many say that all illness stems from dis-ease (disease), and that the causes have nothing at all to do with what's physically or medically underlying. I have found this to be true as I have slowly healed myself from many things, only to watch them flare up again in the face of wheat flour, sugar, not enough sleep, too much improper blue light exposure, chronic stress, and other self-imposed hurdles.

This is where it becomes imperative to research epigenetics, neuroplasticity, electrodynamics, and to gain a fundamental understanding that you *are* energy – sand poured into an hourglass. You are water. You are air. Each particle of you is moving at all times. You are in constant motion. You are an open closed system.

Bravery is not courage in the absence of fear. It's being scared to death and carrying on in courage regardless.

For all you youngsters who rely on your looks, understand that they are transient. Not just with age. But anything can happen. And the most beautiful people I've met were not very outwardly beautiful at all by conventional standards. Perhaps that is how beauty is created, by a deep journey within necessitated by a shedding of the outer shell.

If you lean heavily on the mind and that flashy intellect, know that it too can change in fundamental ways you never expected. If your brain is your greatest weapon and best tool, what happens when you wake in a fog? Or angrier and sadder than you ever fathomed due to chemicals and changes beyond your control as a disease ravages what's left?

For those who depend mostly on their physical fitness, that can be taken in an instant. Like when you find yourself paralyzed from the neck down?

And what is left for any of us then?

The Spirit.

That's where the next chapter of my life's work has taken me. Within.

Dying to Live

Let's talk about some important stuff, now that we've decided to live rather than die.

Some of you already know this, some of you don't.

There is a world all around us, a spiritual one.

Literally laid *overtop* us. Through us. Weaved into our very cells. Existing as we do on this plane and many others. Almost as if there were two earths at the same time in minutely different realms but the same precise spot. Except there are infinite earths. Infinite everythings.

Death is just the passing through a Veil.

But you're still here. Just elsewhere. And the Veil is not some other place, either. It's the here and now. The all the time.

The spiritual realm is inside every fiber of your body. Every leaf. Every newborn. Every drop of blood.

And the battle of Good and Evil is real, even if the terms themselves do not exist in the way most conceptualize them. Both internally and externally to each human life, this spiritual warfare does rage.

But let's talk about death for a moment.

Many speak of crossing "to the other side."

To the other side OF WHAT?

And when someone is shot or seriously injured, we tell them to, "hold on."

Hold on TO WHAT?

As someone uniquely positioned to be close to death but still alive, allow me to tell you after *everything* I have experienced that the Veil is real. You can feel when it's near. I got so close I could touch it.

Now I cross regularly, and on purpose – except it's hard for me to explain how I don't have to go anywhere except into the moments between seconds to get there. And you can also feel when you're fully alive and it's not as close.

Some of you are so totally healthy or unhealthy you have no idea any of this is going on all around us. All around you. I had two rapid response team interventions during my last hospitalization, one of which caused my Spirit to leave my body for eight minutes and cross the Veil unintentionally. You almost need to be in an in between place to experience that which is in between. For instance, if you are under the influence of addiction to heavy drugs, you will almost appear energetically to me as invisible. The unseen. Faceless. Those who are very Dark or would wish deep Harm appear to me as fast moving black scribble scrabble faces.

One day you will feel it too. All of it.

That's the only guarantee.

In fact, not even all Spirits make it to Life. It might be arguable that the purpose of Life is Death, because it is the only Universal guarantee to all. Is it not possible, then, that the experience of it is the opposite of what so many presume? Ever-present in my mind, Ram Dass related that death is the experience of taking off a tight shoe. I believe this strongly.

I can hear and see things I cannot explain to you. Except that they are neither seen nor heard.

Human words cannot adequately describe the mystical, or it wouldn't be mystical at all. If we could understand the notion of "God," it wouldn't be God. When you can fit God inside of your mind, you do not know them at all. It is an energy, a flow, a frequency. Not a man on a throne in the clouds.

Now I talk to people and access their deceased loved ones for them – and I know things I have no way of knowing. That your grandmother smelled like roses and drank sweet wine. That your husband doesn't like that the wood box was moved from the right side of the porch to the left, and items were taken out. About the brown leather dream catcher still hanging in his office. That she had a red and white checked table and loved baking. How and where and when they died. So much more.

If all around us, all day long, exist spiritual forces we cannot usually see nor quantify, is it so hard to believe that energy radiates from every action, every word, every thought? That our entire existence is essentially a video game, a matrix, with energy flowing all throughout? A quicksilver? A sliph. A bodach. The Wakinyan. The Heyoka. Meteors crashing to earth, fire from the sky.

That what I do today could inadvertently cause a tidal wave of cosmic force to set in action a chain of events that profoundly affect a random person on the other side of the globe? That the butterfly effect is real? And if so, then does it not stand to reason that there are things which are not commonly known yet by many, so that the few who do see them seem crazy to the blind?

If you had explained the concept of a cell phone a thousand years ago, you'd have been laughed out of your village. If Jesus, the Buddha, or Muhammad themselves came back today, they'd be locked in an asylum until they stopped insisting on their identity and were sufficiently drugged to silence.

When someone you love dies, no matter your belief system, I can tell you this for sure – for a time, however brief, they are right here. Right next to you. Right past the Veil between life and death.

I know this because I'm dying, and I can feel it. And I'm telling you, I can feel and see and hear it; but not in the way those senses are typically utilized. I use my other face.

Whether I succumb to this particular illness or another down the road or an 18-wheeler plows into me tomorrow... it doesn't really matter. For a brief time, my Spirit will remain.

Here. With you.

And once I cross, you will always be able to access me. Well, some of you will. And I you. So when you think it is me, it is.

It also means your loved ones who have gone are never very far. They are closer than you can possibly fathom.

Why does any of this matter? That there is a spiritual world invisible to most laid over and around and within the one we currently inhabit?

Because.

Not only does this mean the ones you've loved who've crossed were briefly still here, it means you have an opportunity to create great, earth shattering, ground breaking change. It means you can tap into those forces all around us and literally use that to save lives or alter the course of history.

ALMOST ALL OF THE THINGS YOU SPEND MOST OF YOUR TIME DOING DO NOT MATTER AT ALL.

There is so much I am not writing about. The abortion I was pressured into at 17, how I then felt I had to lie and tell everyone I had a miscarriage so nobody would get in trouble. Coming out, and how horrific that was. The tremendous wrongs done to me by abuser after abuser. The horrifying way the medical system and doctor after doctor tortured me. How for five years they said I was crazy until they found cancer that I was estimated to have had for 7-8 years. How when I filed for divorce from one of my marriages, a smear campaign so vicious it almost cost my life was centered on the lie that I was a con artist and never had cancer. How when I stood up for transgender residents at a homeless shelter I worked at, the CEO awarded me with a recognition of exemplary service, but my direct supervisor there managed to target me until I left; and those people continued getting marginalized and abused. How the university where I had a 4.0 on my Master's degree "didn't invite" me back to tutor because I reported that my boss was selling drugs to students and they verified this, fired her, and just didn't ask me back after doing the right thing.

Why am I skipping so much of my story? Here's why: People who've harmed you don't deserve an instant of your *thoughtlife*, of your time. What's written about here which has already passed is only in service of your highest and best – just enough trauma to let you see that you can heal. I don't dwell on anything, not a moment of pain, that happened to me, anymore. Healing and reliving pain cannot coexist because each time you walk yourself back down memory lane, it is experienced by the body and mind as though it is happening in the here and now.

There are so many pathways to peace that it's unfathomable.

This Summer, I came the closest to Death since this cancer and autoimmune journey started for me so very long ago. I danced with her. She told me some of her secrets. Secrets about life and the living.

We decided I have a little more work to do, but I could have gone with her. I could have stepped to the Other side and remained; I was that close. I see and know things now I didn't before. I went with her and could have stayed.

And the entire course of my life has changed, however brief this life may be. Insert bumper sticker here: There may not be a lot of years left in my life, but there has been a lot of life in my years. Do not grieve for me when I go. Dance. And sing. Maybe tattoo my name on your ass and drink whiskey?

When I'm ready to lift the Veil, I now know I will realize it. As will you. And so on. Ad infinitum. Buddha's Middle Way. Aristotle's Golden Mean. Go there. Remain. Then exit gently, like a soft breeze. You don't have to slam the breaks and come to a screeching halt at the end of your life. Socrates. Plato. Meet all of them here. Get balance. Take her with you.

It is not my time yet. Do not be afraid for me. I have no fear.

Perhaps you're drinking your morning coffee. Pondering how much longer you can go without an oil change. Trying to figure out why your teenager won't act right. Thinking of whether the lawn needs to be mowed. Or how you'll make your rent payment this month.

You have so much more power to tap into than you realize. I only just recently figured this out myself.

That tingly feeling you're getting at times while reading this? That's that Other world laid *overtop* ours.

That's those who've gone before us telling you they're here. With you. Right now. And also, elsewhere. But I want you to pause today and think of the Veil. To sit quietly and ponder the Spirits around you. Just briefly. Because one day it will be your turn to see what's behind there. And I want you to go into that knowing you have lived the life you were meant to live.

Are you?

If not, start now, before the last drop of blood evaporates from your veins.

Someone recently told me that blood is made of light, and you can see it in the land if someone has died a violent death, that it rises like smoke.

Did you think that was leading somewhere? It wasn't. Just a random thought.

Like life. A sentence with no period at its end

Death

She comes
Death
Curling smoke fingers
Around me
Trying to get in
Through my nose
I'm not ready

Hold my breath

Cold hands
Ice around my heart
It stops
Then beats
Stops

Wait
I'm not ready

How many heartbeats do I need
To write a hundred thousand words
And is that enough
To explain the
Razor
Scars

Death doesn't knock
But stands
Silently pressed to my door
Her ear against the glass
Waiting for me to draw a breath
Fogging up my window in her
Impatience

Don't breathe
Until the air hurts my lungs
Until she turns away

A brief reprieve

Until tomorrow

*We dance again
Thrust
Parry*

*A victor
Only one*

Section Three: Relational Malfunctioning

When despair for the world grows in me
And I wake in the night at the least sound…
I come into the peace of wild things…
I come into the presence of still water…
I rest in the grace of the world and know that I am free
 -Wendell Berry

What Is Love

Love isn't the carat size of your ring.

It's driving across town to sleep on a hospital couch when your comfy bed was three minutes from work.

Love isn't perfect; it isn't what you thought it would be. But in the best moments, it's better than you imagined it could be.

Love is knowing when to call a therapist. It's making them go even if they don't want to, but you know they need it.

Love isn't pointing out each mistake. It's knowing when to speak up and when to remain silent. It's failing at this concept but trying anyway.

Love is dealing with the weird ass things they do around the house that you know won't change and accepting them regardless, and possibly because of, these quirks. Or at least not killing them for it.

Love isn't some perfectly choreographed dance, everyone moving to the tune of the same music. Sometimes it's a messy house. A messy life. Late bills. But nobody jumps ship. It's everyone shoveling together when you're taking on water. It's rowing in the same direction, a team.

Love is getting her very complicated coffee order right.

Love isn't a competition.

Love is a smile shared over a toddler face-down on the ground while screaming in Target. A toddler who just so happens to belong to the two of you. It's Rock, Paper, Scissors to decide who has to pick up said toddler and which one of you gets to go to Starbucks instead.

Love isn't endless pain. There will be pain. Of many kinds. I used to think love shouldn't hurt. But sometimes it does, for various reasons. A lot.

Love is letting them listen to their music on road trips even if it sucks (unless you're driving – then you're the deejay, no exceptions – this is a spiritual law called "dealers' choice").

Love isn't a sieve. There are no gaps left for anyone to slide through. Even on the worst days. Especially on the worst days. It's tightening any loose bolts to make sure a sympathetic outside ear doesn't turn to more.

Love is making a decision.

One single decision.

To never change your mind.

To always make your way back to that person.

Even when it's dark.

And even when you're lost.

To find your way home again.

Love is a home you always return to and are safe inside of

Vows

Your clit stimulator
Sits between us
A testament to
The empty hallways
Of a stretched out
Marriage

Sleeping in the other room
Hungry for the feel of another body
Underneath mine
Always mean and starving
She'd be lean and marveling

Loving you is like drowning
Unseen

I used to think the death of a union
Of two
Was a thousand little cuts

But it isn't

It's blood that can't flow
Through blocked arteries
Numerous injuries
Left to rot

All the words dammed up inside of both us
Where sex used to be
A connection
A flame
Sealing us together
Searing our bodies
Pressed as one

I should've known we'd land here
When you had no vows

Now continents apart

In the same room

Our bed
A wasteland
A desert

The place where love lays
Dying
Gasping for air

What Is Marriage

It's someone telling you to close the cabinets when they're only open because you're cooking for them. Then closing them anyway, knowing you're about to need to reopen.

It's unpacking your childhood and previous relationships and throwing out ideas that don't work.

It's pulling someone else's hair out of the drain. Every. Time. You. Shower. And keeping quiet about it, because they matter. OK, keeping quiet about it 70% of the time. Fine, 40%. Let's just forget this one. 0%.

It's knowing the grass is greenest where it is watered.

It's staying when you don't want to because you will want to again later.

It's wondering what the hell they spent all that money on, only to realize it was your Christmas gift.

It's growth. Together in the same direction, not apart.

It's failure.

It's working 16-hour days end to end to pay for medical treatments that aren't even yours.

It's choosing their child. A child you didn't have. Loving and raising them.

It's why they say "Congratulations," at 50th year wedding celebrations; and "Happy Anniversary," for 1st years. Because 50 years with one human is an accomplishment.

It's packing their lunch every day, so you know they don't sneak to Whataburger and feel tired.

It's not deleting your messages. It's also not being asked what they say.

It's not finding someone perfect. And then me being perfect. And it all being rainbows and unicorns with glitter rain falling down around us. It's more like, "WHAT DO YOU MEAN, THERE'S AN OVERDRAFT FEE?"

It's dealing with the grouchy ass morning attitude of a fire breathing dragon.

It's I'm sorry I'm being an asshole today.

It's letting them pick the music. Even if they want to sing The Little Mermaid soundtrack and you prefer Tupac.

It's telling them their life is in danger if you find one more inside-out sock. It's laughing when you find six more tucked under the bed a few days later and texting them a chainsaw meme with corresponding evidence.

It's hugging someone you want to shake half the time.

It's being stranded in an airport when they couldn't breathe on a plane. Then driving them 1,800 miles home when a straight shot flight would've been 3 hours. It's having the best road trip of your lives anyway.

It's cheering the loudest when they win.

It's catching them when they lose.

It's dragging a screaming child out of a theme park in solidarity then binge eating ice cream together while saying, "Thank God," the moment said child falls asleep in the car.

It's standing back to back, not toe to toe.

It's not letting anyone slide into your inbox.

It's keeping your personal business to yourself. It's solidifying a union by not exposing cracks when they appear so that something else can come in.

It's being so tired once you get on a week-long cruise that they forget the vacation sex.

It's them thoughtfully leaving a hot towel on the sink while you're in the shower. Some days, it's running around the house wet and naked and screaming, "WHERE ARE ALL THE TOWELS!? Do you EAT them?" at that same person.

It's always coming home.

It's being knee deep in the struggle and still choosing that person every day.

It's service.

It's seeing their worst and saying, "You're worth this. We're worth this." It's letting them see your worst too.

It's picking your battles. *Motherfucker* is it ever picking your battles.

It's emotional fidelity.

It's going to bed angry sometimes. But waking up to try again.

It's, "good morning beautiful," when they look like a swamp monster.

It's sending texts like, "Don't touch the clothes outside the door. They have shit on them. The cat got put into the bathtub by the baby and freaked out and shit. I set the clothes outside because I'm late for work." And receiving a response like, "What? Jesus. OK. I love you."

It's teamwork.

It's a wild ride you wouldn't trade.

And it's also all that stuff you see in movies. Sometimes. Except the "crying in the rain" part.

That's usually more like yelling.

Come Back

I didn't come here
To sleep alone
I brought all my things
In these weathered hands
And I laid them at your feet
But it's your tone
And that look in your eyes, girl
That makes me wanna go home
Home
Just take me home if you don't want me
Take me out into the sea
If you really don't wanna do this
Just please stop screaming at me
I know my brain doesn't work
Quite as fast now
As it used to do
I know my legs won't walk
Quite as well now
Like they did when I first ran to you
Ah, but I still need you babe
Yes, I do
You know it's true
I'd cross a thousand oceans
Just to get to you
To hold your hand
To have another night
In the sand
Under the stars
Looking at them with you
I'd walk through fire
To get to someone who hurt you
I'd work 100 hours a week
If you asked me to
If you asked me to
But I just can't stop making you cry
I can't stop
I'm sorry
Just come back to bed now, bed now
Lay down your pretty head now, head now

You weren't made to sleep alone
I know you said you'd rather
But I was thinking
You could make me into your home
And bury your face into my shoulder
Because I am nice and warm
Come back to bed
Come back to me
Come back

Five Tools to Always Take with You

1. Everyone is doing their best even at their worst. They can only do, moment to moment, what they are capable of doing. We cannot possess skills which we do not yet have nor can we behave in a manner that is more advanced than what we have learned thus far.

2. The key is to be grateful for where you are and what's occurring while simultaneously expecting and being ready for more. When what you're wanting happens more quickly than intended in the grand design, it will not be as honed as your experience can allow it to be.

3. The more you row when you are going backwards, the further you go along an unintended route. If you struggle around too much, you inadvertently head off on a journey you didn't mean to take. Acceleration and directionality are key.

4. Shift all expectations.

5. You must reach for and pull back from in equal amounts to create space for your new design.

Boundaries + Cleansing

Survivors of childhood trauma often see the world in absolutes. Life may appear to us as a place where there are only two choices: Warrior or Victim. This can be problematic in that we then spend most of our lives angry or sad instead of seeking balance.

Experts charge. "Normal" requires a distinct absence of courage. Don't let boring ass people judge your wild cool self. Or do, it doesn't matter what they do, but don't inhale it. Don't consume it. Let their judgment bead off of you like water from a waxed car. The responses of other people to you are none of your business unless you are directly harming them. Play that track on repeat: Whether people like or dislike you, approve or disapprove, love or hate – your clothes, your parenting, your style, your body shape, your sexual orientation; is none of your concern.

Some of the people I work with apologize incessantly for even breathing. The other end of the spectrum contains those who are so mad they can see nothing positively. These are two sides of the same coin.

No is a magic spell you can cast. No is a complete sentence. Anyone who cannot respect your "no" is not really of and for you. That's that. Simple. Your "no" should never engender anger in another person.

Boundaries work like this, and it's not as complicated as it seems. If you have children or a best friend or just anyone you dearly value and want to protect; then scan as you go through each and every person, place, and thing in your life and ask, "Would I want this for them?"

Those of you who can't see your own intrinsic self-worth, place someone you do love in the position of yourself and ask if you'd tolerate the behavior, because rest assured? What you allow is what will continue happening. We teach people how to treat us.

Many of y'all think you have dark entities in your homes or around you, and for a few of you something similar to a negative vibrational web or dark residue may be there, sure. But it's easy to get rid of it if you so choose. And it sounds similar to the human boundaries we just discussed. Let's take a closer look.

All sorts of magical people are out there. Healers. Intuitives. Mediums. Psychics. Sensitives. People who ignite the gifts of others. So. Many. Things. Some use it for good. Some for the absence of good. Some block it all together. Some have no idea what they are doing. Some are plugged into the wrong source, the wrong power outlet. When you are in spiritual alignment, nothing outside of you can harm you. Nothing. *Nothing*.

Just like I can't be an Olympic level swimmer, some of us can't use these gifts because we haven't been uniquely prepared to do so by this life and previous ones. Circling back to the athlete analogy – the equivalent of a lifetime of practice and training plus a unique configuration of muscles and ability to access "the zone" is what differentiates a good competitor from a once in a lifetime talent.

Mine came about by fire – a very difficult early life which resulted in a rather extreme cultivation of these abilities that I then attempted to block for decades. This is a good thing. I was lit to burn, and I have used that flame to light others; and that fire to protect my son. The previous iterations of my being during this current human life would not have used my abilities in their intended way.

And what of those who aren't using their power for Good, as it were? Light workers weaving Dark?

How do we spot them, and once we do, break free?

Narcissists + Sociopaths:
How to Protect Yourself

Well, what about them?

These words really get thrown around an awful lot. Narcissist. Sociopath. All of us (yep, all, sorry – human condition) show transient *traits* of both of these. Just as you may exhibit traits of ADD or OCD and casually toss out these terms; that does not make you diagnosable. Let's get down to brass tacks with actual definitions so we can grasp who and what you may be dealing with. For diagnosable criterion, check out the American Psychological Association's Diagnostic and Statistical Manual, 5. Here's the short of it, more or less:

narcissistic personality disorder (narcissist)
A personality disorder with the following characteristics: (a) a long-standing pattern of grandiose self-importance and an exaggerated sense of talent and achievements; (b) fantasies of unlimited sex, power, brilliance, or beauty; (c) an exhibitionistic need for attention and admiration; (d) either cool indifference or feelings of rage, humiliation, or emptiness as a response to criticism, indifference, or defeat; and (e) various interpersonal disturbances, such as feeling entitled to special favors, taking advantage of others, and inability to empathize with the feelings of others

antisocial personality disorder (sociopath/psychopath)
The presence of a chronic and pervasive disposition to disregard and violate the rights of others. Manifestations include repeated violations of the law, exploitation of others, deceitfulness, impulsivity, aggressiveness, reckless disregard for the safety of self and others, and irresponsibility, accompanied by lack of guilt, remorse, and empathy. The disorder has been known by various names, including dyssocial personality, psychopathic personality, and sociopathic personality. It is among the most heavily researched of the personality disorders and the most difficult to treat.

There are the actual definitions. Here's the deal – there are Covert Narcissists too (research this if you haven't heard of it). That is a whole different animal. This is the passive aggressive, self-aggrandizing silent hero type who will still ruin your life if you let them in. They never apologize. They aren't grand-standing, in fact they are usually humble servants of humanity. The problem is, they're even more insidious than the grandiose narcissist, and you won't realize what danger you're in until their teeth are sunk in deep. But I digress. Back to the textbook narcissists; more on covert narcissism/passive aggressive stuff another time.

These are just two of the Cluster B Personality Disorders. There are two others; and others in different clusters. You might be dealing with one of the above, or perhaps even someone who has Borderline Personality Disorder (research this one too if you are unfamiliar) or a combo of these and other conditions. The main thing is, something led you to keep reading rather than skip this portion, which means you believe that there is/was a narcissist or sociopath in your life, or the life of someone you care about, and want to know how to protect yourself. Let's get to that.

They say love shouldn't hurt. That's never been my experience, but I do believe it.

1. *Love Bombing/Devaluing*

I don't feel the need to write much about this. It's all over the internet. And if you're in this chapter, you've probably already experienced it. In regard to romantic relationships, it feels like the most incredible thing that ever happened. Finally. Your soulmate. The sex is the most incredible part! They just "get" you, like no one else ever has. They'll often say things like, "I've never felt this way before," and, "Nobody before you meant anything to me compared to how I feel about you." Does this mean if your partner has said these things, they're a narcissist? No, of course not. Remember, it's the picture as a whole we're looking at – not specific traits or phrases. But a true NPD/BPD will be the kindest, most romantic, grand gesture partner you have *ever* had – in the beginning. It will feel like the love you waited your whole life for, and you will feel special and beautiful and perfect. Understand this, if you hear nothing else: *They are mirroring you*. They are mimicking healthy human emotions, gathering intel on who you are and your deepest desires, then *mirroring back to you* what they think you want. What does this mean? It means that none of this is real to them, it's a game. And getting you to fall crazy head over heels in love with them is step one; they're winning. And it feels incredible to unsuspecting you. Until. Until they start breaking agreements. Until you find it impossible to communicate, everything turned against you. Until you see all the tiny white lies and wonder what else is hidden. Until you realize that if you ever try to express yourself, that is met with anger or stonewalling, which is worse in many ways.

Until. Until the devaluing begins. Now, these folks aren't stupid. They know if they were a constant asshole, anyone would leave. This begins a cycle – one that can make it feel like you are drowning, stuck inside a whirlpool, and can't quite keep your head above water. It can be subtle, like, "Babe, your jeans are fitting a little tight. Hmm. I wonder if they shrunk or maybe we've been eating out too much. Haha!" Or it can sound like, "Nobody will ever love you like I do. Nobody can take care of you like I can. Who would put up with this shit? I could have had anyone I wanted, and I stay with your stupid ass, you should be grateful!"

Again, all relationships have their ups and downs. Part of love is that we hurt one another's feelings sometimes, unfortunately. We all do and say things we regret. The difference is, you know you are dealing with a NPD/ASPD person when it is constantly *you* who is the one crying, hurt, broken; while they stare impassively on, unmoved by your emotion. When it's *your* sense of identity that's compromised. When it's *you* always making the sacrifices and finding yourself isolated. When it's *you* left doubting your own sanity, shaking your head. When it's *your life* that has dramatically changed, and nothing about them or their circumstance is different. When it's always them who just want to move on and they say things like, "That's in the past. Why do you always bring that up? How can we go forward if you always throw it in my face?"

Here's the rub: They have to stop doing it, show remorse, and actually change for it to stop haunting you, and *even then*, you have a right to discuss abuse you've faced at any time, in any manner, from any platform. Ya dig? This only applies if they are still in your life. You can heal from anything once you are rid your space of the abuser.

HOW TO PROTECT:
You absolutely must, and I mean *must*, comprehend something if you are going to cut the ties that bind to a narcissist. *None of that was real to them*. It was just a game. The person before you meant

nothing to them. You mean nothing to them. The next person will mean nothing to them. I understand, this is a *very* difficult pill to swallow. Know this: It is not indicative of your intrinsic meaning and worth, but more a measure of their capability to value other humans. You've got to get it through your head, like yesterday, that *this person is not capable of love* and does not love you.

And if they spent a lot of time trying to make you hate their "mean, vindictive ex?" Ohhhhhh honey, red flag. One of the first things a NPD/ASPD person will often do is convince you how mistreated they've been; by everyone, everywhere. Does this not mean that normal people don't have shitty exes and life experiences? Absolutely, of course they do. But if your new love interest is obsessed with talking and thinking about their previous partner(s)? Run. Either they aren't over it or they are a narcissist. Period. Either way – they can't love you right now. Look up the cycle of abuse, then take an exit. And if it's your family? If every time you're around them, they're talking shit about family members who aren't present or their own friends or making mean jokes towards one another? *Bet* they do the same and worse to you the moment your back is turned. Bet. Do you really need that in your life? What doesn't grow you has to go. Period.

2. Lack of Empathy

You might see this manifest in a thousand different ways, but it is a huge red flag. Maybe they laugh when you fall and hurt yourself. Maybe they don't seem to feel anything when others are in tears during a moving situation – like a blank face at a funeral of a loved one. Perhaps they are the relationship in your life where they have never, ever apologized. Ever. I have heard this over and over from people I work with. And it sounds like this, "She literally has never said she's sorry! It's like she feels remorse for nothing! She can slap me in the face and the next morning make breakfast and act like nothing happened. What the hell is her problem?" It's a lack of empathy. They are literally incapable of understanding the emotional process of healthier people. They feel nothing during moving situations. They are empty inside. They are unable to process, especially sociopaths, the effects their actions have not only on their victims, but on anyone. They literally do not see, nor does it register emotionally, the damage they cause, no matter how severe. And if they do see it? They revel in it – because it was the intended effect.

HOW TO PROTECT:
Educate yourself. Read everything you can get your hands on. Listen to audio books. Whatever you need to do, do it, but get educated on who and what these people are so you understand they truly lack empathy. Without empathy, nothing will change, and will in fact only continue getting worse. You will be stuck daydreaming about the person you met, who was perfect and amazing, and get into a cycle of, "If I just..." they'll love me again like that and everything will be perfect. Listen to me: They will never treat you the way they did in the beginning, consistently, again. That is over. And it was not real. And if it's your family? And they perpetrated or looked the other way as you suffered abuse? Nope.

3. Isolation

This one is simple and requires very little explanation. They will try to isolate you from anyone who might spot their behavior. Do friendships, family relationships, and other types of connections change when we get into a serious relationship? Sure. You might stop talking to that buddy who always seemed to have a crush on you or quit hanging with your always a little too drunk friend who can't accept you as you grow. But if you see that the person you are with is slowly eradicating *everyone* you ever knew and cared about? Nope. Nope. Nope. They are hoping to get you into a proverbial echo chamber – where the only voice you hear is theirs. Your hobbies, groups, school, and even job may disappear. Hell, your home, car, bank account – nothing is off limits. You might still have resources, but they will subtly and slowly take control. Durable Power of Attorney? Check. Adoption of your children if they are a step-parent? Check. NO.

I wish it was direct, so you could spot it easily. But it isn't always! Sometimes it might be like, "Your friend Tina really seems bad for you. All you guys ever do is binge on junk food and Netflix. Don't you think it's time you started living your highest and best life and found some more mature friends? Maybe we could make couples friends and do art galleries and such." Then you slowly stop talking to Tina without even realizing it, because you have now been programmed to seek your abuser's approval at any cost. The couples friends never materialize. And bam. Years later, when you are tear soaked and on the ground, you call Tina, begging forgivingness for your absence and desperate for some McD's and Orange is the New Black because you've kicked out your narcissist for good. It's very important to a NPD/ASPD to get and keep you isolated from the people, places, and things that used to matter so that nobody can tell you this relationship isn't healthy; and so you have nowhere to turn once you are ready to leave. Conversely, if they're *very* smart, they may go the opposite direction – and become so enmeshed in your life and entangled with your activities and friends that you have nothing left that is only yours. Even *worse*, covert narcissists are expert at isolating *themselves* and in their silence making it seem as though you, in fact, are the isolator – when you've actually been isolated yourself to be tortured at their hand. This way their sick friends and family will attack and blame you for their absence; so you neither have your own family nor any support from them and theirs.

HOW TO PROTECT:
A *healthy* relationship between *healthy* people will sometimes cause some friends and family members to fall away (ie you don't hang out with old dancing buddies as much once you have a baby, or your therapist recommends you stop speaking to that family member who never accepted you as gay until they change). What we are talking about here is total one-sided isolation and identity theft, essentially. The NPD/ASPD tries to take you over completely. They may even try to become you or become more like you, in appearance, habits, hobbies, and more.

Or they'll expect you to become like them. Explain to other people in your life that they matter to you and tell them you are going through some things, but would they please stay in touch? Try to remain as connected as possible. And as we have already, and will continue to discuss, get the hell out of there as soon as possible. And if they are a best friend, family member, or someone else? It doesn't matter. Toxic is toxic. Nobody has a right to be in your life if they can't treat you right or try to control and isolate you! Your time, body, and privacy are inalienable rights. You can revoke or invoke consent to any of those at any time. Insidious invasions of your boundaries can even be as innocuous as, "Hey, what's your new address so I can send you a gift?!" (Gives mailing address.) "Oh, no… I was going to send flowers! What's your home address?" This way you look like the asshole if you say no. No never makes you an asshole. And is a complete sentence.

4. Mind Games (gaslighting + triangulation)

gaslight: to manipulate someone to the extent that they question their own sanity

One of the number one things you'll hear from a NPD/ASPD is how wrong and terrible all their previous partners, bosses, and family members have been. *Everyone* has just done them wrong (classic martyr), *or* the opposite, they'll maintain inappropriately close relationships with everyone they've ever been with to satiate the constant need for attention. It is a red flag if the person you're dating thinks everyone they've ever been with is the problem, as discussed, but it's also a red flag if they are best friends with and keep in constant contact with all their exes. Another one? If they can't seem to get along with anyone, anywhere for a long period of time and have no long-term relationships with friends or family to speak of – where did all the people go? This isn't the same as someone who naturally keeps to themselves. That is healthy, and normal, for many. This is someone who will provoke you to reacting, then point at that for all to see; never disclosing their abuse caused your self-defense.

The classic example of gaslighting is the dude in that old movie loosening all the lightbulbs or turning down the gas or whatever to make his wife think they aren't working. Then he makes them work right as she asks about how dim the lights were to make her seem crazy. Or something like that.

Has this ever happened to you? It sounds like this:
"You're just overly emotional. I wouldn't have to get so mad if you weren't so sensitive and didn't make such a big deal out of nothing all the time."
"You just told me it's my fault that you get so mad!"
"No, I didn't. You're crazy. I said you just experience your emotions really strongly. That can even be a good thing. You're passionate."
"That isn't what you said."
"Honey, are you OK? That's exactly what I said. Maybe we should talk about anti-depressants since you always think everyone is against you."

(You: Internal dialogue: "Is that what he said? Am I losing my mind? Did he not just blame his abusive behavior on me then act like he didn't even say that? Maybe I AM the problem.")

triangulate: to manipulate someone by not communicating directly with them, instead communicating via a third party to relay information (hence the triangle); can also refer to splitting; which is manipulating a relationship between two people by controlling their communication

This one might look like this:
Narcissist brother-in-law to you: My mom says that you should feed the baby breastmilk, not formula.
You to husband: Your brother told me your mom said I shouldn't be using formula...?
Husband to his mom: Why would you try to tell my wife how to feed our son? It hurt her feelings and she's really worked up about it.
Mother-in-law: What? I just said if she was having trouble latching or with anything that I am available and want to help.
Mother-in-law to Narcissist son who started this mess: Why did you tell them I said they were feeding the baby wrong?
Him: I never said that! I told them you offered help. I think she's (you) crazy.

Do you see how this goes? The net effect of the triangulation is to get everyone to turn on the victim of the narcissist. One person like this can wreck an entire family and all the relational ties therein, and all the while nobody really understands how it's happening. A huge red flag on this one is if you have an ex who contacts your previous exes or friends – trying to establish friendly relationships with them, or to get them to see their side of things. *That is not normal behavior*, and indicates you may have been dealing with a NPD/ASPD person. Example: M's narcissist ex even went so far as to invite *multiple* other exes of M to their previous home after M filed for divorce, then sent pictures of them all together. Creeped out yet? Yeah. Me too. They're expert at getting someone else to do their dirty work so they never have to take responsibility for anything. Gross. Move along.

HOW TO PROTECT:
To stop the gaslighting, use direct phrases and language. *Do not participate in any mind games* whatsoever. Monsters do not go where they are not fed. Look for patterns. If there's a pattern where

your partner gets mad, withdrawn, disappears, hangs up, turns their phone off so you will chase them, or any other related behaviors; refuse to participate. If there's a pattern where they flirt with or cheat on you with other people then deny and hide evidence, but you know what's happening, refuse to participate. You can be direct and call them out on their behavior, but they will usually just laugh or call you crazy.

To stop the triangulation, do not participate in any third-party conversations, go no contact or grey rock if you can, and seek advice from a therapist about this.

A NPD/ASPD person will often do something like this:
To you: I don't know, Jennifer said it seems like you have a drinking problem and is worried about the kids, but don't tell her I said that!
You: What?! How could she? (Stops speaking to Jennifer)
To Jennifer: I don't know what's wrong with her. She said she was going to stop talking to you because she thinks you are judgmental, but don't tell her I said that! (Jennifer stops speaking to you)
And boom. Friendship done. You're mad at your friend. Your friend is mad at you. And the narcissist wins; and truly derives pleasure from this manipulative process. You find yourself isolated, with no idea what people are saying, whether it's true, or why. The way to *stop* this is to talk to your friends directly. A true friend will *always* tell you if someone contacts you about them and what was said. And more importantly than that? Ask them what their response was, to determine if they are actually a true friend. And if they're not? Poof. Be gone. Just like magic.

But again, the best way to protect yourself from these people is to *get them out of your life*. A truly disordered person will come by unannounced, come in uninvited, even plan entire trips and so forth that you did not agree to so that you feel guilty enough to see them once you have set boundaries. They will contact all your friends and people connected to you; such that you end up losing all of them too. When exiting completely isn't possible, like if you're stuck co-parenting due to a court order after a divorce, keep everything very clinical and simply emotionally detach. Divorce yourself emotionally from them, their feelings, their reactions, and definitely their provocations. Remember, they know where your buttons are to push them. Move your buttons. Be as neutral and limited in your responses and only answer when literally legally necessary. Over time, gaslighting and triangulation can have you in such a mental fog that you lose your own identity.

5. Total Control

This can come in the form of financial, sexual, educational, custodial, physical, emotional, spiritual, and literally any other way imaginable. Remember, this is a game to them. It's like cat and mouse. Or "breaking" a wild horse. It may not always be overt or direct. You might look around and realize five years have gone by and you no longer speak to friends and family anymore, no longer have your own vehicle, have stopped working or going to school, do not get to make decisions regarding your children, quit going to church, whatever.

A true narcissist or sociopath wants total control – but it's no fun for them if they demand it and you submit. The enjoyment and fulfillment they get is usually through getting you to give up that control voluntarily, gradually; in a process by which your psyche is finally so worn down that your tank remains empty, and you don't have the energy to maintain control of anything, so it is ceded to them. Then they can add insult to injury and say, "I never told you to do that!" They may withhold sex as a form of emotional punishment. They may ask you to sign over your checks to them so they can "handle" all the finances. They may talk you into taking a break from school, because after all, it's just so stressful for you. Then you turn around and suddenly your entire life is different. Many people meet, work through past damage and baggage, and totally change their lives *together*. This is different than when a narcissist or sociopath gets their claws into you. It will only be *your* life that has changed. *Your* control that has slipped away. Not theirs. You'll find them holding all the reins and not even be sure how it happened.

HOW TO PROTECT:
That's all well and good, but what the hell do I do now, you might be asking? If it is or was a romantic relationship, you slowly build back up your support network, whatever that looks like. It could be church, family, school, friends, a therapist. Immediately.

A. If you are still in the relationship, you begin documenting abuse of any kind. Record them, video them, save evidence of infidelity, keep texts and social media posts – whatever. Be as surreptitious as possible about this and do it only for your own protection. A true

NPD/ASPD person will lose their ever-loving mind if they find out you are trying to get help, to break away, or doing anything that may expose them. Make a safety plan. Keep a "go bag" or even a box somewhere else – copies of everything like birth certificates, social security cards, bank information, titles, etc. Make sure you have a spare set of keys to a vehicle and some cash hidden in case things escalate. And get immediate help of any variety to find out why you haven't left yet if you feel unable. GET. OUT.

B. If it's a past relationship and they are still trying to have control via manipulation, take them back to court and modify custody/visitation. Enforce it with police. Have no other contact than is absolutely necessary. If you are in the middle of any type of divorce or custody battle, keep track of every communication by any means necessary. Tell your attorney the truth. Get professional counseling for your whole family immediately. If you can't afford a lawyer, you can present your own case if necessary. It's hard, but not impossible.

C. Friend/Work situations: This one is easy: Just stay *the fuck* away from them. Period. Full stop. Once you realize a friend is toxic or doesn't have your best interest at heart, just let them go. You don't owe an explanation. If it's a very important relationship, you can try talking it out, but if they are truly NPD/ASPD, they will not change no matter how sincere they seem or what they promise to do. If you have a boss or supervisor who is one of these and like your job, that's a totally different ballgame. Again, documentation is key. Keep track of everything they say and do to you that isn't right, dates and times, and so forth. Report up the chain of command if you must; but know that often if there are sick people within an organization, the whole damn place might be sick, and you might just run into another crazy. If you feel you are retaliated against or treated unfairly, report this to the appropriate organizations in government and elsewhere. But be prepared for the shitstorm that will come in the workplace if you do.

6. *Magnetism to Empaths/Vulnerability*

You might find yourself going, "Yes, yes, and yes," as you read this. And your next thought might be, "Does this mean I am weak?" NO. They are *only* attracted to a challenge, so they often pick the strongest, brightest, and most sensitive to energy people they can find. It's more fun for them to break down a victim who is powerful than one who is already weakened. *There is nothing wrong with you.* You did nothing to deserve this. I often work with clients who will come in and say things like, "I am abusive. I shoved my wife to the ground." After getting more of the story, it sounds like this, "My wife was trying to stab me with a broken wine bottle, and I tried to push her away, then she hit the ground. I was reacting to abuse and trying to protect myself." People who are abused by NPD/ASPD persons will often become convinced they are the abuser, because they are usually highly empathic and sensitive. When you lash out in anger or self-defense, you decide you are, in fact, the problem. This is all part of the narcissist's rodeo. It's exactly what they want.

Ever had someone hurt you and find that *you* are the one apologizing? Yep. You've got a narcissist or a sociopath on your hands, for sure. They will home in on your deepest desires and vulnerable spots and capitalize on those. They will use the secrets you've told them against you, whether that is with other people or during arguments. And as far as vulnerabilities go, it looks like this: Single mom? They'll step in as the dream second parent you always wished for, until they're not. Be cautious with everyone new you meet if you have a pattern of letting NPD/ASPD people into your life. Take things slowly. Slooowlyyy. Set *firm* boundaries. Those who are safe within your circle will respect them and respect you for openly and honestly setting them.

HOW TO PROTECT:
Watch for those red flags – whether it's new friends, coworkers, a romantic interest, or even a family member. Look for the warning signs and trust your gut. A lot of times people I work with will say, "I feel like I have been in the same relationship with the same person in different bodies over and over. Why do I attract assholes?" Listen up: The common denominator is *you*. Only you can stop the cycle. Get into coaching, get some help, vow to stay single awhile, figure out the pattern, then break the eff out of it. With practice, you'll be able to spot these folks from miles away and protect yourself! What you allow is what will continue. *Hear that.*

7. Violent or Extreme Reaction to No Contact

Obviously, things are going to escalate when you try to exit this relationship. They do not want to lose control. It's not about whether they lose you or not, so don't get it twisted. It's that when they are ready for their next victim, that needs to be on *their* terms, not *yours*. Their reaction to you trying to exit the relationship or going no contact will usually be extreme, and can often trigger a smear campaign, which is written about below.

HOW TO PROTECT:
Especially if it's a romantic relationship, you have to exit, the end. Most of the tips on how to do this safely were covered above. Be very careful, with everything from text messages on your phone to browser history. If you are making a plan to get safe and get away from an abuser, and they find out, it's your life that's on the line. Once you are safely away, *no contact* is a must.

8. The Smear Campaign

And now we come to my favorite part of writing this entire thing. The smear campaign. I suffered one of these that was so severe it literally almost killed me. Because I was "online famous" for various viral writings I had done, and because I was extremely involved in a huge group of people focused on addiction recovery, my abuser had access to an *infinite* resource to perpetuate this. Fake Facebook profiles were used. Government agencies contacted. My job was emailed. My family was involved. My son was stalked and harassed at school. We've covered this in some detail already.

I am not kidding when I say these people tried to ruin my life. The smear campaign is when your abuser paints *you* as the abuser or tries to get allies to "buy" their version of the story. If they can't do that, then they try to discredit you, and convince anyone who will listen that you are evil, a con, and a liar – and whatever else they can think of to make people (from their lives and yours) change their minds about you. If you have a strong public or social media presence, this will be used against you since you have a wide audience for them to access. They can even weaponize this against you – for instance hunting out people with views opposed to yours or former friends so that they have minions ready and waiting to help spread their lies. They assassinate your character because they are afraid you will reveal the truth.

For instance, in my smear campaign, things I had written were in the international press and A list celebrities had shared them. My abuser enlisted the help of friends and said horrible things on those posts, exposing me to numerous threats and even a home break in and vandalism. A NPD/ASPD ex is most dangerous right after the relationship ends, before they find their next victim. They will be hellbent on discrediting you and will often organize an entire behind the scenes campaign to do so that could literally ruin your life and cost you everything. Sound dramatic? Don't doubt it for a minute.

It happens every day. Vicious lies were spread about me everywhere – ones easy to disprove, but nobody bothered to tell me what was being said. I didn't know who to trust so I kept to myself and stopped talking to everyone I cared about. It was one of the worst periods of my life; but it led to one of the very best once I overcame it. They will reframe everything they ever said and did and try to paint you as the abuser. Don't be hurt by the people who choose to believe them. Be thankful the Universe moved those fake friends and family right on out of your life. The narcissist will weave their web of lies sewn by seeds of the truth; so that even some of those closest to you may turn on you because it "seems" like there is enough truth to their words that the rest might be true as well. This is the intended effect. They'll cleverly manipulate those who love you into thinking you have said or hold bad opinions of them so they gain credibility when your "own" people turn on you.

HOW TO PROTECT:
Again, no contact. If you have to or it fits your situation, file a restraining or protective order or even a civil lawsuit for defamation. You absolutely cannot respond to *any* of these people, because that's what they want. Attention. Positive. Negative. Doesn't matter. That's what your abuser wants. They want attention, to know they still effect you, and to have hooks in you, via any means necessary. Document. Document. Document. Do not be surprised if they contact a new person you're dating, everyone you ever knew prior to your relationship with them, or try in various ways to wreck your life.

But protect yourself. No contact. That's it. Don't let someone take up precious and priceless space among your thought life. Don't let what they are doing or saying matter. The truth always comes out, and the cream always rises to the top. And people who do bad things always get what's coming to them. Period. It's not your job to mete out that justice. It's not your job to "prove them wrong." It's your job to live your best life and move on. Instead of fighting my abuser and the squad of flying monkeys, I used that year to obtain another graduate degree, and completed a Master's in Education. Devote yourself to what's best for *you* and utilize any legal protections you can. Don't spend all day every day talking, thinking, or worrying about them and what they are saying and doing. Worrying won't change a damn thing.

PS If you've ever wondered whether *you* are a narcissist? A sociopath? You probably aren't. Sick people don't realize or care if they are crazy and they sure as hell wouldn't admit it. They don't have the conscience to recognize they're a problem, remember? Crazy making behaviors that cause us to react in ways we normally would not and reactive patterns we pick up from insane, toxic, abusive relationships *do not* make you an abuser. What you *are* responsible for is whether you choose to break the cycle.

Are you ready?

For freedom? For peace? For safety?

All are within reach.

Haters

Rest assured, as your life begins to evolve and shift, you gain momentum in the direction of your goals, and things change beautifully in your favor, there will be those who are none too pleased. *Pay attention* to who isn't clapping when you win.

What of haters, then?

Every single human being is imbued with light, the power of creation, and has the same ability you have to connect to all that Is, Ever Was, and ever Will Be. Let me say that again. Every. Human. Being.

Some of us just take a very long, painful, unnecessarily circuitous route to get there. Some of us will not arrive there in this lifetime, or ever, by choice. Some of us are buried too deeply within ourselves to even see the light breaking through the hard-packed dirt we're under.

If you have been the target of gossip, bullying, lies, and so forth; it can feel like the whole world is against you. But one person who is in touch with their own spirit and the power of the universe cannot be struck down by a thousand who are not. And no persons who are in contact with these things can be a hater.

It isn't you they're hating. It's themselves.

I suggest that you must be very shiny, beautiful, talented, and incredibly important – or they wouldn't talk about you or try to hurt you.

I have a radical proposal for how to address any smear campaign you're the target of.

Do not struggle. Do not fight back. Do not argue nor attempt to set the record straight. Do not give it a single moment of your time – not reliving it by discussing it, not thinking about it obsessively, not acknowledging it all.

Appreciate the God inside those people, and there is God in every single one of them; even if the spark is very difficult to see, extremely dim, or buried very deeply.

Be grateful for every person who has ever been unkind to you or made things harder.

What?

Yes. I mean that. Be thankful they exist. Then build a bridge, get over it, and decide to move on.

Sound harsh? It isn't. Your attention and focus on them and what they say can only bring about more of the same negativity. Focus on every single person who loves you, appreciates you, and says wonderful things about you and your spirit. Trust your intuition.

Why is the human condition to focus on one complaint in the face of 100 compliments?

What differentiates a professional athlete from the rest of us? An Oscar winning actor? A brilliant award-winning inventor? A famous composer? The painter who has work hanging for $70,000 versus a starving artist?

Focus. Intention. Being in the zone. A perfect combination of traits – both mental and physical – which culminate in extraordinary talent. This can be seen in certain songs, that bring you to tears, versus records which never make it to a producer. All things bright and beautiful, strong and incredible, are created on the other side of the veil. And never, ever, has a famed painter, incredibly impactful writer, or dynamic speaker not experienced condemnation, character assassination, and widespread hatred as well as love.

It's a requirement of the universe, for balance, that as much love as you receive, so too will obstacles in the form of human ire be placed in front of you. Your experience is 100% determined by which you focus on. It's like if you were in a mansion, surrounded by a buffet of delicious food, watching the sea crash against its shores, with a beautiful companion and happy family surrounding you, yet complained of the rain. Focusing on "haters," if you will, will bring more attention from them and others like them. The rain on the windows of your castle can't change its contents unless you throw open all the doors and windows and let it into your mind and reality. Then you have a flood, and it's hard to dry once everything is drenched, permeated. Keep yourself on high ground so it cannot affect you. If you do not think about what "they" are saying and doing and so forth, then it literally doesn't exist.

This would then stand to reason that human beings who are consumed with inflicting pain on others are themselves in incredible pain. What they "do" to you or "say" about you can only make you stronger.

I'm not suggesting you remain in unhealthy situations, but I am recommending that you turn all of your attention off of what anyone thinks or says about you – positive or negative – completely. Similarly, rather than focusing on becoming happy, aim for a middle ground of peace.

I'm also suggesting that if you are burdened by guilt or shame if your own behavior has been less than desirable in the past, that this is a good thing. It means your conscience is present and shines forth. Be so very glad for this. Without it, you'd not have a care in the world regarding your effect on people. Those who hurt you often suffer from this. It is, however, imperative to let it all go. You cannot get onto the right frequency when you're bogged down in yesterday. Yesterday is gone forever. Does that mean we don't make things right if we've harmed or wronged other people? Of course not.

Can you arrive in a place where you feel compassion for how much misery someone must be in to talk about and lie about and attempt to destruct the life of another? Because don't we all know that when we are happy, fulfilled, and rocketing forward in love and our life's purpose – there is no time for judgment, gossip, and the like? Only unhappy people have the time and energy to do these things. Happy people are busy doing the things that make them happy. Busy surrounding themselves with other happy people. Happy people are busy creating, enjoying, laughing, and basking in how incredible life is.

Can you move yourself along the scale of anger, reactivity, and so forth towards turning your awareness to literally anything else that brings you peace? Can you use the fuel of pain their words and deeds caused to burn a fire in the direction of what you do want? Can you ponder, just for a brief moment, how horrific it must be for them to feel trapped in that existence of pettiness? Then can you totally and completely shift what you think about each and every time to anything, literally anything, that keeps you happy instead? Can you attempt to go from anger at the injustice of it to compassion? Not pity, but compassion? Your emotions determine your reality. Your thoughts create your experiences. Why give an instant of you to what is not of and for you?

Can you love them – the God part of them – and see how far things must have gone awry for them to behave in such a way? How sad it is that they cannot dream large, or worse; cannot achieve those dreams, and thus are stuck trying to get in the way of the happiness of other people?

I propose this: The more haters you have or the more vicious the hate you receive, the closer you are to knowing your true self, bringing forth your real purpose, and experiencing the extraordinary fulfillment you desire. If someone's goal is to hurt you, keeping them foremost in your mind and words and deeds is the surest way to help them achieve that end.

I submit for your consideration that they aren't hating you at all. They're hating themselves.

Don't get stuck in that undertow of negativity. Hold fast. Stay your course. No human opinion of you has significance when the creator of universes holds you in high regard. No person's judgment of you will stand in the court of all that Is, Ever Was, and Will Be. Don't you see? Can you see this? That you are loved by the highest of high, by the actual energy flow which made the oceans, every single grain of sand on their shores, by the power that built the human body and every creature walking this earth and so many other infinite realities about which you are unaware? And really, how can any human opinion stand in opposition of that love?

It can't.

How do you know when you have a problem with your home's foundation?

Well, at first, you don't.

Eventually, you'll notice cracks in the walls.

And you sure as hell notice it when a home inspector or appraiser comes in if you're ready to sell it.

What does this mean? This means that even the most beautiful, pleasing home can have a flawed foundation. This means we cannot judge others based on what they look or even sound like. Not that we should be judging, anyway.

Perhaps discernment is a better word. We have to discern who and what we'd like to cross our paths – and we learn this by progressively editing our ideal as experience teaches us – often the hard way.

Everyone is a teacher.
Listen to me.
Everyone is a teacher.
Some show us what to do. Some show us what not to do. It's that simple.

Step back, quite a ways back, like perhaps all the way into the sky or even stratosphere. From here, observe all around you. People. Places. Things. Take inventory. What seems to be working for you and what does not?

Who resonates with you? What speakers, teachers, coaches resonate deeply within your Soul? Which people can you *hear* most clearly? Find them. Follow them around as long as they'll let you. Learn everything they can give. Every single thought matters – have you heard that part yet? The way it applies here is that each thought given to those not of and for you is detrimental. You might as well let them punch you in the face every instant they occupy your mind. It would be less detrimental, actually.

Your frequency is literally all that matters. Your thoughts lead to your emotions which lead to your vibration which is what calls about *all* that comes into your path – that to which you are attuned.

You can drive 500 miles on the wrong road and still not get where you're going. Conversely, sometimes where you want to be is a short walk as long as you're on the right path. Are you going 'round and 'round in circles wondering why you aren't getting what you want? Why everyone who crosses your path seems to be difficult AF? Why everything is so freaking hard and your wheels are constantly spinning, yet it feels like you're getting nowhere?

Maybe it's time to take an exit.

PS No one will make you famous as quickly as a hater. Keep that in mind. They're really your biggest fans. Why else would they devote so much time and energy to you? Take it as a compliment.

How do you think my book hit #1 new release in its category over a week before it was even available?

Let your haters do the leg work.

Impenetrable

Nelson Mandela said, "May your choices reflect your hopes, not your fears."

That about sums it up.

Peeling the layers of your own onion is painful. They say pain is the touchstone of spiritual growth, and I always hated the fuck out of that phrase. It reminded me of the toxicity and sickness I found in the rooms of "recovery," but that's another story for another time. You don't have to experience pain to grow, but it seems the human condition consists of not changing until the pain of staying the same becomes greater than how much it would hurt to evolve.

Out of desperation, from hunger; growth. Seeking. Searching.

Once I wrote a post, and it went viral; like *viral*, viral, and I had no idea what I was in for at all. I was just ranting per the usual on social media. I didn't intend for that to happen; for it to spread around the world like wildfire, it just did. It was viral on platforms I wasn't even on – like Twitter and Instagram. It had more likes and shares than the statuses written at the time by the President of the United States. I was wholly unprepared for the backlash I would receive. I went to sleep like always and woke up with hundreds of thousands, millions, of fans and haters.

Everyone who I had ever hurt or who secretly wished me ill came out of the woodwork to harm me. A deep and wide network was formed, and a narcissistic spear campaign almost made me kill myself. It was horrific. They used the comment section of my own activist infamy to create a platform none of them would ever be prolific enough to achieve on their own. Be careful when someone is on deck that they are there to help you sail, and not dropping anchor when you aren't looking.

Typical of those suffering from personality disorders, harmful people I had previously removed from my life used my own platform to say I was a fraud, a liar, that it never happened, that I never had cancer, that I lied about having any formal education, that I was actually 45, that I was transgender, that I never had any degrees, that I never owned a tattoo studio, just total untruths – all easy to prove false – many weren't even insulting. It was so bizarre. They called my job. They called the local, state, and federal government and tried to get benefits to me stopped while I was undergoing treatments. They attempted to have charges pressed against me as a fraud, tried to get a GoFundMe campaign taken down that a friend had started for my expenses. I was emailed death threats. They used a registered sex offender to harass me about my child. MTV tried to have me on some show.

The most ironic thing was that I had been a very widely known and respected speaker in Alcoholics Anonymous, served on Boards and Committees, created and chaired meetings, and was well known in these circles in many parts of the US and even abroad. This same network was used to convince strangers I was some sort of evil con artist, all easily disprovable, all headed up by a few individuals I'd removed from my life. Because there are so many sick people "in the rooms," it was easy for the cruel and unsuspecting to be weaponized in this manner against me.

It was a nightmare, as previously discussed.

It was the worst time of my life, easily, as I was terrified that I would somehow lose my son in the melee. Luckily, he is the best cared for and protected, loved and provided for little guy on the planet, so that didn't work. I could have pressed federal charges and they would have stuck, easily. But I took the high road. This is important.

It blew my mind how someone could assemble a crowd of minions to do their dirty work, and that strangers would jump on the bandwagon; that friends could be so easily manipulated and turned, and that such cruelty could be hurled, totally unfounded.

I sued for defamation.

Then I realized, and this is when the tide truly turned: Give them nothing. Give them no ounce of yourself. Pay them no attention. None. Them hurting me was the best gift I'd ever received.

And during that time? I earned a Masters' degree with a 4.0 after dropping my lawsuit. A lawsuit I could've easily won.

You cannot create while using both hands to fight back.

Fight by building, not by engaging in combat.

Small minds do small things. Speak on small things. Live small lives. Bored tongues wag because they have no purpose. Cockroaches scurry for corners when lights are turned on. Make of yourself a light.

Ignore people like this, and you can create something incredible by turning your energy to positive.

Then you'll have a fortress.

Hell, you'll be a fortress.

Impenetrable.

Alcoholics Anonymous

Take my will
Take my life
Is what you say in them meetings
But those people ain't there for sobriety
They're there for feedings
And when you show up for god
But get only their beatings
Where do you turn
When the man at the table
Touched you when you was a kid
How's he gon be a lawyer now
You have to hold hands to pray with
And what do you say
To the felon at the counter
When she lies in your name
While she sniffs up that powder
So you do that fifth step
Like they told you to do
But who you gonna tell
If they use it against you
Just admit your part
In your childhood rape
Says the man at the table
As he plays the god tape
You can put down the bottle
You can put down the bag
But what happens to you
When you wave the white flag
Just surrender it all
To a god you can't see
Or even the doorknob
Is what they told me
What about that thirteenth step
It sure is steep
How do you close out those meetings
With the secrets you keep
My sponsor said hey
Can I borrow some money
It's the least you can do

*It's service work honey
Oh that ten o'clock meeting
Is a zoo for lost souls
They go eat at Denny's
Then they smoke up some bowls
I don't get how
You're gonna work with those guys
Then cheat on your wife
Go home and tell lies*

When He Was a Baby

Son,

Someday, I hope you realize:

That when the world is just too heavy, I place my hand over your heart as you lay sleeping and know I can make it just one more day. That when I can't sleep it's OK because I just watch you sleep and it's like dreaming of an angel.

That when you slip your little hand in mine, pat me softly on the back, or raise your arms to be held, I breathe just a little more calmly. I see things just a little more clearly. I feel things just a little more deeply.

That I'd rather be with you, even on the days when you're very much a toddler; kicking and screaming, than any other human. You're my person. I made you. With my body, heart, and soul. Me and God. From scratch. I'll always belong to you. I'll never make you belong to me.

That the tears silently roll down my cheeks from the other side of the wall from your room as I sit defeated; but you don't see this. You don't see how worried I get. How tired I am. How hard all of this is. But I work and I do and I trudge and I go and one day we will get there. I will build you a home with my own two hands if I have to, and you will have anything you ever dream of, anytime you need.

That when you nuzzle my neck with your nose and snuggle down into the crook of my arm in the early morning as you are still asleep; I stay awake on purpose. To smell your baby smell just a little bit longer. To hold you while I still can. I am keenly aware of and looking forward to the day you walk right out of my arms. But for now, we snuggle. We cuddle. We giggle.

That I sob hysterically when I have to do surgeries and radiation. Not because I'm afraid or cancer. Not because I'm afraid of dying. But because I need to be here with you. And I don't know what to do with you or how to plan for you if I don't make it.

That I will raise you. I won't always be your friend. But I will always be your parent. You will know respect and you will have values and I can promise I'll teach you how to navigate this world so that you develop the skills you'll need for both war and peace.

That the man you will become is destined for greatness. Never allow anyone to say differently. Never back down. Temper your wealth and fame with humility and generosity. Don't deny your roots, my love. They'll keep you strongly planted, so that no wind can ever bowl you over.

That when they told me I wouldn't make it through the pregnancy while having cancer and I should "terminate," I told them no. And I meant it. And it was never a second thought. My life for yours would have been a fair trade. I'd do it again.

That even though I knew I was sick, and that we would be doing this alone, I don't regret it. I am afraid and we don't always have all the things I want for you, but we don't ever go without the things you need. That won't happen. That is my promise to you.

That there isn't a moment in the day where I'm not in awe of your humor, brilliance, musical talent, strength, handsome face, nor sweet demeanor. Never ever let this world make you hard. Do not be broken.

That when I say; I love you son, that's a covenant between us. To never place anyone before you. To never allow anyone into our lives who isn't healthy. That nothing I want will ever be more important than what's best for you, should those two things ever happen to not be the same. I swear I will always be there. Always. Unconditionally.

Now That He's a Big Boy

Son,

As you begin kindergarten,

You took a complete and total stank face to Meet the Teacher, the other day, by the way. Are you dying laughing, reading this at 25 years old? I hope so, because it was funny as hell. You might have my DNA, but that face was *all* your other mama, just saying.

For the parents, uh, there is no way to prepare for your baby to start Kindergarten. Sorry. There just isn't. What you feel will be so overwhelming you might not make it. Excitement. Relief. Fear. Happiness. Pain.

I bought all the right stuff, monogrammed what was necessary, carefully selected pieces for his wardrobe all summer, shopping sales and using coupons, so he would have the very best things at prices I could afford. I got books to read him on what happens when you start Kindergarten. I tucked him in tightly and kissed him goodnight and fled his room before he could see the tears start flowing. I signed all the forms and checked everything approximately twenty times. I made sure he had the perfect lunch in the perfect dinosaur lunch box, with a note tucked inside. I checked and ran through protocol on his big boy water bottle to make sure he knew how to use it. I fixed his hair more times than necessary and told him about 30 times how smart, strong, handsome, kind, capable, and giving he is.

Son, I know you can do this. You can do anything.

But here's the deal. For a long time, buddy, it was just us. You and me. And it was my job to take care of your every need, my job alone. You clung to my neck like a monkey. I made sure your nails were clipped perfectly and that your face was always spotless; and God help us all if your hair didn't get cut regularly. Even that I started doing myself because the barbers couldn't "do it right." I got you all the best programs and taught you everything I could and spent every waking moment taking you to every single theme park, splash pad, playground, other country, camping trip, zoo, and museum I could imagine. You've been on planes, trains, and automobiles all over the freaking world. You've even been on a cruise to Honduras, Mexico, and Belize. You have legit had the most amazing life a 5-year-old could fathom, starting with a trip to Hawaii at 2 months old. You've been 700 feet up in the air parasailing with me at 3, jet skiing all over the ocean, and even zip lining. In fact, we met your other mama on a tiny island in Honduras because you couldn't wait to get in the water, so you jumped on her head. You're a good wingman.

I have packed your five years with as much fun, adventure, and love as I could fathom – probably because I knew my time with you would be limited in this earthly realm, cut far shorter than it would be with my current terminal diagnosis. But that's another story for another day. I have tried to give you what I felt I missed out on; I started my first day of school homeless from a tent. I understand now that we all just do the best that we can with what we have and know at the time. Poverty made me stronger, gave me a lifelong practice of gratitude for even the minute; and I have no regrets. I have stroked your hair nightly as you fell asleep. I have held you as much as you ever wanted, stopping whatever I was doing to fill you up with what my heart has inside it for you.

Because I knew this day would come.

The day you would walk out of my arms and open the door to manhood.

Look, I get it. I'm being a bit dramatic. You're only five. And you just started Kindergarten. But my *entire* job as your mom (and therefore my entire existence on this planet, since being your mom is the most important thing I do) is to prepare you in age appropriate steps for complete independence. And hope that one day you walk right outta my life and FLY BABY FLY.

But.

But letting you go into that big shiny school today in your fancy new clothes with your little bag over your shoulder you still looked so impossibly small. I wanted to scoop you back into my arms, throw you in the truck, and haul ass.

I didn't want to let you go.

But I have to.

That's the true ecstasy and agony of motherhood – that the entire thing is rigged so that they are 100% dependent on you and by the time they're 18, they need to be 0% dependent on you and able to stand alone. It's not like you can't call home, come back, let me know whatever you may need. But my job is to make you ready for this world. Motherhood is a slow slope of letting go until you completely set them free. One day I will look back and realize you no longer sit on my lap. One day I will look back and realize you don't need hugs every day. One day I will look back and realize it's been a week or a year since I've heard from you (hopefully the former, but whatever). We've all seen the effects of what happens when mothers try to parent their 20-year-olds like they're still five, or don't bother parenting their five-year-olds at all; letting them mother themselves like they're 20. There's a delicate balance to strike here. And I'm still finding my footing.

Look, son, this world is hard. People can be horrific. Bad things may happen. But I was reminded the other day that some way, somehow, I still see the good in people and have an unwavering faith in humanity. I still find a way to stay positive and wake each day with a smile *no matter what.*

And that's what I want you to know. As you try to figure out how to do the lunch line. As you get in trouble countless times for leaving your seat. When some little asshole says, "I don't want to play with you." When you get in trouble for defending someone being bullied, but all they see is what you did, and so you stay in trouble. As they tell you to, "stop scribbling, and write properly."

Never color inside the lines, son. Well, maybe in Kindergarten. But not in life. If I had followed that advice, you wouldn't be reading this. Some rules really were made to be broken. Adhere to a higher moral code, and nothing else – abandon the laws of man if they do not match your core beliefs. Forge your own path. Be your own self. Don't let school or anyone or thing break your wild spirit, my little man.

Because here's the deal. You will get your heart broken. You will experience tough times. And I may not always be here. If you should somehow one day find yourself totally alone, walking this earth solo, as I have? You have more strength inside you than you can possibly imagine. And I'll always be nearby, this I promise.

I'm rethinking every parenting choice I ever made. Did he have too much red dye? Too much flour? Too much sugar? Will he be comfortable in those shorts? Can he get them off to go potty? Will they notice I forgot one thing off the list of like 100 that they wanted to be ready for today? What if they don't know that Play Doh calms him down? Or what if he forgets to ask for water and is thirsty? Will he make friends? Will other kids be kind? Will he be kind? Even now, as I write this, I am wondering what you are thinking, son. How you are feeling. Are you scared? Of course you are, and any new endeavor you ever undertake will be terrifying.

Do it anyway.

Let me tell you a little bit about who you are and where you come from. You are made of steel and iron. You are forged from fire. Getting you into this world almost killed both of us – which means you have a purpose. You came with a month early inducement then emergency C-section after a day of natural labor and the *only* reason either of us is alive was because we had a fantastic high-risk pregnancy physician. He saved your life. And mine. Do you know you managed to wrap the cord around your neck several times and tie it in knots? Did you know you spent a week in the NICU with a hole in your heart, among other things, even though you were ten pounds, three ounces? Did you know I had you after cancer and radiation? Did you know you stopped breathing twice? And that I was so worked up I ripped out my IV and stormed down to the NICU against all advice and doctors' orders with a fresh hip-to-hip C-section incision and in critical condition myself? To make sure you were OK? I will storm your enemies from the heavens in just this way.

You were the happiest baby. You never fussed. You never cried. Even when you had tubes put into your ears, you came out of that surgery like nothing had even happened. And I worry about that too, my love – don't ever let this world make you hard. Stay kind. Stay humble. Stay open. Be careful who you trust and keep your inner circle tight, but don't let the pain and betrayals you'll experience close you off to the possibility of love. And by the way? You stopped that perfect baby ish by 3 and by 4 I wasn't sure if we would survive raising you in the day to day – you gave us a run for our money, big time. I wouldn't trade a moment, but God Bless America, son, did you ever raise hell with us. Five seems to have brought some sanity back into the picture, thank goodness.

There isn't a time in your life you won't remember having two moms. You were still in diapers when I met her. But there was a time, I remember, where it was just us. And now it's just you – out there in this big world trying to navigate a whole host of new people and rules and structure. We literally moved so you'd have the highest ranking, most forward-thinking schools in our entire state. I've given you the best chance I can. I've prepared you for this the best way I knew how. You can write your name. You've been walking since you were only seven months old, knew your alphabet at 18 months, and can do math problems in your head when asked out loud. You have every single tool imaginable at your disposal. There is no expense or effort I would spare to get you anything you could ever need.

And more importantly than any of that; you are truly a fantastic fucking human being. You just are. You're empathetic. You're hilarious. You're already a criminal mastermind. I honestly cannot *wait* to see who you become. I don't think it's our job to mold our children into tiny versions of ourselves. You aren't my legacy. You are your own human being, your own little Spirit. I have not instilled any dogma of religion, philosophy, or politics in you. Instead, I have exposed you to all schools of thought about all things, so you can make your own choices. Become your own person. That way you won't have to struggle, like I did, to figure out if you are really who you were supposed to be.

Everything you need is already inside you. I started crying once we were a few blocks away after letting you go into the school. You seem so impossibly small to navigate this whole big world all "by your own." But I have unshakable faith and unwavering belief in you, my boy. I know you can do it.

And for all you mamas (and daddies, and grandparents, and anyone raising a little starting school) out there; just know your worries are real. Them starting Kindergarten is opening a door to their adult life. They will never not be in school again until they are adults, or at the very least, they will never be a baby again. They will never need us in quite the same ways they did as babies. Those days are over. And it's our job now to figure out how to guide them while keeping the reins loose. Nobody wants to be led around by a collar. Our mission as mamas and guardians in general is to progressively let go while still holding on.

I'll let you know when I figure out how.

PS You were fine once we got you back home and you didn't have to wear "those serious clothes, moms, for real." And by the way? I'm so glad we have my wife, your other parent, in our lives. She *picked* us. Every single day she *chooses* to love and take care of you. Y'all may not have the same genes, but she's the other one who wipes your little nose, holds your sweet hand to cross the street, wakes when you're afraid in the middle of the night, makes sure you have the best kicks in school, and never gives up on either of us on our best or worst days – not by obligation or because of DNA, but by choice. Every day. That is a parent.

Bubbaisms

A collection of just a few of the hilarious, sweet, and insane things my son does and says. The joy of my life. My reason for breathing. Selected musings of a 3 + 4-year-old:

Cue 5am dog walking. My child had questions about sunrise and sunset and wanted to know why it's not called moonrise and moonset. Then, per the usual, we got into a heady academic discussion regarding time zones, the hemispheres, and the rotation and revolution of earth. This somehow (IDK, I really don't) led me to spinning on my axis while circling the dog and now I'm on the ground and I'm also fairly certain my kid already knew about this process. This child is 100% wild and I am all the way here for it. Got played.

PS? He concluded the discussion, while I was still on the floor no less, with, "Perhaps, then, me spinning all the time isn't so dangerust after all... maybe it's only dangerust if you're too old. And, also, mom, if the urf is already spinning twice ways, I can too because three is a luckier number anyhow. But I also think something in the middle of urf is spinning too." Whoa. Checkmate.

Old folks, don't spin. Even in the name of science.
Maverick Academy, indeed. Perhaps I am the student. Aren't we all?

Let me set the scene for you: Trying to drag my son outta the house to breakfast so his other mama can rest after coming home late from a longer than usual night of catching bad guys. He wants to stay home and play with his toys. Interestingly, his rationale for eventually and reluctantly deciding to accompany me was this:

"You're a girl! You can't go sit at breakfast by yourself. How would you get into the restaurant if I'm not there to open the door? I want to be here but I'm coming with you because that's my honor."

(Duty? I don't know, but I'll take it.) Today I'm going to let him be chivalrous and not explain I've been kicking doors in for decades. Sweet kiddo. Get your booty in the truck before mama wakes up and we're both in trouble.

Him: Mommy! I love your squishy tummy.
Me: Yeah... but you made it that way; growing you in there stretched it out!

Him: But... I'm four. So. You could've prolly stretched it back by now.

THE TRUTH HURTS

(Son runs out to wife's squad car, naked as a jaybird)

Her, from inside car:
Responding to a disturbance about a nude person approximately 3.5 feet tall. Blonde hair, blue eyes. Last seen wandering around hunting doughnuts. Non-responsive to lawful commands. Official statement, "Let me explain." May try to set up Play Doh trap to entice subject indoors.

Me: We will have wonderful schools at the new house.
Him: Mom, can you homeschool me? (Before I can answer)
Wife: Aw hell naw. I've been waiting for you to start kindergarten my whole life.

He and wife weren't at the playground alone for five minutes and he'd already found a "girlfriend," *by the way*. Lawd, I ain't ready for this!

Me: Bubba, can you go grab my phone off the charger and bring it here?
Him: (Takes approximately 30 seconds too long per rubric of previous devious behavior)
Me: Bubba?
Him: (Runs in with phone)
Me: What happened? How did you break my phone in thirty seconds!?
Him: A tiger bit it.
Me: YOU BIT MY PHONE!? Omg I totally can tell. All the way through the shattered screen protector. The screen is damaged. Son!
Him: I'm sorry. It was a tiger.
Me: ...
Him: Mom! You can't be mad. I'm coming from a point of power by taking wesponsitility.
Me: That doesn't mean I can't be mad! You BIT my phone!
Him: (shrug) I thought it was bacon.

I can't make this stuff up.
The apple doesn't fall far.

Four-year-olds are totally weird. Are teeth protectors a thing? Maybe we should go back to naps.

Think "tiger bite" is an appropriate phone insurance claim? I did file one on a phone I dropped into actual lava flow, so I reckon anything is possible.

Him: This robot has laigs.
Me: Legs?
Him: I know what you mean, but no. Laigs. It's Texas, mom.
Me: What do lions eat?
Him: Lambs (horrified facial expression)
Me: Uh... spaghetti?
Him: Jesus, mom.
Also him: Why is your face all wrinkly?

Gosh, I don't know, Son; they just started to appear mysteriously APPROXIMATELY FOUR YEARS AGO

My four-year-old: Do you like me?
Me: I love you more than anything.
Him: But do you think I'm pretty?
Me: Um. Yes. And handsome. But most importantly you're kind and
Him: (interrupting) Ok, ok. I got crumbs on the chair and just wanted to make sure you and me were cool before I let you know. I make mistakes sometimes. It's my fault but I'm taking wesponsitility.
Me: There's no fault in that. It was an accident.
Him: Well there may be one other mess.
Me: May be? And what might that be?
Him: I can't tell you right now.

Me: (cooking and so forth but hear some grumbling and rumbling headed up the stairs) Hi my love
Bubba: (wakes up all sleepy eyed, shuffles in here all cute) I know you're really busy but maybe you could take care of me for a little bit (THIS CHILD! We are legit together 24/7)
Me: I'm working babe so I can't just stop at the moment, but you know you're the most important thing. Sure, honey what do you need?
Him: You to just do those mom things.
Me: Mom things?
Him: Like pet my head and snuggle my neck.

Me: (*Ceases all things immediately*, literally hangs up on client, heart melting, heading toward him to pick him up)
Him: (holds up hand in a stop motion) "Not right now, mommy, but you can have three hugs later."

Y'ALL I CAN'T EVEN

"Mama got you flowers decuz you don't feel good. When I have my own truck and my own house by my own, I can do dat too. Until den, here are flowers so you feel happy in your heart."

Best flowers I've ever received.

Him: Can I have a sip of your Diet Coke?
Me: No babe. How about some juice?
Him: What? That's not fair. How about you drink juice and give me the Coke? Only grownups get Coke? Not kids?
Me: Well, Diet Coke contains carcinogenic phenylketonurics which produce phenylaniline. It negatively affects neurotransmitters like serotonin, dopamine, acetylcholine, norepinephrine, and their reuptake inhibitor processes in the still developing brain. This could literally change the way you later make decisions by permanently damaging your synapses, like a broken train track. Your mind is still growing.
Him: Mom, it's not that serious. When I grow up, I'll drink all the Cokes I want, and nobody can stop me.
Me: Here's the thing though... grownups still need to have discernment and utilize their best judgment to remain healthy. So, you'll have to regulate when and how many Cokes to drink and the optimal number is zero.
Him: WHAT!? GROWNUPS HAVE TO USE GOOD JUDGMENT TOO?! (literally crying at this notion)

I know, son. I know. It's a letdown.

Son: (slams toy and growls)
My wife: If those guys can't be kind to you, they don't get the pleasure of playing with you.
Son: This guy just needs to eat some carbs so he can act right.

I mean, he ain't wrong.

Him: When I grow up, I'll be able to do whatever I want, by myself?
Me: More or less, with some exceptions.
Him: Well then; I want to go to work. And use my money to go buy groceries. I want to do all this by myself. And bring you oatmeal so you feel better. I can tell you don't feel good.
Me: ...
Him: It's OK, mommy. I'll keep you forever and never leave you. And when I grow up, I can take care of you.
Me: Your only job is to take care of you, once you grow up. But that is so kind. I love your sweet heart.
Him: It's just what boys and mamas should do. Besides, if I'm big, you can't stop me.

Four-year-old: (puts bottle cap on the right side of his chest and leaves it there, goes about his business)
"Son, what are you doing?"
"Oh, that's my superhero power center. It's so I can be strong like you."
Me: (looks down, realizes his bottle cap is in the exact spot on his chest as my port is on mine)

(((melting commences)))

Stardate: 3am, child has awoken from nightmare

Explained to said child he has to be very quiet if he wants to come onto the patio as it's the middle of the night and our neighbor dogs are crazy and bark all the time but they're sleeping so shhhhh

Child: (contemplative, premeditated one-minute silence)
Commences barking AT THE DOGS

Send help.

Update: He fell asleep shortly thereafter, thank Baby Jesus and Tom Cruise. Dogs still barking.

Son, working on riding his bike, speaking to the air:

"OK everyone, be sure to like this video. I'm about to take off! We're about to get started with the bicycle, I can show you how. It's even cooler. Let's try it out and review it. Hey, do you like this video and want to see more? Then check out my page! Let's get started. Now, let's take our bicycle for a spin and play with it! Mom, we have a lot of customers who will really like to go for a ride. So, let's get moving!"

(no video currently occurring)

The apple doesn't fall far from the social media famous tree. Guess it's time for me to finally learn other platforms and get this kid his own page. Or, perhaps, run away off the grid with him. Sigh.

Little girl to my son on the playground: Is that your mom and dad?
Son: That's not my mom (confused did-he-just-disown-us glances between parents). I mean that's not my dad. I mean that's my mommy and my mama. She's cooler than a dad. She's another mama.
Little girl: Oh, OK cool!
Son: Moms might try to tell you my name is (name), but it's T-Rex (roars in her face, stomps feet, shows claws).
Her: Whoa. Cool. I'm a princess (commences climbing a pole).
Guess this whole "worrying about him being judged for having two moms" thing is fruitless – turns out it's no big deal.

Hate is taught.

Me: Lay down; no more shenanigans. The bath and bedtime routine has never changed; you know the drill.
Toddler (in the calmest, most exhausted middle-aged tone): I'm tired of this bullshit.

Spirited children tho, amirite?

Mommy, can we wear our boots to the playground?
Sure baby.
Oh I'm so glad you want to go play. I just knew it.
But wait I never said
Oh

Well played son. Well played

The essence of motherhood:

Holding a snack he can't open away from your toddler to be offered only in exchange for him getting a Diet Coke from the fridge for you.

Giving him his now open snack. Him running off maniacally laughing. Looking down to realize it's a janky day old almost empty Diet Coke. Hollering at him, "YOU TRICKED ME,"
Him screaming, "I DON'T MEHGOSHEEATE WIF TERRISTS."

This bee can't make any honey if he's dead. I've got to hurry and put some water on him so he can make honey again or we won't have any flowers or trees. And his whole hive will die! They all depend on the king bee! Awwww poor mister! I'm so sorry you died. Hang on. Help is on the way.

(Dramatic pause. Stopped in tracks. Serious face.)

Mom.
Yeah bubba.
What if his plan is to sting us later?

Him: When I grow up, I won't have to ask if I can have a treat.
Me: That's right.
Him: Well, I'll still have to say thank you, I guess.
Me: Yeah. How will you know how to not eat too many treats?
Four-year-old: Well, maybe if you learn about not eating so many treats you can teach me. But you eat a lot of treats.

TIME FOR A NAP.

Him: I'm not sure, but it's possible there's a monster in here. If there is, I'm going to trick it. But we need a plan. Do you agree to help me if I need you?
Me: Yes?
Him: Hmph. Well the plan is to be very smeaky and quiet and I'm not sure you can do that. Also, you don't really have fighting skills? I need mama actually, not you, for this trick. We may need to set off an eelarm and fight them. You need to stay back, where we can keep you safe. If you hear fighting, just stay in your room because you might get in the way. What I really need is my pleece oppisur mom right now, not you. What you are good at is cooking, not fighting.

THIS CHILD

Me: I'm gonna dress up today and look nice.
Him: Like a pancake?
Me: Um. Not exactly. Do you want to dress up with me?
Him: Sure. I'll dress up like Batman, but I don't know where you put my suit. You shouldn't hide my suit, because then how will I fight bad guys?
Me: I think we're veering off track. Can't we just wear nice clothes today?
Him: Fine. I'll be a dinosaur. And that's my final offer. But you gotta be a pancake.

Him: Can you fix my car?
Me: No baby. The wheel is broken.
Him: But fixing things is your job.
Me: I know love, but it broke at the axle. It's just a Hot Wheels. We can get you another one and throw this one in the trash.
Him: (gravely and deeply offended that I'd suggest such a dishonor for one of his 3,471 cars) MOMMY YOU DO NOT JUST THROW SOMETHING OUT BECAUSE IT IS BROKEN. This car depends on me to take care of it. I can't just give up. Don't you know about mechanics? Can't we call one or find something on YouTube?

Oh my. Guess I better locate some tools?

Me: What are you doing? (He's holding up blocks to his ear and talking into the "phone")
Son: Well, mom, I'm on the phone with my girl. What you have to say is very important to me, but I need you to not interrupt right now. (Turns back to "phone," resumes convo.) Yes, I'm sorry. I won't do that again, gurr. Don't be mad. It's just my mom.

JUST MY MOM! WHAT! I CAN'T

I bribed him away from his "girlfriend" with the waterpark and ice cream but have a sneaking suspicion this may not work for too many more years.

Wife delivering food for our restaurant. Son went with her because I'm t i r e d. I've had lots of chats with him about food safety and why we can't dilly dally or leave things out and so forth.

Client comes out of her house for her order. My kid doesn't realize it's been frozen and kept cool for delivery.
Him, at top volume, to our CLIENT: YOU CANNOT EAT THIS FOOD. IT WILL MAKE YOU SICK AND YOU WILL DIE.
Then he smiles at my wife like... See? I listen to mommy.
Wife (unaware of previous food safety convos): :o

Four-year-old: Mom, I want to talk to you.
Me: OK. About what?
Him: Animals.
Me: OK. How about elephants?
Him: No. Cats are fine.
Me: Sure, baby. What do you know about cats?
Him: That they're machine washable.

Um

(going through and doing his sticker achievement chart)

Me: Bubba, did you listen and mind today?
Him: No, not at all, but I will tomorrow, so you can give me a sticker for that now.
Me: No fronts. You wanna be hard? Welcome to the street.
His other mom: (jaw dropped)

Me: What are you doing baby?
Him: I'm stretching my muscles for more swimming.
Me: Oh, that's good.
Him: Right. You should probably do that too. You look sort of old right now and I want you to swim fast, not slow.

MMMK

Me: Babe did you have a bad dream last night?
Four-year-old: There was this wild pack of bears. And they came to the house. They arrived without warning; utterly infuriated.

That vocab tho!

Family dynamics, 101, four-year-old edition

"Get that cat off the counter, son."

"But he wants to be there."
"That's against the rules. Enforce his rule kindly and calmly by getting him down. You're the boss of him."
"And you're the boss of me. And mama's the boss of you."

That escalated quickly

Son, why are you sitting in the dark?

I turned the lights off so I can be Christmas.

Four-year-old: "Where's our cupcakes?"
Me: "Mama took them to the other police officers."
Him: "But what about me? You said police officers eat donuts, not cupcakes."

Oh my

Pediatrician: It's time for us to check your privates as part of your exam. It's ok only because I'm a doctor and your mom is here. OK?
My son: My TEETER is FINE.
My wife: (OMG face)

Me: Good morning! Did you have sweet dreams?
Four-year-old: Yeah! About lions and tigers.
Me: Aliens and tigers?
Him: No. That doesn't even make sense. LIONS and tigers, mom.
Me: Oh my. I need coffee.
Son: About those lions and tigers, mom? I didn't finish my talks with them. We can either go to the zoo or stay here. What's your option? It's your choice today.
Me: Hmm. Let's go to the zoo?
Him: That's a great idea.

The monkey has taken over the circus. Bet your ass, we headed to the zoo to finish the discussion.

"Alright, son. What are you going to tell the mean kid at school if he is hurting other kids?"
"Try me, bro."

Well I reckon that'll work just fine.

What is your name? T Rex and (Name) and I always make a boy sound and a robot sound.
How old are you? Firteen and fourteen.
(Me: Can you shut the door? Him: Yes, sir.)
When is your birthday? (Him: (no answer) Me: Is it (says birthdate)? Him: Nope)
How old is Mommy: You're firteen and fourteen but older.
What is your favorite color? I like black and yellow too (yes, like the song lol)
What's your favorite food? Strawberries and chicken and 'nola bars and yogurt and peanut butter jelly sandwich
Who is your best friend? The whole world
What's your favorite animal? You. All of them
What are you scared of? A beetle timer that eats bees
What makes you happy? Horses and cowboys and grandmas
Where is your favorite place to go? Sea World
What do you want to be when you grow up? A big, bad wolf giant
What does love mean? It means to dance
How old is Mama: Firteen pounds
What are your parents' jobs? Protect everyone
Where do you want to go? Sea World

Are we done wif our test yet?
Yes, honey

———

(About to chew wife's head in public restaurant while she's in uniform)
"I thought she might taste like a doughnut."

Best thing I've ever heard in my life.

———

Cop's Wife

Laying here beside her
I wish she could feel my need
She hears my words
Hot
Like fire
But you never meant
To punch my closet
Tangled in my head
Are memories of us
Imaginary thoughts of you with someone else
Missed phone calls
Deleted messages
Girls sliding into your cruiser
Police siren cutting
Into the freezing night
Lights flashing
Red and blue
Across white snow
A car I shoved out of a rut
With a broken leg
For you
And I wait at home
Waking at the drop of a hat
Worrying
Is tonight the night
A bullet tears through your heart
You are so small
A giant fist
Smashing your perfect face
Just right
I am terrified
Quaking water
Waking nightmares
Shaking awake
Will she make it back tonight
Will I be handed an envelope of your things
The ring I gave you
Or will you walk through the door
Stomping snow off your boots

So I can holler at you instead
Jealous for no reason
My own insecurity
Don't take my lasagna to that bitch
She ain't your work wife
And I'm not your "side piece"
That ain't funny
Does she even know
How I feel
How could she realize
That this is real
I'd kill someone for hurting you
But what if it's you
Hurting me
I lay awake
And sit up a thousand times a night
A third shift wife, alright

Viral Post

When I was 19, I was driving home erratically, crying. I did a rolling stop through a red light. I was a mile away from my house. I got pulled over. There are wonderful police officers in the world. This wasn't one of them. He was of the psychotic variety, of which there are also quite a few. Demanded I sign the ticket. He was being scary. I didn't know, nor was I advised, that you can go to jail for not signing a ticket. Usually an officer just lets you go because you have to appear in court regardless of whether you sign it. When I said I didn't want to sign it (not understanding any of the aforementioned stuff), he demanded I get out of the car. My father died three days later; it's what I'd been crying about. I was 150 pounds soaking wet (at 6'2", that's pretty slight), halfway through a BA at a private school with a 4.0, and terrified to be on the side of the road in the dark with a very angry man whom I didn't know. Instead of getting out of the car, I locked the door. I was afraid. I didn't know better.

He kept screaming at me to, "Stop f***ing crying!" It would have been so easy to deescalate the entire situation.

He drug me out of the open car window and onto the ground. He kicked me in the ribs. He fractured my wrist cuffing me and picking me up by the link between the cuffs. He held his boot to the back of my head with my face on loose gravel, leaving what would later become scars. He bounced my head off the side of the car when he was putting me in, all while laughing. He called for backup and none of the other officers would touch me. One even said, on camera, "This is wrong, man. She ran a red light." I, understandably, was hysterical. Crying. Screaming. Huge bruises starting to form on my face and body. Clothing torn. High heel even broke off.

Do you know what I was arrested for and charged with that day? Resisting arrest. Can you imagine? Resisting arrest.

Fast forward to the jail. I'd never been in trouble. Had no idea what to expect. I couldn't stop crying. I couldn't breathe. I told them he'd broken my wrist but they wouldn't believe me. They strapped me in a chair when I wouldn't calm down. Strap on your forehead. Strap on your chest. Strap on each arm and each leg. Like a beast. I remember begging for someone to scratch my nose, hysterically sobbing. I remember being in that chair for hours, topless, because I'd gotten "unruly" during the strip, cough, and squat procedure and refused to do it. So they ripped my shirt off and as I fought them, they put me in the chair. I tried to fight back against a female guard when she tried to rip my pants off. I didn't understand why I was there. I didn't understand what was happening. I didn't think I should have been arrested. I was livid. And loud.

Then they parked me. For five hours. In that chair. Strapped down. In front of a men's holding cell. I was literally losing my mind. It was a black man who, for five hours, while incarcerated himself, talked calmly and softly to me. Sang to me. Said every kind thing you could imagine. I finally stopped screaming and trying to head butt or kick anyone who passed. He said, "Stop, or they'll kill you. Just stop baby girl. It's ok. You'll be ok if you stop." He was an Angel. Straight from God.

I didn't get to use the phone for a full 12 hours. No one on the planet knew where I was.

I was so crazy after being in that chair by the time they placed me in a holding cell that I began to bang my head off the cinderblock wall. They had to let me sit in the hall, on the ground, because I almost broke my own nose. I was muttering incoherently and rocking.

They mailed me a charge six months later saying they'd found a joint under the back seat of the bolted in police car and that it belonged to me. How do you hide a joint from an officer while cuffed with a broken wrist and get it underneath the bolted in backseat of a cop car? You don't. They offered me every plea in the book on the two charges, all the way down to a misdemeanor. I would not enter a plea. I went to trial on a felony. Because I knew my innocence. Because we had the money for a good attorney. Because the justice system wasn't already systemically stacked against me and my color and gender were in my favor, as my lawyer pointed out.

During the trial they "lost" my videos. My attorney threatened the city with a lawsuit. The tapes magically appeared. My jury came back in four minutes with a not guilty verdict. They were crying after seeing the videos of my arrest and the videos from inside the jail, of me in that chair. My jurors all hugged me. They told me I should sue. My dad had just died. I was a college student. I was tired. The prosecutor dropped the resisting charge when I beat the possession rap; meaning I legally and literally should never have been arrested in the first place. How do you get arrested for resisting arrest?

During my trial, my attorney asked him if he kicked me in the ribs repeatedly while I was already cuffed. He laughed and said, "Yes." My attorney asked, "Do you think this is funny?" He said, "I do."

A week later police in the same town shot an unarmed and senile very elderly black man in the face because he wouldn't come with them. There were no videos. There was no social media. You haven't heard about him. But he's dead. You won't hear his story.

This arrest is still on my record. It doesn't prevent me from anything but I do have to explain felony charges when I get pulled over or apply for a job.

I have never publicly told this story.

I tell it to you, today.

And here's why:

If I were a black man, I would be dead. Plain and simple. Pretty white girls don't get shot during wrongful arrests. Not any that I know of, and certainly not me.

You can't deny white privilege and what it affords you. To deny it is to acknowledge it exists, that you are privy to it. You don't see it because it exists for you.

Something is very wrong in this country. There is a sickness. Black men (and sometimes women) are dying. They are being gunned down. For no discernible reason, and at an alarming rate, by white officers.

You may read my story and think, "She should have signed the ticket." Perhaps I should have. Certainly. But should I have been beaten and stripped and jailed and shamed and prosecuted for not doing so? Certainly not. Saying someone shouldn't resist arrest when being forcefully unnecessarily detained is insane. Did I fight? Damn right. It's instinct. When someone is hurting you for no reason, your fight or flight response kicks in. It just happens. I truly believe I am alive today in part because of the color of my skin. He shouldn't have gotten away with what he did, but it's the reason he didn't have the courage to do more. Two unarmed black men have been killed during routine arrests by police in one day. Happens all the time. Why?

Of course they riot. What else are they supposed to do? Watch their brothers, fathers, husbands get gunned down in complacent silence? How many stories have we not heard because there is no tape? How many more deaths are there?

How do we protect our brothers and sisters of color? What can we do? We need to move. We need to make something happen. This is unacceptable.

#blacklivesmatter

Aftermath

Oh, lord.

At the time of this book's writing in 2019, I have the prior post set to private, because you may have noticed I married a police officer somewhere along the way. But before I did that? It had 80,000+ reacts and 55,000+ shares on Facebook alone a few years ago. You can search "Molly Suzanna," and still find articles about it. Everyone from Ashton Kutcher to Brad Takei to Young Money shared it – A List celebrities and politicians around the world felt the message resonate with them. Most major media outlets covered it, internationally.

First, just let me say this: My life is confusing as fuck. I am a tattooed lesbian who lives in the red state of Texas. I am a liberal Bernie voting outspoken civil rights activist whose first Trump protest drew over five thousand RSVPs in less than 24 hours. I am a woman who is married to someone who "doesn't care" about politics yet is a cop's cop and lifetime member of the National Rifle Association. I wrote possibly the most viral thing in history on police brutality; then I fell in love with one. A good one. The best one.

To further complicate matters, it turns out police officers have been violent with me both in life and in my personal relationships. She acknowledges this. The decent ones always do. They don't pretend there isn't a problem. They actually know precisely what it is, but I can't speak for her or any of them. They are a confusing breed. I have no convictions, yet no one has paid for the harm that was done to me in any way. I never even filed a complaint.

There is no excuse for abuse folks, none. But if there's a verbal equivalent to punching holes in the wall, shoving folks, and kicking doors in, it's what I used to do, long ago. My child is the only person I have never done this with no matter what. We re-enact our childhoods and take our scars out on one another.

The partner who was an officer would beat up the house when I'd threaten to leave. I'd threaten to leave because their attitude sucked and they had, in my opinion, untreated Complex PTSD. I didn't mind the PTSD part, just the total unwillingness to get help for it. It's hard for me to understand, because I have the exact same thing, yet do not behave that way as a fully-grown ass person. I can't even say that's really why I threatened to leave. I guess the truth would be that I had no other tools. But a fear of abandonment is real and an unfair way to gain the upper hand emotionally, even if unintentional. Don't do that. I did. It doesn't work, and it's mean. Just leave. I did that too, and it also didn't work.

I felt, when I was with this person, that they were obsessed with me in the most toxic of ways. The disapproval was always felt, a look of contempt or disgust. I remember annoying them by simply waking up, being happy, existing. I felt like the life was being sucked from my bone marrow by that relationship. I felt like they were a well with no bottom, and I could never fill them up, but they were willing to let me die trying.

But on the job? When this partner worked in a huge and majorly dangerous city for over a decade? Not only did they never have an official complaint; they were in chases, shot at frequently, and encountered sometimes thirty different runs alone at night in a rough part of town, yet never had a use of force or any formal complaint there. I actually went in their pocket for hundreds, if not thousands of hours. I'd put the phone on mute, and they'd take me with them. I'd fall asleep to the sounds of their call sign and radio traffic.

What does that mean? It means that on the job, they were 100% one of the good guys. One that puts up with more than most would. One that sacrifices all. I was in their pocket the night they saved a man's life by administering Narcan over and over. This is a good person and a damn fine cop. And God knows that's been true with me, too; the service and loyalty they felt was extended to me and mine. They would have sacrificed their last dollar for us, their last drop of blood. Leaving isn't always black and white. They even laid on the floor in my hospital rooms, so I'd never be alone. They didn't drink. Didn't party. Always wanted to be with us, their family. They were loyal to a literal fault. They never pulled someone over without a strong reason and followed the law in their own life to a T, minus the parts where they would lose their shit because of the family they were born to and the job they felt called to choose. Then again? I don't know what happened in the back of their car or down dark alleyways. Perhaps they were precisely the type to abuse those who were powerless, as they did me. I'll never know. The other things they did were unspeakable, and I never imagined they would make me feel terrified and trapped; imprisoned. Who knows? Do any of us really know any another? Do we? They were a deeply good, yet troubled person. So am I. Honestly? We were perfect for each other at that time. Please know this, though: Like attracts Like – and this? It is the Law. Not the Law of Man, but the Law of Source.

The direct aftermath of that viral post was a whirlwind of death threats and vitriolic hatred, getting loosely more or less let go from several important to me things once they found out, and the realization of the power of my words. So how do you write a book of your darkest secrets; secrets that must be kept in order to safely move forward, yet which comprise a story that demands telling? What do you do with the knowledge that you can fire a shot heard around the world with a single verbal bullet?

How do you write something like that about the police, stand up for the voiceless, date one, marry one, let them have raffles for your medical expenses, visit you in the hospital, become part of a blue family, allow them to bring you cake as you recuperate, meet so many who are decent and wonderful, selfless human beings, then write this book? How do you get tortured at the hands of a monster in uniform yet still love? I don't know.

I don't know, but we're going to find out. I'm hoping what I've experienced is true: That the culture of silence is as painful to them as it is to anyone. That the good cops despise the bad ones more than anybody else ever could. That the endemic sexism, harassment, and racism extends its roots into and beyond the actual police force itself. That sometimes it is a machine eating its own heart in front of itself. And that the epidemic of domestic violence and untreated mental health problems as a result of being on the watch in broken government systems can finally get addressed, from the stage, by the two of us holding hands and explaining to you how many found their way out of the storm so that others might follow.

So how? How do we heal? Where is the white buffalo? How do we find its woman?

I'll tell you what I'm doing.

Take what you need and leave the rest.

Blue

And what if somebody gunned her down tonight
Down tonight
What if someone messed her around tonight
Around tonight
And they don't know that it's my girl
All you see are lights and sirens
I know you think that badge is sexy
But we are hoping she comes home
Before she makes it in the morning
God only knows what she will see
But she is brave enough to do it
To lay her life down for you and me
Would you?
Would you take a bullet
Could you stand behind that thin blue line
Would you wear a badge and go right through it
You should know that she is mine
Before you make her draw that gun
Before she gets out of her car
You should know I'd hunt you down
And find you no matter where you are
Don't hurt her
She isn't yours to break
That officer's heart is ours
And it's not yours to take
She's a person with a family waiting back at home
And who are you
What are you
How have we become this
Fighting in the street
If you see her tell her we love her
And then sit your ass back in your seat
Because we aren't ready to let you have her
No
It can't possibly go your way
She is out there keeping us all safe
And today is not your day
Did you know
I packed her lunch tonight

She's having salad
Her uniform has wear spots
From working those long shifts
I dust the lint from off her shoulders
And I send her out to fight her way
Please send her back tonight
Back tonight
So we can have just one more day

Poisonous People:
How to Block Toxicity

Chances are good there's someone in your life's energy field who is having a negative effect on your overall sense of well-being. Maybe it's a narcissist or sociopath, like we just discussed. It doesn't really matter what label you slap on it, if you've got an energy vampire in your life, you need to do something about it. Like, yesterday.

Perhaps it's that coworker who always tries to coax you off your diet with cupcakes. Maybe it's the family member who never fails to remind you at Thanksgiving that you look a little thick around the middle. Or the friend who says, "You aren't wearing *that* are you?"

Or maybe it's a bit more sinister than that. Perhaps you are in a relationship with a narcissist or sociopath; or have one or more of these as a parent, boss, friend. How do you avoid the negative effects of all of those little energy zaps you, if you are an empath, feel all dang day long?

1. Wash it off, figuratively or literally.
Use your shower or some time swimming to visualize the water cleansing off any unwanted energy, residue, or vibes from your body, inside and out. My favorite trick is to imagine a fire extinguisher, essentially, and it's full of cool, blue, spiritually pure light. I spray my body from head to toe with it in the shower, while taking an only cold shower at the end of my normal routine. It creates a powerful visual and physical energy cleanse with the added bonus of stimulating some really cool stuff your body needs to happen anyway – like reawakening the vagus nerve! Or dive into a pool, and imagine as you are gliding under water that all of the bad or toxic things you have said, done, encountered, heard, or dealt with that week are flying off with each stroke, rising from the water like smoke, and back to the clouds to dissolve.

2. Set actual, physical, earthly boundaries.
We teach people how to treat us by showing them what we will accept. If you have someone emotionally draining in your life who can't respect your boundaries, try no contact for a bit if possible. If this isn't an option, be very clear about what you need, want, and will accept from this person. For instance, if Aunt Zelda is always

pinching your cheeks and saying, "Aw, just as chubby as the day you were born," and you are now a 23-year-old female college student... this might ride on your nerves a bit. There's a lot to be said for picking your battles. But if someone is really hurting or bothering you with their commentary, let them know. Keep it about you, rather than an accusation. I feel _____ (crummy, worthless, whatever) when you say _____. If they laugh at your boundary, you've got a bigger problem. If they get angry with your boundary, you've got the biggest problem. Bet.

You can use the visualization of a chain-link fence and see anyone toxic or negative as too big to fit through, with the smaller openings still allowing love, peace, and freedom to flow freely to you. Fence yourself in or fence out the toxic person if you cannot avoid the situation. Every moment spent worrying or obsessing about a person or situation you cannot change is another moment things cannot resolve. It is literally a total waste of time. Staying angry with someone is like lighting yourself on fire and hoping they choke on the smoke. Find yourself rehashing what you "could've said," over and over and fighting with that person even when you're all alone? Or begging for hours for them to see the problem and you're the only one with tears running down your face? They're sound asleep as you watch the clock's hands go 'round and 'round and you're still upset? Love yourself enough to walk away if they don't want to change. Just like with kids, if you set up boundaries with consequences that are ignored and they see you'll put up with it, you're actually setting yourself up for worse behavior down the road...

3. Put up a shield.
Some of us are like literal beacons to other people, whether those people are powerfully good, powerfully bad, or neutral. Like moths to a flame. If everywhere you go, you can feel the energy of people around you, imagine yourself in a literal bubble. Set up a permeable energy field around you in a full spherical shape; so that whatever is of the light or of God (or whatever you believe to be the equivalent to "good" or positive karma) can get through, but anything negative like people's fear, sadness, or anger bounces right off. Visualize yourself as a stone in a river when negativity is headed towards you and let the black smoke flow around you – not permeating nor remaining near. Think this won't work? Athletes performed better on actual scientifically researched experiments when they visualized themselves training. This is really good if crowded places are too

spiritually or emotionally "loud" for you – like grocery stores or concerts. There is a lot of information on the internet about how to cut energetic ties to people, but my one piece of advice I've learned from multiple trusted sources is you never want to "cut" their tie to you – you want to pull out the hook completely. And you can send it out into the universe or back to them, which I never knew until recently when I encountered a really cool spiritual guide who helped me find my way back within. Here's the thing when you cut a line, the hook remains within. Sacred geometry tells us all is conneted, so realizing that you must fully unplug their psychic hook to you *and* yours to them is critical here.

4. Get them help.
One surefire way to address what's going on is to be direct. Obviously, you may not want to let your boss know you've armchair therapist diagnosed them as having Borderline Personality Disorder; but if it's a sibling or someone else like a best friend, telling them you think they might benefit from support for depression, PTSD, or the like is not a bad idea. Do you see the difference between telling someone they "need help" and "might benefit from support?" The need word implies lack. The help word implies weakness. The word might allows wiggle room so that they can own their truth, and can say, no, thank you. Benefit implies addition rather than lack. Support sounds like building instead of adding what is missing. Clearly, do not attempt to diagnose someone yourself, but if they have a known issue they've shared with you or if you suspect they may be suffering, letting them know you're holding space for them then pointing them in the right direction can't hurt anything. One of the hardest pills you may ever have to swallow is if you're dealing with someone active in their alcoholism, drug addiction, or who is truly abusive, they (LISTEN TO ME) will. not. change. until + unless. they. ARE READY. Did you hear that? God, I hope so. It'll save you unending pain.

No amount of begging, pleading, or "good reasons" will convince someone to seek mental health or addiction help if they are in denial. Period. A true alcoholic will often find themselves under the bridge before they are willing to reach out. You cannot love someone into wellness. This is painful and awful and if you are just realizing that for the first time, I'm so sorry. But it's the truth. And the sooner you realize it, the better. I'm not saying that if someone significant in your life has a struggle this big you should just brush them off your hands and walk away; only you know what you are willing and able to handle. But firm boundaries, mind + body + spirit help, and professional guides are essential lest you find yourself so empty trying to save someone drowning that your own head ends up underwater too as they climb you to get some breaths from the waves. Remember, if you're an empath or a rescuer type personality not to lose yourself in this endeavor. It's very easy to try to save someone from themselves only to realize all too late they never had any interest in being saved.

5. Learn to say no.
No. No is a complete sentence and requires no explanation. Also, stop apologizing. "I'm sorry, but..." No. No sorries. No feeling guilty for saying no. When you take care of yourself, and are full, you can give. When you allow those around you who are toxic, whether intentional or not, to drain you, you are empty. The consequences of remaining too empty for too long can be drastic. If you are an over-scheduler or find yourself constantly surrounded by people who aren't good for your highest and best, change your circle. People in your life, overall, should lift you up rather than drag you down. Period. I'm not going to tell you love doesn't hurt. I used to think that. Love can be painful. Raising children is hard as hell, and if you're doing it right; letting go of them just enough as they grow so that they can find their own wings is even harder. Letting them learn from their own mistakes and become humans without steamrolling their every move is very difficult, and sometimes painful, especially when you know that by exercising control you could prevent them from a painful life lesson. But sometimes you just have to say NO, you make the choice, son. And watch him make what he knows to be the least optimal choice and hold him while he experiences those consequences. Obviously, don't let your kids run into the street, but you get the drift. One way to avoid toxicity is to remember that everyone is entitled to their own experience. If they choose to be miserable, unhappy, angry, stressed, and just overall negative all the time, give them the respect, dignity, and space to make that choice.... far away from your happy ass. And for you over-givers? "Can you bring all the cupcakes for the party?" Yes. "Can you also clean up afterwards?" Sure. "Oh, and do you mind coming early to set up?" No problem. Bullshit. It is a problem. Say no when you mean no and yes when you mean yes. Real friends will understand. Nobody likes a martyr, Karen. How's that for some Realness Pie?

What does all this result in?

Well, for many of us, toxic family and relationship systems leave us with limiting beliefs about ourselves, the world, other people, and worse; can feed the pipeline to systemic dis-ease. We end up with a broken framework from which we operate; which then lends itself to the question of whether everything we say, do, think, and feel is from a faulty foundation. We try to please one another and desperately toe the line, never journeying inward to heal bleeding emotional and spiritual wounds.

Next; we explore how to see past trauma to regain your footing.

7 Limiting Beliefs and How to Overcome Them

1. I am irredeemable

This is the notion that a lot of us get that we are unforgiveable, that we've done things that cannot be redeemed; or that things have been done to us which have made us unworthy, unforgiveable, unlovable, whatever. You are not the things you've done. And you are not the things that have happened to you.

Do you hear me? You are not the things that have happened to you. The rather unfortunate, for some of us, flipside of this, is that no human, even the most despicably behaved ones, aren't redeemable as well. The good news is this naturally requires us to question justified anger and righteous rage.

If we're all redeemable, yes all, then that sort of leaves anger out in the cold as a useless answer to any problem.

If you feel like you've created an erroneous life that can't be righted or turned around, then you're going to have to start behaving like someone who never did or said those things. It doesn't mean staying in denial. It doesn't mean not correcting wrongs. It just means that you've got to turn around, you've got to do an about-face, a one-eighty in the middle of the road, and go in another direction.

Sometimes you correct with that person directly. Sometimes you correct while going forward with other people. There are infinite options. But if your limiting belief is primarily that you are irredeemable, just know that it's not true.

How to overcome:
Develop a redeemable pattern of behavior
Create self-esteem by esteemable acts

2. I am unworthy

A lot of us have this manifest in the notion of imposter syndrome. We are incredibly talented, able, and uniquely capable individuals and yet we feel as though we're fake, we're not real, we're not good enough to deliver a message, create a project, live our dreams.

There's a really bizarre notion that many of us get that we're imposters if we're not perfect all the time. I have news for you: You are a human being, and not a single one of us is perfect. Sometimes, and maybe even especially the ones who seem the most to have it all together, don't at all.

Anyone whom you find to be particularly inspirational or motivational will have flaws. Don't look to closely at anyone or you will not like what you see. There are two types of people who seem like they have it all together and appear perfect. One: It's more or less true, and they're so far on the other side of the Veil and have been there so long and go there so often that they are genuinely peaceful, good human beings almost all the time because they're barely here on human earth. Two: They're hiding the more human and flawed parts of themselves because perhaps they think it would lessen the *impactfulness* of their message.

There is power in authenticity and vulnerability, as we've seen via the incredible rise to stardom of Brene Brown. What she most specifically was terrified to speak of is why she is now a world-famous leader and coach.

This idea of, "I am unworthy," proliferates because it means you think, "Good things will happen for them, but not for me." It's like punching somebody in the face and then complaining about their bloody nose dripping all over the carpet, except that somebody is you.

You don't have to suddenly believe you're worthy. It doesn't happen that quickly. But you can act like you believe it. You can say you believe it until it feels true. You can put Post-Its all over your house. I stand naked in the mirror every day and I tell my body how grateful I am for it, that I'm so glad it's healthy, and that I'm so glad it's beautiful and perfect. I tell it I know it's going to continue to work in my favor. Whether these things are true in my current reality matters not at all. Don't sacrifice the ending you may now create simply because you cannot go back and change the beginning.

How to overcome:
Create an environment of worth
Remove, like surgery, anyone and anything that does not support feelings of worth, worthiness

Add, like building a house, new people and things that do support
Eject old tapes, make new ones
Can be in the form of affirmations, meditations
Turn focus completely onto what is wanted, not what is unwanted

3. I cannot overcome anger

When we are deeply hurt or feeling some other negative emotion, anger is simply the easiest behavior pattern to grasp, as we've discussed. At least then we are feeling something. It's why people who suffer from extreme depression are so often overcome with anger.

Aside from all the chemical implications of not having the correct balances for reuptake of serotonin, dopamine, acetylcholine, norepinephrine, and other feel good neurotransmitters; some of us have actually burned out neural pathways. How do we balance these levels so they serve us rather than harm us?

Anger exists because it makes us feel more powerful than acknowledging what's really going on inside. Anger is only the absence of something else, not the presence of itself. That absence is usually caused by fear – which as we already learned is composed of: "I won't get what I want," or "I will lose what I already have."

Would you stand over a spot where you need to dig a hole yet not use a shovel, ask anyone for help, or hire equipment? You can't just stand around and attract a hole to you. If you have extreme anger, depression, anxiety, or any other clinically significant thing, you may need professional help and there's nothing wrong with that.

Have you ever spent a significant amount of time around a baby? It takes almost nothing to make them happy. You tickle their toes and they laugh like it's the best thing that ever happened. And to them, in that moment, it is. So living in the moment, then, would be one aggressive way of overcoming this belief. In each and every moment you can find at least one thing to be OK with. Life is lived one breath at a time. One heartbeat at a time. One way to overcome anger is to become childlike again, and do those simple things which bring you immense, pure joy, effortlessly. And just like a baby – scream when you need to, cry when you feel like it, and learn to let things out.

How to overcome:
Get busy with literally anything else
Consider professional help via any avenue holistic or medical
Review tools and prior beliefs for what is faulty
Rediscover hobbies and fun

4. Where I am is too far from where I want to be to ever get there

This is a limiting belief because it just isn't the truth. If I decided right now, "I have to go to Australia. I must be there in the next hour." Depending on your mindset and the way you look at things, you might tell me, "That's not possible."

When we change the way we look at things, the things we look at change. I could be in Australia right now, through video chat, through text. Or I might already be there, and you simply assumed I am not currently there.

If where you are is too far from where you want to be, you just have to change the mode of transportation you're using. You might be slogging through the snow on foot when really you just need a plane ticket. We outgrow this the same way we overcome the need to travel. Find a different method that's faster and more efficient than the one you're using now. Finding and following efficient travelers is a brilliant way to implement the strategy of closing the gap between current reality and future desire. Envy won't get you what someone else has; but if you admire it and want it, do what they did to get it and you will create your own.

Then all of a sudden, where you are isn't that far from where you need to be at all.

How to overcome:
Get new tools
Find new guides

5. I do not have a purpose

Oh yes the fuck you do.

You just don't know what it is.

Have you ever just taken a drive somewhere, anywhere, and found that you ended up having a really exciting adventure? Or better yet, gotten lost, when you definitely were on your way somewhere and ended up doing or seeing or finding or meeting really cool people or places or things?

That's how you figure out your purpose. You have an emotional GPS already installed and it is perfect. All the time, every time. Things that don't make you feel good aren't what you're supposed to be doing.

What does this mean? It doesn't mean if you have a child who throws tantrums that you set them outside and hope they get raised in the wilderness.

It does mean that when you feel a disconnect, when you feel a deep emotional dissatisfaction; you've got to do something about it. If what you're doing, saying, and thinking does not align with your core values, then you know you're not on the right track.

Discovering your true purpose, what your Soul intended for you in this lifetime, is about eliminating what doesn't work more than it is about searching out what does. As you chip away at what you know doesn't work, what is of and for you will begin to take shape.

If you have a loss of your sense of purpose, and this is the belief that's limiting you, all you need to do is suss out all the things that aren't your purpose, and what you are meant for will become crystal clear.

How to overcome:
Get a map
Eliminate everything that isn't of and for you
What is of and for you will then be revealed

6. I have bad luck

You don't have bad luck. You're going in the wrong direction. Correcting this is as simple as turning around. I tell my son all the time that there's an emotional scale of behavior – which has a "no" end and a "yes" end. This looks like, perhaps he's trying to earn a new toy or something that he'd like. If his behavior starts to deteriorate or devolve toward the no end, which might look like tantrums, I let him know, "You're at a yes, but you're heading towards a no."

Having bad luck is the Universe telling you, "You're heading towards a no, you're going in the wrong direction. TURN AROUND!"

Life isn't fair. People will treat you badly.

Accepting accountability for every aspect of your life, in all areas of your life, is how you get your power back over what you're perceiving as "bad luck."

If you focus on the unfairness in life or the badness in people, that's what you'll get more of; period.

It's kinda like this: Say I spilled some milk.

Shame says: I'm such a bad person for spilling this milk. How clumsy of me.
Guilt: I should've never spilled this milk, and I'm going to spend all my time thinking about how wrong it was that I did.
Blame: I wouldn't have spilled this milk if you weren't bothering me while I was trying to pour it.
Responsibility: It's my fault I spilled the milk.

The most powerful position from which to overcome this limiting belief is accountability.

Accountability says: I spilled the milk, but I'm going to clean it up, and I'm not going to focus on that – I'm going to move on to my next task. Having spilled the milk taught me how to be more careful and deal with the milk in the future.

This is different from shame, guilt, blame, and even responsibility and the ways in which those limit you and can contribute to feeling like you are powerless over your "luck."

Accountability says, "Yep, this happened, but I'm moving forward; and I'm going to do what I can to keep it from happening again."

How to overcome:
Own accountability for every single thing in your life

7. My mind, body, and spirit are disconnected

The thought that these things are somehow disconnected or unrelated can hold you back from reaching your full potential in all ways. Everything that impacts one of these will have a ripple effect into all other areas.

This is the most limiting belief of the ones we've covered. Believing this can result in utter misery.

It's like having a totaled car that you've wrecked into a tree, and somebody saying, "Oh God! Do you need a tow truck?" And you say, "No." And then somebody else saying, "OK… well, do you need a mechanic then?" And you say, "No." And still somebody else saying, "A body shop? Do you at least need a body shop?" And you say, "No, I need a manicure," and walk away.

Thinking that anything that you want or any state of desirable mental, physical, or spiritual well-being are not connected is the worst thing you can do for yourself. Nothing outside of you can affect you, which might sound really, really bizarre to those of us who are still privy to the last idea of, "I have bad luck."

If what you're doing is working for you, and you're happy, then keep on doing it. You are guaranteed to get the same results. But if it's not working, and you're unhappy, then something needs to change. Yes?

Nobody can make you do this. I can't tell you how many people I've worked with who tell me all about their miserable lives, all about the problem. And I understand. I've been there. But the minute I try to tell them what some of the solution might be, they immediately return back to the problem, back to the issues, back to the story, that is so true and real and painful in that moment that they don't want to see the solution. For some of us, chaos and pain are much more comfortable, if only via their familiarity.

Also? Unrelated, still important: Be conscientious who you let into your innermost life sanctuary. Not all who smile in your direction mean you well, friend! You might be chemically depressed, or you may just be surrounded by assholes. Figure out the difference and respond accordingly. This life is not about pretending to be perfect (anyone who seems to be is lying or a space alien). It is also not about wallowing in pain or any other negativity. Go, but don't stay too long. It's about finding a healthy middle ground where you are OK when you are not OK, where you are just more or less alright. It is about not staying too long in ecstasy, either, or the fall is too far. Taking care of yourself is also imperative. Our culture has decided this means long baths and chocolate, mani pedis and shopping trips. Self-care is really the act of saying no, scheduling yourself accordingly, getting rest at any cost, and knowing how and when to reach for help.

There are a lot of things that are painful.

Having a baby.

Running a marathon.

Overcoming cancer.

But they're worth it.

How to overcome:
Reconnect, journey within, level up

Ah, lookit what's next:

Section Four:
Level Up Program

Far and away the best prize that life has to offer is the chance to work hard at work worth doing.
-Theodore Roosevelt

Preparation for Level Up

This program is ONLY for:
Anyone willing to become willing
Anyone desperate for change or hungry for more out of life
Anyone teachable

The purpose of this program is to become able to create any reality you seek, to become aware of the soul purpose of all that is, to become aligned to design an existence that is to be celebrated rather than tolerated, and to become awakened to the full potential of your soul and experience/create the most good on a universal spiritual level.

The Promises:

Become able
Become aware
Become aligned
Become awakened

Sacred Covenant 1

I WILL: make a decision to journey within

JOURNEY – engage in the lifelong process of becoming

Make an agreement to journey inward to my deepest self, no matter the cost, placing these actions as priority above all.

You must become the life you wish to live, move towards the person you would like to become, and speak to the truths you have hidden to move forward.

MAKE A DECISION – simply make a choice, requiring no struggle, happening in an instant

1. become willing to look within
2. become willing to make this a priority
3. become willing to avoid excuses and begin the process of

Action Step 1: List everything you think you have power and control over
Examples: Make action lists over the top five things from this list which are easiest to repair

Action Step 2: List of all the qualities of a best friend or ideal partner
Examples: Begin to construct your own God by listing all ideal qualities, and their opposites

Action Step 3: Definitions from dictionary, hand written – power, control, manage, addiction, obsession, compulsion, choice, freedom, manifest, truth, mind, body, spirit, map
Examples: Using these precise definitions, determine whether you have a new understanding; then map where it is you would like to go

Narrative:

Making a decision is as simple as that.

Turn left or turn right?

Then the wheel moves the tires, the tires move the truck, and off you go.

When following a map; you don't pull over, bite your nails, call someone and yell, cry, pull apart the truck, put it back together, fret about whether it will be the right turn or the wrong one, worry about what might happen the instant you do turn, and so forth.

You trust that when you press the gas, the vehicle will accelerate in whatever gear you've chosen. You trust that when you press the breaks, forward momentum will cease. And you don't have to know the inner workings of it before you become willing to press the pedals. In fact, you give it no further thought. You just go.

Decisions are like that. When you flip the switch, the lights come on. You don't wonder about the process nor do you need to understand how or why electricity works to attempt to hit the switch.

Unless, of course, you're an electrician. And some of you are. Masters of connecting to the other, the black, what's beyond the Veil.

Some of you flip the switch, yet nothing happens.

So, you replace the bulb.
Still no light.
You flip the breaker.
Still no light.
Then what may you do?

You call an electrician. That's sort of what I am – someone who has a little bit more information than most about how all this works – who can give you that information, so you know it too.

So you can become your own electrician.
So you can become your own everything.

But this requires a journey within. Where all that Is, Was, and Will Be resides.

Where every thought, idea, inspiration, feeling, emotion, action, and behavior in all of humankind is accessible to you.

When you're going on a hike up a mountain, you don't wear flip flops. You wouldn't go without water. You wouldn't want to venture into the unknown with no sort of guide. Unless, of course, you're an experienced hiker and you know that trail like the back of your hand.

And such is the manner in which you must get to know yourself to achieve all you ever wanted.

It is the only way.

I don't claim to have the only map – there are many routes by which you may achieve the same destination. I don't claim to follow it perfectly – there are certainly other teachers more adherent to their own espousals than I am.

But I will tell you this: I have defied death. I have risen from ashes. And I know a peace and prosperity that cannot be described in words.

Some of the most intelligent minds alive today insist we use only a small portion of our brains.
Some of our most prominent scientists say the rest of the mind is always active yet have no clue its purpose.

The rest of the human mind contains all that is; the perfect design of the universe, infinite potentiality that can be easily accessed if so desired, and perfect guidance to any destination. An always reliable map. A vehicle that never breaks down. A switch that turns on the light for all of the people, all of the time.

I want to show you metaphysics. Epigenetics. Neuroplasticity. Your Soul. All that's left is the decision, which is yours alone to make.

Are you ready to level up?

Then let's ride.

Sacred Covenant 2

I WILL: adjust my perception of timelessness

TIMELESSNESS – the other side of the veil

Decide that everything is constant change, and the only place to live is in the moments between seconds, where time does not exist.

You must be in a fluid motion with the human concept of time, going with the flow, and learning to be still and move in perfect harmony with the entire universe. Only in attempting to go nowhere can you unlock the ability to travel any distance to any location; moreover, in attempting to go nowhere you will go all places at all times and do all things instantaneously.

CHANGE PERCEPTION – begin the process of my soul's (r)Evolution by changing my experiential reality

1. become willing to adapt & overcome habits
2. become willing to adjust preconceived notion of time
3. become willing to immerse myself on the other side of the veil

Action Step 1: Connect spiritually by selecting any 3 mentors and studying them intensely. Examples: Sadhguru, Abraham Hicks, Wayne Dyer, Eckhart Tolle, Deepak Chopra.

Action Step 2: Select 3 practices you will adopt to create new habits. Follow basic discipline. Examples: Make bed daily, take brief walk after dinner nightly, drink half weight in water fl. oz.

Action Step 3: Create your outline for wellness; not remaining in past nor jumping to future. Examples: Create monthly schedule for sleep/wake times, turn off phone 2 hours before bed.

Narrative:

A couple things –

One, as I was filming the beach on the day this video was shot, I kept thinking, "C'mon God, let a butterfly land on the camera or make a bird do something neat! Show them that you're here!"

And what I heard in reply was, "The ocean isn't enough?"

Holy smokes. The ocean isn't enough? The ocean isn't enough.

It's the human condition that even when faced with overwhelming evidence of incredible and miraculous things, we seek more. We overlook the proverbial forest, and all its majesty, for the trees.

Even just now, I am impatiently waiting for something to upload, and my mind has been on a repeating track of, "I need a drink. I need a drink. I need a drink." (Not that kind of drink, you heathens, it's 8:31am.) I got up to get the drink, and as I came to sit back down, saw that the same exact drink was already behind my laptop.

I had been sitting there thirsty all along, when exactly what I wanted was literally within reach yet out of view.

It is how so many of us live, yes?

If you only knew what you are capable of, friend. Good God, if only you knew.

You would never be buried beneath fear again.

Sometimes we have to shift the position in which we are seated to get a better view. You might be directly in front of a concrete pylon. Perhaps things look hard, bleak, gray. But shifting even an inch to the right could reveal the most glorious sunset you've ever beheld, the love of your life, or even… a pile of money.

What's. Blocking. Your. View?

This covenant is all about that concept, of reconsidering all we were taught, and the very essence of spirit, time, good and evil, and even reality. But how on earth do you do that?

Sometimes all it requires is a gentle tap on the shoulder, someone standing in full view of the rest of it saying, "Hey buddy, maybe scoot over a little bit so you can see this too. Have this too. Be this too."

Sometimes, we have to get knocked the hell off our chairs, and only then, from the ground, from the very bottom, do we look up. Some of us stay behind that concrete pylon, and for them, the view is never more than hard, bleak, and gray. They never know what's on the other side – what they could see, have, or be if they only shifted perspective.

You might now be thinking, "Sounds great, especially the pile of money. How do I lean over so it comes within view?"

Well, it isn't quite that simple. You have to get out of your own way. It's not tremendous effort or work on your part that's required for you to gain all you desire.

It's more like the fullness of a lake that is overflowing with that which would fulfill you on a Soul deep level. It is just waiting for you to turn the wheel and release what's behind the dam.

You don't have to collect it a drop at a time in a bucket.

You don't have to wait for rain and try to catch a few drops on your tongue.

You simply need to change the frequency you're emitting so that you can allow the dam to open, and what's already there will flow so quickly and deeply that it will flood you with well-being.

Sound awesome?

Good. Then, are you ready to level up?

Sacred Covenant 3

I WILL: activate momentum towards abundance

ABUNDANCE – the lack of scarcity or need, fear + worry, or unnecessary pain

Come to know that all needs and wants will be provided for always; when I meet these conditions, there is no lack or scarcity not self-created.

You must design, make room for, be thankful about, and look backwards upon your desires as though they have already occurred; indeed, in the infinite other realities and worlds as well as possible versions of yourself which exist, they have.

ACTIVATE MOMENTUM – trust that by moving forward, I have begun an irreversible process

1. become willing to experience discomfort and release fear
2. become willing to reconsider perceptions based in childhood and families of origin (or lack thereof)
3. become willing to make decisions regarding what I take with me and what I leave behind and shift my energy accordingly towards that which I bring forward

Action Step 1: List dreams left behind, select 3 variations, create action plan towards those.
Examples: For each dream, list related jobs that remain possible in a circular pattern.

Action Step 2: List hierarchy of needs, create visualization schedule.
Examples: Physically make representation of this via vision board, set meditation schedule.

Action Step 3: List every person, place, thing, situation, event, emotion, or relationship which ever caused you pain or in which you caused pain, then burn it.
Examples: If there are none, that was fairly straightforward. Be safe in the burning.

Narrative:

If I told you that you needed to get from Florida to California, would you lace up your kicks and head out the door walking?

Most likely not.

Yet that is what we do. We do things the hard way; the way that requires the most effort. And in such a manner that we often waste *a lot* of time and energy.

A vehicle might be a faster option. A plane even faster than that. If you were really creative, you might realize that the quickest way would be a phone call, by which you could be there instantaneously, through whatever mysterious process via which voice travels through air and time.

Think of all the things that could happen if you tried to walk from Florida to California.

Would you make it? Maybe. But it would take *forever*. You'd have blisters. The expense would be tremendous. You'd be utterly exhausted. A mess.

And that's the state in which many of you come to me. You've got most of what you want, things are pretty much the way you'd like them, but *dang* are you ever tired.

Here's the good news. You can catch that plane or make that call anytime you want. And the even better news? All that unnecessary and *slow* walking has just prepared you for where you've arrived in this exact moment. Your muscles are stronger. You know you can survive anything. And God knows; where there's a will, there's a way.

What if I told you that your life could be so much easier?

That the things you're reaching for are not as far away as you imagine? What if I said that the energy which creates universes is on your side, rooting for you every step of the way; but wondering when you'll realize there are planes?

Better yet; wondering when you'll realize you can fly?

This third step is all about reactivating your momentum. When you came into this world, you were full tilt ahead, full speed – bombs away.

Life, trauma, to do lists, other people, pain, bills, and the unexpected may have thrown you off track. But if you're on your way to a meeting and you make a wrong turn, do you just park your car and say, "Well, I guess I'm stuck here forever. That's that?" Or do you re-route, turn around, and head back in the correct direction with just as much speed as you were going in the wrong one?

This covenant is all about that.

For some of you, it'll mean taking an exit off of a never-ending loop that isn't getting you anywhere. For many of you, it could mean learning to drive in the first place. For others, it might be overcoming a fear of being in a relatively tiny hunk of plastic while it's hurtling down the highway of life with other unpredictable vehicles.

Regardless, it's time to get momentum flowing in the right direction.

It's time to tune your frequency to what you actually want. It's time to take the quickest and most effective route to where you are going, in the least painful and resistant way possible.

It's time.

It's time to level up.

Sacred Covenant 4

I WILL: accept all accountability for my life

ACCOUNTABILITY – complete ownership

Realize that all of the power of creation is inside of me, every other person, in every inch of nature, and during all moments; and behave accordingly to the best of my ability and knowledge at any given time.

You must begin to respect every living thing, creature, plant, and substance with equal reverence to achieve balance so that what you do not want stops arriving.

ACCEPT ALL – completely and totally agree without condition to welcome

1. become willing to experience the veil
2. become willing to connect to and revolutionize the way I treat self/others/earth
3. become willing to create a new inner and outer dialogue

Action Step 1: List 100 things you like about yourself, enlist help of others if necessary.
Examples: Consciously revise self-talk by identifying better thoughts in which to reside.

Action Step 2: Consciously revise behaviors which can level up your spirit.
Examples: Identify patterns that need better actions from you towards others, the universe, and self with viable alternatives.

Action Step 3: Adopt personal mantras. Try transcendental meditation. Re-consider all substances.
Examples: Embrace and cultivate consciousness by developing and creating constant visual and audio reminders. Evaluate and appropriately discard any harmful foods or products.

Narrative:

You're so stupid, why did you do that?
God, you're fat. It's disgusting, honestly.
Everything you try to do fails, you're such a loser!
Nobody will ever love you; you aren't worth it.
You'll never make enough money; you aren't talented at all.

How did those words make you feel?

Would you talk to a friend that way?
Hell, would you talk to an enemy like that?
What about your children – is that how you'd speak to them?

No?

Then why do you speak to yourself this way?

Interesting question, yes?

What you think, feel, say, and do comprises the frequency you emit which then creates your reality.
Your thoughts are the foundation of this. The foundation of all that you may have.

How does chocolate cake taste if you forget to add the sweetener?

Like actual dirt.

It's sort of like if you dress the right way, have all the right things, jump up and down trying to please those around you, sit in the front row of church; then turn around and say and do harsh things to others and yourself.

There is no place for guilt and shame in forward momentum.

Forward momentum is all that is required to live the life you desire.

And if the goal of that life is to help others? If you're on fire with the need to help people but can't seem to heal yourself?

It's crucial that your cake have all the ingredients – that your house have a firm foundation, or any wind can and will come along and blow it over.

That's how important the thoughts you have are to every single aspect of your life.

Your money. Your relationships. Your body.

The flipside of this is keeping *all* accountability for what comes into your path. Yes, all. This is a very hard pill to swallow for many, but it is necessary if you wish to be truly free.

Does this mean if bad things have happened to us that they are our fault? No. This isn't about blame.

It *is* about setting your frequency to the exact wavelength of what you desire so you can lift the veil of creation and realize what is all around you, all the time.

It's about revising your inner dialogue in such a way that it revolutionizes how you treat yourself, which will then naturally bring into alignment everything else – from the quality and strength of your connections to other people, the health and wealth you desire; all the way down to how you treat the earth.

Every thought has a consequence.

But how do we change them when the process feels so involuntary, like being swept out to sea by waves much larger than we are, carried into the undertow by negativity all around us?

It begins with accountability, and I can show you.

Let's level up.

Sacred Covenant 5

I WILL: release all that is not of and for me

ALL THAT IS NOT ME – all that is not Source, or however I choose to see it – all that is not in the highest and best

Become willing to release all history, thoughts, emotions, actions, relationships, and situations which do not serve my highest and best good.

You must cease the momentum of any memories, ideas, feelings, behaviors, connections, or influences which do not serve your highest and best good.

KICK OUT/RELEASE – totally let go of

1. become willing to tell myself the truth
2. become willing to seek out what it is I truly want and am
3. become willing to disregard all that does not support my journey

Action Step 1: Polar dip meditation practice of gratitude, freezing guilt + shame.
Examples: Jump briefly in cold water or do a snow angel – shock system back online.

Action Step 2: Identification of blocking patterns; sabotage of self.
Examples: Deeply examine ideas brought forward from childhood for truth, discard untrue.

Action Step 3: Do one thing that is terrifying, songs and art, breaking things.
Examples: Ax throwing at a designated place, taking a new creative class, shattering an item.

Narrative:

I jumped in a trash dumpster today.

Dug around in smelly, nasty garbage. Rubbed it all over myself. Even ate some of it – put it straight into my body. Then I really rolled in it to make sure it was covering me thoroughly. I made sure to bag some of it up so I could take it with me, too!

Does that sound insane?

Well, good. Then we're on the right track.

But that *is* exactly what we do when we relive trauma, get into unnecessary arguments (and spoiler alert: they're all unnecessary, even when you're right), or trash our body with terrible food, products full of chemicals, and so forth.

It's like carrying garbage with us everywhere we go. Not only is it heavy, it's an extremely unpleasant experience – for us and all who are exposed to the experience of us.

But what if I told you it was unnecessary? All of it?

The reliving of trauma. The unnecessary arguments. The absence of health? Wealth? Love?

What if I told you that you *never* had to feel that way again?

What the actual eff?

Look, forming new habits isn't easy. I get that. And I'm not expecting you to shoot rainbows out your rear while prancing around on a unicorn 24/7. That isn't how humans were built. We were built to experience both ends of the spectrum and all shades between.

Pain. Total well-being.
Heartbreak. Ecstatic love and belonging.
Illness. Complete health.
Poverty. Total financial freedom.
Feeling trapped. Never letting the ties that bind get hold of us again.

But some of us, oh *some of us*, will hold onto our anger with tightly clenched purple fists until our last ragged breath whooshes from our bodies. We will light ourselves on fire hoping the person we are angry with chokes on the smoke coming from our still burning bodies.

Ever replay an argument over and over with someone who isn't even there? Thinking up rebuttals and retorts and all the things you could have or might later say?

We already learned that our thoughts literally become reality, so having these memories and wasting these precious seconds is like literally praying all day every day for more of the same.

Ever pray for patience? *The whole world slows down.*
Ever pray for humility? *Life will bring you to your knees.*

We get what we ask for, and every single thought is an ask.

What's next, then?

You tell yourself the truth, not the most convenient version of memories in which you are presented well, finding an accurate mirror and facing what you see in it with neither praise nor condemnation.

You seek out everything that is of and for you – your highest and best good.
You totally disregard everything that does not support this endeavor. In this way you make space for what's to come next, and boy do you *ever* want to do that.

Trust me, you really, really, *really* want to do that.

Because what's going to come after this will blow your freaking mind.

Level up.

Sacred Covenant 6

I WILL: embrace all that is of and for me

ALL THAT IS ME – all that is Source, or however I choose to see it – all that is in the highest and best

Become willing to make of myself a doorway and speaker through which all light may gather, remain, and flow freely.

You must decide to light other candles in the ways in which you are called to do, which never dims your own flame; then you decide to pursue your life's purpose.

INVITE IN/OPEN – totally and radically embrace and welcome

1. become willing to allow in new truths
2. become willing to accept and love in total radical positivity my entire self and history
3. become willing to find and exuberantly pursue all whom and that which supports my journey

Action Step 1: Outline all the ways you wish someone had been there for you.
Fxamples: Identify each space in which you were not protected, gather up prior versions.

Action Step 2: List any problematic behaviors from past that you have carried forward.
Examples: Unhealthy coping mechanisms, relationships to food, smoking.

Action Step 3: Make a list of all fears.
Examples: Determine whether rational/irrational, how they control your life, exposure plan.

Narrative:

This is where things get really, *really* good.

Man do they get good. *God, I hope you get here.* I want this for you so much.

No worries, everyone gets here when they die.

And we all die. So, one way or another, you'll arrive. It's just a matter of whether you want to get to this awesome feeling place while you're still breathing.

Do you? I do. I can show you how.

This is where you glimpse the face of creation; of all that Is, Was, and Will Be. This is where, for brief moments, you know every thought ever to have existed, feel every feeling ever to have been felt, and are all that could possibly be. This is where you have everything that can be had.

This is where there is no lack. No suffer. No fear. No pain.

This is pure, delicious, unfiltered, *God* – for lack of a better word – and there really isn't a better word.

Don't freak out on me now, atheists and agnostics. I'm not talking about some guy with a white beard in the sky on a throne deciding if you're good or bad.

That's more like, um, Santa Claus.

What we're discussing in this covenant to self is literally how to get in touch with what you are, which is a designer of worlds, a maker of life, a unifier of all. This is where the answers are.

Ironically, it's also where the questions cease.

Even religion says God created us in his own image. Could that not mean that perhaps we are God and God is us? There exists a symbiotic relationship in which the world *is* because we see it and we *are* because the world *is*.

I can tell I lost some of you there. Down the rabbit hole. Stay with me; this gets really, *really* awesome.

This is where you fall totally and completely in love with yourself, almost by accident. It's where all of the steps you've taken before this one culminate into the top of the freaking mountain. It's like the end of a long, long, *long* hike.

Yet now you can finally see the view; and off in the distance? An even taller mountain to climb once you've rested a bit.

Imagine the best day of your life, or even play yourself a movie of those moments now. Perhaps it was holding your baby in your arms for the first time, being moved to tears at the sight of the ocean right before going totally blind, a delicious meal in a foreign place full of wonderful sights and smells, tastes and feels.

Whatever it is; imagine it, hold it in your mind. Know that you can go there any time you want. From anywhere. Your couch. Your desk at work. Even a jail cell.

Know deeply that freedom is completely yours if you so desire. That reality is a construct. Then decide to embrace all that feels good. All that is of and for you.

That's it. It's that simple.

This is the place in which all inspiration occurs, this is the place where millions of dollars can be made, this is the place from which terminal illness may be overcome; if it is not yet your time.

It is infinite power. Wisdom. And love.

You can't stay here, I'm sorry. Humans weren't made for that. But you can come as often as you like, create as much joy as you choose, and rest solid in the knowledge that this is where you'll return when your heart has pumped its last beat.

Only one more step remains.

And then you will have leveled up.

Sacred Covenant 7

I WILL: break through the veil to perfect healing

HEAL – reparation of any wound which has completely been resolved as though it never took place; with the exception of scars which remain to remind us where we have been and warn not to return (a brief glancing over); mind, body, spirit cohesion

Accept that you can be freed of any illness or dysregulation of mind, body, heart, or spirit; that perfect harmony can be restored to all systems at any time and anything other than is a choice.

You must enter into an entire soul (r)evolution, and be totally open to the notion that all you have thought to be true may be false, all you have thought to be false may be true, and that neither universal truth nor falsehood actually exist.

BREAK THROUGH VEIL – pierce the worlds, knowing in my deepest that I have accessed the divine, and carry that forward with me back to this current physical *timespacereality*

1. become willing to seek out all dysregulation
2. become willing to identify and dismantle pattern
3. become willing to create and maintain (r)evolution

Action Step 1: RAOKS – don't tell anyone – get out of your comfort zone.
Examples: Take food to a shelter, donate money to an animal welfare society, mow a lawn.

Action Step 2: Totally reroute life and patterns.
Examples: Break free from all you are doing by making a new plan and acting on it.

Action Step 3: Clear out all chemicals and unneeded items; medical, physical, + food plan to follow for habit breaking.
Examples: Select a protocol to follow – whether whole food, therapy, gym time, so forth.

Narrative:

Here we are at our seventh sacred covenant to self – synergy past perturbation.

Did you know I didn't even write anything for this one? I just began speaking and here we are.

Did you know I don't have any fancy editing skills or perfect timing?

For the previous steps; I wrote them once, read them once, and I filmed all these in one day because I am a medium, a channel, a psychic; whatever one who holds the gap and stands between worlds just long enough to tell you what they see is called.

All of the videos have been five minutes and nine seconds, and that wasn't intentional. When I read about what that means, there you go. Apparently, it's a prompt to put your focus towards beginning or expanding your spirituality as light working skills and talents you have are greatly needed by the world. It also means that Angels are asking for you to illuminate the way for others.

I think that's why I decided to go off script; because this *is* the final place. When something is divinely inspired; it's easy, free-flowing, and everything else is hard, frustrating.

We have been given an emotional GPS that was installed so that we can tell when we are on the right track. If something sucks and feels awful, we're not. If something makes us happy and feels good, we are. This seventh step is elusive but it's not impossible.

Think about everything that this means for the Hindus. The seventh chakra, Sahasrara, is rainbow colored and at the crown of your head. It is thousand petaled. It is the final place of enlightenment. The seventh sin in the Bible is "Thou Shalt Not Commit Adultery," which applies here because when you are not true to yourself, *when you are not true to yourself*, is when you fall out of alignment with peace. In the Kaballah, the seventh Sefirot is eternity. This is a space of timelessness. For Muslims, the seventh sin is not performing pilgrimage to Mecca and the literal meaning of all that, to my limited knowledge is, going to the house of God for a visit. My son was even born on the seventh. My life purpose is to speak this information.

All the signs point in the same direction and the seventh covenant is the final one, the one we carry forward with us. You can get to the same destinations by so many different roads, religions, or schools of thought.

It does not matter how you get here; it matters only that you do, and you will go in and out of all these different stages and steps. It is not a progression. There is no graduation. You may find yourself in any one of these places at any time.

No one expects you not to be human. But the important thing to remember is all religions and most schools of spirituality talk and say the same things. Huston Smith's perennial philosophy is that there is one Source.

You may wonder why I haven't shown you my face or told you my name in the videos, and that is because this simply does not matter. In 300 years, none of us will be here. Our children won't even be here, nor in almost all cases; theirs.

Nothing of us will remain. I have no need for recognition.

The seventh step is the resonance of all the divine, the continuance of existence, the dwelling within – perfect peace inside and out. It is when you run around smiling and everyone thinks you are crazy. It is the place where you can heal any mental, physical, emotional, spiritual, heart, chakra, or other wound; as though it never took place – where only a scar will remain to remind you of where you have been.

It is where an entire Soul (R)evolution can take place. It is where you seek out dysregulation; it is where you dismantle old patterns. It is game over; it is smooth sailing. You do not need to level up once you're here. It is the last level.

Did you know

Conclusion to Level Up

Are you now willing to become willing?
Are you now experiencing change or more from your life?
Are you now teachable?

The world is your oyster, then. You are your oyster. You are the world and the world is you. Therefore, anything can be created by your innermost self, and your innermost self can be created by anything. Taking captain-hood of your ship is always the priority, because only then can you steer towards desirable outcomes rather than crashing unknowingly again and again against unfriendly shores. This program has not installed any new software into your spirit. It has simply unleashed what was already contained within you. You are freed of guilt and shame when you honor these sacred covenants, and are released to your greatest purpose, joy, and freedom.

Are you now able, aware, aligned, awakened?

Section Five:
Meditations + Affirmations

*The best way to take care of the future
is to take care of the present moment.*
    -Thich Nhat Hanh

I Love
(Morning – Rated PG)

I love that I have had more days healthy than I have sick.
I love the incredible power of my body.
That my heart pumps blood throughout my organs.
That everything works in perfect concert, just like the machinations of the universe.
I love that when I don't feel well, that always gets reversed.
I love the power that I have to heal myself, the power that I feel flowing through me at all times.
I love that I get to be happy.
I love that I can feel things.
I love that I can move about in this world in such a way that I cause good.
I love that good comes to me.
I love that I am good and all that is of the light and of what is best crosses my path.
I love that I am always in the right place at the right time.
I love that when things don't appear to be going my way, I trust that in the background, there is a movie playing about which I am unaware; which is still what is best for me, what is working out for me
I love that there are people who I have yet to meet who are wonderful and will teach me much
I love knowing, deep in my knower, outside of my thinker, that I am made of light, that I am made of air, that I am made of what the stars are made of
I love knowing that when I need to rest, I can sleep deeply and peacefully
I love knowing that when I need to be awake, I can become aware and function with pure concentration and energy
I love that anytime I need it; I have the insight available to me of Universes, of Worlds, of the Creator of All
I am so excited for what will come next
I am so happy to be here
I am so glad that when I am experiencing something that feels uncomfortable, I know that it is temporary
I am so relieved that pain never lasts
I am so, so grateful for all of the things that are in my current reality
And really, really excited to know that my reality can change in all the best ways, anytime

I love knowing when I'm on the right track
I love that I get to feel clearly and distinctly when I am not
And that I will be given information about which way to turn so that I can get on a better path if I need to
I love my body
I love that my organs, right now, are keeping me alive; that my heart has endured so much
I love what my eyes have seen and yet they have chosen to keep on looking
I love what my ears have heard and yet they have chosen to keep on listening
I am so sorry; body, heart, for what I have sometimes put you through, but I am so thankful that you continue to live and beat for me each day, each moment
I am very much looking forward to what this day has in store
What my life has in store
I know that as I am awake, I will encounter so many magical and incredible things
And that as I sleep? I will find them there too
I love being alive
And in those moments that I don't love being alive?
I love the knowledge that I will once again; sooner rather than later
Just as I always have
I love knowing that the best things are right around the corner
I love feeling deeply accepted by All that Ever Was, Is, and Will Be
I love

For Bad Bitches
(Morning – Rated R)

You are one bad motherfucker
Everything that has ever happened to you has built you into something strong, something incredible
Someone who is capable of doing anything that you put your mind to
Every scar, every stretch mark, every hurdle, every setback, every hardship; has prepared you
To become whatever it is you wish to become
To do whatever you want to do
To accomplish all
And not one of those obstacles took you down when it was meant to
Good people will cross your path today
Things that you want will flow freely in your direction
Everything will run smoothly
Because that's what happens to bad bitches who do good things and have good karma
You are beautiful just the way you are
You don't need to put your life on hold because you don't think you're skinny enough or pretty enough or young enough or loved enough
Book that ticket, go on that trip, call that person back, buy the shoes; whatever it is you've been waiting for
You don't have to wait for it; you can do it now, you can do it today, this instant
You can turn entire tides in your favor
You can move the sun, the moon, to your orbit
Don't wait until you're perfect; it's the enemy of what you could have in this moment
Embrace the power of authenticity in your story
You are made of stars and motherfucking light
And within you, universes are contained
You come from All that Ever Was, Is, and Will Be
And you can tap into that knowledge at any time
You need to look yourself in the eye in the mirror
And say, thank you, body
Thank you, heart, for pumping blood all throughout my system
Thank you, skin, for remaining a healthy organ
Thank you, all organs, actually, for running in concert with one another

Thank you, cells, for copying and regenerating, and doing what you're supposed to do
Thank you for this magical, magnificent fucking amazing human skin encased temple that I'm in
Thank you, extra fat cells, for protecting me, but you will go now
Thank you, illness, for warning me of when I'm going too hard or headed in the wrong direction, but you will go now too
Nothing that is not of and for me may reside or dwell in my body or my home
Only those who belong and are of my highest and greatest good may cross my path
In God's name, in all of the names of the different ways that God is called upon
I ask that light and love only may enter my field, enter my day, enter my mind – enter me
And I ask that a filter be placed, so that I only say what is necessary, true, and kind
I am one bad bitch
I am a spiritual gangster
That's what you need to be telling yourself today
You will find so many opportunities to do good and impact other people
And anything that gets in your way?
You'll overcome it
You got this
Today is your day and you are gonna make it your bitch
You are gonna own this motherfucker
Good morning

Sleep Meditation
(Evening – Rated PG 13)

Hello. I am delighted to be with you as you drift peacefully to sleep.
You are never alone.
Let's take some cleansing breaths together.
Place your hand on your stomach so you can feel your breaths.
When you inhale, do so in such a way that your stomach expands.
Breathe in through your nose, 1234
Breathe out through your mouth, 1234

It's a good time.
It's the perfect time.
This is such a safe, clear place.
The day has come to a close now.
All momentum can cease.
Thought can cease.

Listen to my voice.
As you hear the sounds of my voice, you'll feel your body progressively relax.
The longer I speak, the more relaxed you will feel.
Hearing my voice will gently lull you to sleep.
Once you are asleep, you will sleep deeply.
Peacefully. Soundly.
You will travel and dream and love and feel total safety in your sleep.
All your visions are possible there. It is a place of infinite manifestation potential.
Breathe in through your nose, 1234
Breathe out through your mouth, 1234

Now:
Snuggle down into your covers.
Tuck yourself in perfectly.
Wiggle your toes.
Wiggle your fingers.
Turn your head from side to side.
Stretch out your neck and back.
Sink down.
All the way down.
Feel your body getting heavy, impossibly heavy.

You are sinking down through your bed or resting place.
You are melting into a perfect energy cocoon.
This cocoon is made of magic silver thread.
As you rest, every cell will be copied in perfect health and harmony.
All unneeded materials, energies, thoughts, feelings, worries, and fears will fade; then leave.
Blood will flow and organs will perform in the most magnificent ways.
You can close your eyelids.
They are so very heavy.
They are too heavy to hold open.
Breathe in through your nose, 1234
Breathe out through your mouth, 1234

Tighten the muscles in your neck and shoulders.
Now release.
Feel the day's tension and stress behind you now.
All motion ceases.
All activity has come to a stop.
There are no bills to pay.
No worries to ponder.
Nobody to take care of or talk with.
It is time now, the most perfect and peaceful time, for deep, deep rest.
Breathe in through your nose, 1234
Breathe out through your mouth, 1234

Your brain waves will be in a perfect pattern for the deepest sleep and restoration.
Love envelops you.
Perfect acceptance surrounds you.
All errors and problems are behind you now.
Tomorrow will mark the beginning of an entirely new life.
Each day it is so.
You will wake brand new, ready.

Travel back to the most serene place you have ever been.
You are there now.
Recall the most peaceful moments you have ever known.
Those are with you now.

Press your knees together, then release.
Furrow your brow, then release.

Crinkle your nose, then release.
Breathe in through your nose, 1234
Breathe out through your mouth, 1234

The wind is blowing gently.
The clouds glide slowly past.
The stars, moon, sun, planets, and all of creation have aligned to make you in this moment's perfection.
They have conspired in your favor to bring you to this peaceful time of rest.

You may imagine a roaring campfire.
A babbling brook as you sleep in a comfy tent.
The sound of train tracks beneath you.
Waves crashing to the shore of the ocean at your feet.
The weight of your body sinking into a gently swaying hammock.
The rocking of a boat in the ocean.
Typing on a keyboard.
Whatever you like.
And that sound, feeling, place will carry you gently to sleep.

You are so very tired.
Your work is done for now.
You are so very ready to rest.
Settle your body all the way down.
Breathe in through your nose, 1234
Breathe out through your mouth, 1234

There is nothing which needs your attention now.
You may let go.
Totally release.
Allow rest to come over you like a heavy blanket, like the sun that warms your face, like the rain that washes away all the troubles of the land, back to shore.
Allow sleep to enter the doorway of your consciousness like a gentle lover caressing your brow until you are so relaxed that you simply cannot remain awake.
It just isn't possible.

Hear the sound of my voice.
Listen to my voice.
Breathe in through your nose, 1234

Breathe out through your mouth, 1234

Your skin heals perfectly from the dents or dings of daily life.
Your eyes rejuvenate as they are shut, to see clearly both in this world and the next.
Your jaw relaxes, the stress slowly leaving each joint and bone.

Your autoimmune system kicks in and comes online in perfect harmony, protecting you while you dream.
Your nervous system is a symphony, working in concert with your entire body; the brain its conductor.
All of this happens as you enter the deepest and most calming place of deep, healing rest.

While here, you may choose to dream in lucidity, meet your spirit guide, travel to destinations unknown, or enter the great black for deep restoration while floating.

Your body hums with the vibratory effect of total healing and motion cessation.
Your entire cellular makeup rejuvenates down to the atomic level.

Everything returns to its natural homeostasis.

You are free.
You are so tired, ready for sleep.
You will wake refreshed and ready to face anything.
You will be made strong and brilliant by this rest.
You will know the power of creation resides within you.
When you wake, you will move mountains. You will be focused. You will be renewed, energized.

But for now, you rest.
Let's take some cleansing breaths together.
When you inhale, do so in such a way that your stomach expands.
Breathe in through your nose, 1234
Breathe out through your mouth, 1234

You are perfect. You are worthy. You are loved.
You are an incredible piece of the moving wheel of creation and you are terrifically important.

Feel each part of your body with your mind.
Feel your feet.
Feel your legs.
Feel your hips.
Feel your back.
Feel your stomach.
Feel your chest.
Feel your neck.
Feel your face.
Feel the crown of your head.

Imagine white light coursing through the top of your head like electricity or lightening, cleansing every inch of you until you are full of light and glowing. Carry this with you as you arrive on sleep's shore.

Goodnight earth angel

Today is Going to Rock!
(Morning meditation for kids – Rated G)
have them "hollaback" each line or just read to them

You are such a magnificent kid!
You are going to have amazing experiences today.
You are full of light, made of stars, and going to encounter so much magic all day long!
School, play, friends, learning, meals – everything today is going to go smoothly.
And if it doesn't? You will know exactly what to do!
I trust your judgment and am so thrilled I get to be your parent.
It makes me happy to be your mom.
It makes me smile to watch you grow.
I love that your healthy, strong body is going to be there for you all day long!
I know that your brilliant, wonderful mind is going to lead you on amazing journeys today!
Your smile makes other people smile.
If you cry, I am here to hold you. I am here for you, always.
I love you when you are sad. When you are mad. And when you are happy.
I love you when you win. I love you when you lose. I love you when you make mistakes.
Go out into the world and try new things, and know home is always right around the corner.
You are more than enough.
Making mistakes is how you learn, so be excited when you get to learn this way.
It's OK to be afraid, and I love that we walk through our fears anyway, together.
We do the right thing, especially when nobody is looking.
We use our kindness, our gentle hands and feet, and our integrity!
Your body is your body.
I know that you can do nearly anything that you set your mind to do.
I know that you are capable of so much.
I know that you can reach your dreams.
I know that you are trying so hard. I see this, and it makes me so proud to know you do your best.
I know that you can always take a break if you need to rest, and that's OK too!

This is going to be a beautiful day.
This is a good morning.
This is a wonderful chance to start over, brand new.
I can't wait to see what you become today!

(Hollaback)
I am strong!
I am smart!
I am capable!
I am kind!
I am funny!
I am good!
I am resilient!
I am honest!
I am talented!
I am giving!
I am dedicated!
I am fun!
I am friendly!
I am loving!

Sweet Dreams, Angel
(Evening meditation for kids – Rated G)
read quietly and slowly to them

As you lay down, snuggle deep into your comfy, comfy covers.
Wiggle your whole body, feet to finger tips.
Feel the warm blankets like love enveloping you.
You are safe. You are home. You are with people who will always take care of you.
Let's let our eyes drift closed together, eyelids fluttering down slowly, like butterflies on our faces.
Can we take a deep breath together?
In through our noses, making our tummies rise – 1234
Out through our mouths, slowly – 1234
That was really good! I bet you feel so relaxed, calm, and ready for rest.
Let's imagine we hear the ocean waves nearby.
And look, into the distance, what is that?
Keep your eyes closed so we can see it together.
Squeeze your fingers and toes so tight, then let them go.
Listen for the sounds of birds on the sand and look for the bright spot in the distance.
I think it's a hot air balloon!
Lay back in my wagon, and I'll take you there.
We set off… headed in the direction of the hot air balloon… you are riding in the wagon.
It's a nice, slow ride. You are so relaxed, hearing the ocean sounds, riding along.
Can we take another deep breath together? You did so great the first time.
In through our noses, making our tummies rise – 1234
Out through our mouths, slowly – 1234
We are going along here, near the sea, and feeling so sleepy.
We know that when we sleep again, we will have happy dreams about wonderful things.
There's nothing to worry about. Today is done. Tomorrow isn't here yet.
The only thing we have to do is get to the hot air balloon
And you're just riding along, calmly, as we head in that direction
I see a little more color in the distance
Of the clear, blue sky, as the sun is setting

You can let your whole body relax totally, melting down into your bed, sinking into the comfy
Can we take a deep breath together?
In through our noses, making our tummies rise – 1234
Out through our mouths, slowly – 1234
As we get closer, I can see the air in the balloon, it's rainbow colored
It's all blown up and ready for us
So we get in and rise into the clouds, slowly
Floating, floating, floating, floating, floating
We are flying, slowly, safely, across the sea, across the world
We can see our home down below! Our families sleeping in their beds!
We relax totally, sitting on pillowy clouds.
Can we take a deep breath together?
In through our noses, making our tummies rise – 1234
Out through our mouths, slowly – 1234

Your Body is Whole!
(Anytime wellness meditation for kids – Rated G)
have them "hollaback" each line or just read to them

You have been healthy so many more days than you have been sick.
Every time you have had a cut or a bruise, your magical body has healed itself!
It can do this again, any time you need it to.
Every cell, organ, and part of your body works perfectly to make you well.
Speak life into yourself, tell your body how strong it is.
Thank you, wonderful body and mind.
Say this with me:
I love being healthy and whole!
Good job!
You are so much stronger than you think, and able to do more than you can imagine.
Every part of you is becoming well.
Anything that doesn't feel good right now is temporary.
You are made of stars and light.
You are perfect and ready to heal.
Thank you for _____'s wonderful heart.
Thank you for _____'s wonderful brain.
Thank you for _____'s wonderful skin.
Thank you for _____'s wonderful organs.
Thank you for _____'s wonderful bones.
Thank you for _____'s wonderful tissues.
Thank you for _____'s wonderful cells.
Thank you for restoring _____ to a state of perfect health, wholeness, peace, and ease.
I am so glad I am alive!

Thank You Body

A mostly Christianity based original personal meditation piece for deep physical and trauma healing. Change names or words where needed to customize for yourself, PG 13 rating, designed for adults. Hold each relevant part of your body tenderly or visualize associated chakra area while meditating.

Thank you.

Thank you, heart, for beating through all the drugs I pumped into my body. Thank you for beating through all the surgery and radiation. Thank you for working for me, even as we underwent trauma. You kept us alive. Thank you for all the miles you let us run. Thank you for growing our baby. Thank you for pumping blood through the veins and arteries and keeping them clear. Thank you, heart. Thank you for enduring the pain and suffering you underwent as I exposed us to more and more trauma. Thank you for enduring the abuse when you were just a tiny heart and staying beating, living, for us. I am sorry I hurt you. I vow to take better care of you. Please keep beating. Thank you for deciding to live.

Thank you, lungs. Thank you for every breath I have taken. Thank you for working diligently despite the poisons and toxins I put in you. I'm sorry. I didn't know any better. And once I knew better, I felt compelled. I couldn't stop. I will not put any more poison inside you, and I am deeply and truly sorry that I did. I am so very proud of you. I love you for the air you give. I love you for the light you bring to body. I love you for the way you allow energy to move and flow inside and outside. I want to learn more about how to use you to get closer to God. Help me breathe the way you would have me breathe for optimal health and enlightenment.

Thank you, kidneys. I am so sorry you have had to process so much. It is more than any other kidneys could bear. Thank you for filtering all the drugs you have been given. I thought they would heal us. I was wrong. I am so sorry I did not know better. I am sorry that once I thought I knew better; I did not listen. I will not poison you again. Thank you for healing and being willing to work with body so we can live.

Thank you, liver. I am so sorry for the alcohol. It numbed the pain. That is no excuse. Thank you for all that you do. I vow to restore you to optimal health, so you have a chance to heal. I know you are damaged. In God's name, I demand complete and total healing. By the stripes of Jesus, you are whole. You are well. We will take better care of you. Thank you for all you have done. Thank you for helping us give life to our baby. Thank you for the new cells you have had to create time and again. Thank you.

Thank you mind. Soul. Brain. Center. Connection. Thank you for what you have done. Thank you for taking us to school, and for retaining all that I asked of you. Thank you for the words. You can stop fighting now. You are safe. I am so sorry that you were not safe before, but you are safe now. In Jesus' name, I command you to operate only from the highest good and from what is of Christ; to think, feel, communicate, and live in such a way that what you allow in and what you put out is of My Beloved Lord only. I am so sorry for the memories you had to retain. You can release whatever does not serve God. You can forgive. You can heal body now. Thank you for healing body. Thank you for taking our power back. Thank you for all the ways you protected me. I required such fight from you, such spirit, such power. I understand now I drained your power to successfully run body by remaining angry. I am so sorry that I overburdened you with more than what any brain or mind could handle. I ask that you seek calm continually, like the floor of the ocean, and allow life to pass us by like the waves on the surface. Mind, please integrate. You are healed. You are whole. You are safe. Let every word that passes lips be of God, from God, for God. Help me re-dedicate my life to My Beloved Lord by guiding my thoughts, words, and actions. Take my will, and always redirect it to what aligns with that of My Beloved God.

Spirit. I do not know where you have been. I do not know where you are going. You have ruled. You have been beaten. You have been raped. Not just now, but in so many lifetimes. You have led armies. You have lit cities to burn. You have battled. I understand what and who you are. But we do not slash throats in this lifetime. You are not welcome to bring forth that aspect to who we are. We are a mother now. I understand you are eager to return. I know you are being pulled to come home. I command, in Jesus' name that you heal body in its entirety. That you return body to optimal health. Body was sent here for the Soul Purpose of bringing forth life and must remain until God alone calls body home. In Jesus' name, I command you to live in this current life only. To remain here. To be a mother. A wife. And a healer of people and lover of life. I command you to allow body to give breath from lungs, blood from heart, and clarification through all other areas as needed for Molly to follow her highest and best path to me, her God, so she can do my work. I have given her a path and a purpose, and she has lost her way because you, warrior, come forward. You must remain. You will be needed again. But not in this life. Lay down, soldier, and let the nurturing mother I need her to be come forth. You are burning her. From the inside. I command you, in Jesus' name, the name of the holy spirit and holy ghost and all who have gone before, of all ancestors in her line and Angels I have commanded to protect her, to immediately let her gentleness return.

Thank you, Spirit, for keeping her strong. Without you, she would not have gotten to here. Thank you Spirit, for helping her fight. But you can lay down the weapons now. A ceasefire has been called. A peace treaty created; an agreement made. She is needed here for now. I cannot tell you for how long. But right now is not her time.

Lungs, heart, and body are in agreement. Spirit, you may not continue to light the fire. You must let Molly become the child of God she was destined for. Let go of your pain from this lifetime. Release it immediately, in the name of Jesus Christ. Let go of what is hurting you, Spirit, immediately. Release all negative energy or anything taken in, on, or around Molly so that she can heal and mother her son.

Section Six: Guides

*It is no measure of health
to be well adjusted to a profoundly sick society.*
-Jiddu Krishnamurti

Weight Loss / Health Restoration
Mind + Body + Spirit Detox Challenge

An ideal amount of time for this program is one month; but take as much or little time as you may need to do this thoroughly, which is more important than completing it quickly.

START WEIGHT: Date_____ *Now stop weighing!
Optional, not recommended:
Week 1 Wt.____ Week 2 Wt.____ Wk. 3 Wt.____ Wk. 4 Wt.____ Wk. 5 Wt.____

END WEIGHT: Date_____ *Until now, then weigh again if desired.

START Measurements, Date____
Bust____Chest____Waist____Hips____Thigh____Chicken Wang____

END Measurements, Date____
Bust____Chest____Waist____Hips____Thigh____Chicken Wang____

Wake (W)/Phone Off (PO)/Sleep (S) Schedule

Mon___	Tue___	Wed___	Thu___	Fri___	Sat___	Sun___
W:	W:	W:	W:	W:	W:	W:
PO:	PO:	PO:	PO:	PO:	PO:	PO:
S:	S:	S:	S:	S:	S:	S:
AH:	AH:	AH:	AH:	AH:	AH:	AH:

*Use fourth column to record times that these action items ACTUALLY HAPPENED (AH).

Week One Mind/Body/Spirit Schedule

Mon___	Tue___	Wed___	Thu___	Fri___	Sat___	Sun___
Mind	Body	Spirit		Mind	Body	Spirit

Mind Preparation:

Select what will best challenge and expand your mind.

This can be anything from enrolling in classes to learning a language or practicing new recipes. A really neat way to train your mind into new habits is by adopting new behaviors; like washing all dishes daily or cutting out "diet" foods and drinks to clear up your thinking and memory. I recommend eliminating all sugars, alternative and artificial sweeteners, cow dairy, wheat, corn, and as many other potentially inflammatory items as you can tolerate.

If in therapy or any sort of group support, share your homework results with those professionals! Make sure you have scaffolding in place before you embark on this journey. It will be far more intense than you think. I conduct online and in person workshops and seminars. A huge portion of this learning takes place in what participants learn from one another; so please get in touch if you would like to find a way to take your progress to the next level. Make any appointments with health, medical, or holistic professionals you may need.

Make a commitment to get the hell off social media for at least 30 days too. It's a pointless time suck. "Oh my god, but I need to connect to my family and friends," you scream. OK, cool. Do it like we did in the olden days. Letters. Visits. Phone calls. Whatever. Stop falling into the mind numbing endless well of content. It's numbing you to the spiritual experience your Soul is craving.

Select mantras and listen to + say them each day. Write them down, put up reminders everywhere.

Here's an example: I GOT THIS. I WAS MADE FOR THIS. My BODY IS BEGGING ME TO DO THIS. I AM READY, EVEN WHEN I DO NOT FEEL READY. I CAN DO THIS. I WILL DO THIS. IT DOES NOT HAVE TO BE PERFECTLY DONE; IT ONLY NEEDS TO GET DONE. I DO NOT HAVE TO DO IT ALL AT ONCE. BUT I WILL DO IT! I AM GONNA GET DOWN WITH MY BEAUTIFUL SELF. I AM A BADASS, AND ABOUT TO MAKE SOME MAGIC HAPPEN.

Body Preparation:

Select healthy body focus times, schedule minimum 3x/weekly, add to calendar.

This can be anything from yoga, swimming, or dance videos to HIIT, CrossFit, or gym time! One thing that is fun here is to stretch your comfort zone as far as you can. Do something totally different! If you are a triathlete, try a gentle tai chi class. If you are not into physical training at all, consider learning about breathwork and stretching. Just get moving, in any way! Incorporate as much of this into your daily life as you can. Lift up on your toes while cooking, do lunges to the bathroom each time you need to use it, so forth.

Do not weigh. At all. All month. Most of us have very unhealthy relationships with the scale. Weigh only on the 1st and the last day of the month if you must. Record weights if you like. The clearest way to gauge progress is with before and after photos, measurements, and most importantly – how you feel!

Plan out your recipes, meal ideas, grocery lists; and prepare them to refrigerate and freeze so you have an easy time staying on track. Our website and social media have lots of great tried and true ideas to share. Thousands have revolutionized their health, wellness, and weight with our totally free resources. Shop and gather as much as you can ahead of time, and if able, make a 30-day commitment to not eat outside of your home. Purchase healthy and non-processed foods to prepare meals during this time to ensure your greatest chance of success!

Try intermittent fasting; learn about autophagy. Consider implementing 16:8 at least one day per week, more if you can. Widen the window of fasting as you are able, if your health permits. Consider trying One Meal a Day (OMAD) once per week so your body can rest and repair. I do full on three (or more) day fasts, but do not recommend this abruptly; rather ease into it if you are coming off of the standard trash diet most of us consume.

No alcohol for the duration of the challenge! Shortcut: If you must drink, there is a one day drinking maximum exception! This does not mean drink whatever TF you want, either – still no sugar and no wheat friendly beverages ONLY! If you can't stop drinking alcohol for a month, you might want to take a look at what could possibly be a larger problem at hand. What are you trying to drown with all that wine, mama?

WATER, WATER, WATER! Drink at least *half* your weight in fluid ounces of water per day. Get a container and mark it with times if historically you do not meet this goal unaided. Set alarms in your phone if you have to, but make it happen. This is *beyond imperative*! You may need extra supplementation, electrolytes, and even additional salt if you are consuming a lot of water.

Now is the time, if you have the financial means available to do so, to see anyone and everyone you think may help you along this holistic journey – reiki, acupuncture, hypnosis, massage, anything that fits for you. Learn some new shit; it won't kill you. Make taking care of yourself a priority, finally, and you'll be surprised at how quickly your body can right itself of some seriously major problems!

Do all the things! Get your home or living space clean if at all possible – starting from an organized point will help you greatly. If in doubt, throw it out – give it away – have a garage sale, whatever. Declutter! Kondo the hell out of everything, people too. If it doesn't bring you joy, tell it, "Bye, bitch!"

Make your bed daily. Don't ask why. Just do it. Absolutely no phone in the period two hours before bedtime! Plug in to a totally separate room or at least out of reach. Schedule approximations of when you will be waking and going to sleep. Work hard on those sleep patterns and limiting blue light/EMF waves! Spend some time meditating and grounding yourself, getting in the actual sun and sitting on the real earth. It is imperative for your survival and healing.

Begin creating structure if you do not have enough of it, work hard getting free if you suffer from too much routine. Create new art, do a rain dance, or run through the street naked – I don't care – but work on getting free from the ties that bind. Pick a handful of motivational mentors and follow their advice. There is so much amazing free content on the internet it's mind blowing. If something is not a challenge, enhance what you are doing for that portion of your life to maximize your positive results!

Spirit Preparation:

Select the things you will do to enhance your Spirit, add to calendar.

This can be anything from vision boards to meditation to attending seminars. A wonderful way to implement change here is try out other faiths than your own, get to know new communities of people, and learn totally new ways of thinking. Learn a new language. Take an art class. Join a bicycling group.

Sex. It doesn't matter if it's with yourself or consensual partner(s), but sex. Yep. **SEX**. With orgasms.

Mandatory date night is important. This is just as imperative if you are single as if you are partnered; perhaps even more so. Carve out an hour minimum with your partner or alone, even if it is cream cheese and celery in front of a candle once the kids are in bed. Fall in love with your person again. Whether or not you are solo, fall in love with *yourself*.

Schedule a goal smashing reward for each week. So many of us reward ourselves with food that harms our bodies. Schedule yourself a pedicure, new organic product, movie date, or any small reward you can think of and afford to *celebrate the new changes* you are making. Often, we take care of everyone else and forget to take care of ourselves, so be sure to add this item to your calendar. It is just as important as everything else. You are a spiritual gangster! You learn to love yourself by behaving in loving ways towards yourself; doing for you what you do for others.

Get any applications downloaded that you will be using. There are ones which help with everything from water consumption to mindfulness, counting macros to healing frequencies and white noise sounds. Use tech in your favor.

Consider Meditation Mondays. Ideally, you would do this every day, if even for only a few moments. There are lots of guided and helpful tools online. You can find some I specifically have created on our Channel (www.youtube.com/C/MaverickAcademy).

Week One:
Navigational Beacons

Start your 100 things to love about me list! Literally number a paper and put 100 things on there. They can be anything – from your eyelashes to your sense of style to the way you volunteer at shelters. Ask anyone you know, post on social media if you need to, but *find 100 things*. It won't be as hard as you think! This is not optional and *must* be completed; it is the key component to continue successfully on in this program. It must be posted somewhere highly visible once complete and left up for the duration of the challenge (bathroom mirror, inconspicuous spot in cubicle, fridge).

Start your list of 100 things to be grateful for – again, this can be literally anything! The sea. The fireflies. Nail polish. Your cat. Pizza. Doesn't matter. Just do it. I have led thousands down the path to wellness and weight loss and freedom and you would not believe the way some balk at this. JUST. DO. IT. You don't have to like it, but you do have to do it if you want the results.

Get whatever supplements of vitamins and minerals you may need to help you along your journey. As with entire this challenge, I highly recommend you consult naturopathic or medical professionals to determine what supplements or medications you may need, if any, and in what amounts these should be safely consumed.

Get an app for macros and keep your ass on target with your preferred eating plan. I recommend keto for hardcore food addicts with a lot of weight to lose, autoimmune protocol for those with illness from under that umbrella, and vegan or paleo (natural, whole foods only) for everyone else! If you have ever been diagnosed with an eating disorder or feel you may have one, do not track macros under any circumstances. If this is too time consuming, use this shortcut: Omit two days a week that you will not be tracking if daily is too daunting; but schedule which days these are and stay within the parameters of previously tracked known safe foods.

Decide what you want to happen and make it happen. Check out documentaries and information about epigenetics, neuroplasticity, genetically modified consumables, and more – start doing intensive research into food, chemicals, and manifestation simultaneously. Learn more about the body's incredible power to heal itself!

Schedule a polar bear plunge. If you cannot do this, pick something else way outside your comfort zone to shock your system!

In case you haven't noticed, the following challenge can be altered to help with any debilitating addiction or self-harm behavior cycle – quitting smoking, moderating other harmful behaviors if done to excess, modulating anger, and so much more! This is not just for or about weight loss or healthy bodies.

You have A LOT to look forward to for this challenge!

>Week 1: Focus on mental, physical, spiritual fitness via new food plan
>Week 2: Focus on financial and organizational fitness
>Week 3: Focus on goal setting and intentional fitness
>Week 4: Focus on relational and sexual fitness

Week 1 – HOMEWORK 1

In what ways has food maintained a stronghold of control over you? Elaborate

>Eating more than you intended?

>Eating foods you did not initially set out to consume?

How does "eating your feelings" inform your food choices? Elaborate

>Do you use food to celebrate accomplishments/at family gatherings?

>Is food a tool to manage emotions like stress and sadness?

Do you eat as habit, after/before certain events or when bored? _____

>What could you do instead? DEVELOP ACTION PLAN FOR HANDS/MIND:
…Examples: begin knitting, get fidget spinner, plan family game night

Do you stop eating when you are full? _____ If not, why not?
>How will you develop this habit? ACTION PLAN TO DETERMININE FULLNESS:
…Examples: eat more slowly with timer, pause after bites, drink water first

Does your family of origin make healthy food choices? _____
>What habits or ideas about food did you receive during childhood?
…Examples: eat everything on your plate even if full, dessert as a reward

Do you experience food cravings/binges? _____

What foods do you crave?

>Action plan! (Examples: more fat for sugar cravings, salty snacks on hand)

In what ways do you binge?

>Action plan! (Examples: do not binge if you cheat one meal)

How will you regain control over food? Elaborate.

Week Two

GET OUT AND DO GOOD

You *must* commit a minimum of three random acts of kindness this week and remain completely anonymous about them. I am really tired of you guys being like, "I took my sister lunch today!" Cool! But it does not count if it's something you would have already done. Random. Acts. Of. Kindness. With. Strangers. These need to take you fully outside your comfort zone and need not cost a dime. But if you have a few dimes? You bet your ass I expect you to utilize some of those on this project.

LET IT GO

Compile a list of everything that weighs you down – every person, place, thing you have ever been mad or upset with – on slips of paper, place into a jar or container. Also make sure you add yourself to the list, as well as God, if you are mad at them as well. You will burn all of these at the end of this week! Make sure you use safe precautions.

TAKE TWO DIRECT FINANCIAL ACTIONS

Meet with accountant, download savings app, buy book on financial fitness, create budget spreadsheet, make bill paydown plan – doesn't matter – just complete two financial tasks which will be baby steps in propelling you towards wellness in this area.

TAKE TWO DIRECT ORGANIZATIONAL ACTIONS

Make chore lists for your home, clean out and give away clothes, get entire family on synced calendar – whatever – just complete two organizing tasks. Explain to people in your life what you are trying to do and that you really need their support big time! Ask them to get on board and help you with your new project.

EXAMINE PROGRESS

Write about your relationship with the scale if you are having trouble not weighing. Journal if you find you have the time; about the struggles, the excitement, the hope you may be feeling.

REMOVE SCALE FROM HOUSE VIA ACCOUNTABILITY PARTNER IF PROBLEMATIC

Take before and after photos in same clothing, same position, same lighting; each week. Hook up with a mentor! We have free online groups and forums where lots of people who have walked this way before you are ready and willing to help you, coach you, guide you; for *free*! Just be sure you will pay it forward one day when you find yourself further down the road than another person.

Week 2 – HOMEWORK 2

In what ways have you put your life on hold because of weight or food?

>Not doing/wearing/engaging in things you'd do if you were smaller?

>How have negative beliefs about your weight informed your choices?

What are the worst negative self-talk items you believe? Ex. fat, ugly
>List ten negative words you think about yourself:

>What are the opposites of those ten words?

Have you made a concrete decision to change your life? _____
>What areas within need the most development? OUTLINE SPECIFIC STEPS:
>Examples: take financial counseling course, declutter with lists, dr. appts.

Do you stuff down and internalize anger or sadness? _____
>How will you externalize these emotions? ACTION PLAN:
>Examples: kickboxing class, online workshop on feelings, breaking plates

What did you learn from family of origin about emotional expression?
>What negative habits or ideas about relating did you receive as a child?
>Examples: smile even when angry, don't make a scene, crying is for babies

Do you put the needs of others first? _____
>In what ways can you change this maladaptive pattern?

Action plan! (Examples: schedule time for self, delegate to family member)

In what ways does this negatively impact you?

Action plan! (Examples: no time for meal prep/working out, lack of sleep)

*Define, handwritten, using dictionary, the following words:
control, stress, compulsion, obsession*

Week Three

IF YOU ARE SLACKING IN ANY AREA

Take advantage of the "easier" level of the homework this week to recommit to all aspects of the challenge. You can do this. If you stumble, regain your footing. If you slip, hop back up.

IF YOU ARE NOT TURNING OFF YOUR PHONE AT NIGHT

Please get a flip phone with no internet access for bedtime or delete all social media apps at bedtime each night and turn off WiFi to discourage screen time. It is that important.

CREATE VISION BOARD OR SIMILAR INSTRUMENT

If you have not already, please watch information on the law of attraction or similar programming. Please listen to something in this vein daily. Create a visual representation of what you would like to manifest into your path.

REDISTRIBUTION

Finish any other incomplete homework. After last week's emotional boot camp, it's imperative that you give yourself a chance to rebuild and redistribute your energy and attention. Hyper-focus on giving as much attention as possible to your body. Walk, swim, or do other low impact exercise *daily*. Give your body a jumpstart.

PUNCH BOWL

Make sure you have your "punch bowl" burned by now – all the people you'd like to punch. Let. It. Go. This is the previous exercise you completed. BURN THAT MOTHERFUCKER DOWN; release the anger, pain, fear, guilt, shame with the smoke. LET IT GODDAMN GO. We do not overeat or eat in a toxic way when we love ourselves. No judgment, but it really is that simple. The things you are holding onto are why you can't lose weight; the pounds are but a symptom.

IMPORTANT! WHERE ARE YOU "WINNING?"

Remember this is a marathon, not a sprint. What areas have you nailed or done to your satisfaction? Where are you seeing change, or better – *progress*? This is for you to reflect on and does not have to be written down. Find some ways in which you are proud of yourself for what you have done thus far. It is very easy to want to give up when things are not done "perfectly." The goal is not perfection, it's a slowly changing way of life and new habits which will turn you all the way around before you even know it. One day you'll wake up and won't even recognize the person staring back. It's a beautiful, slow, process. Never stop learning. Seeking. Growing. Eliminating faulty belief systems. Embracing new knowledge.

Week 3 – HOMEWORK 3
Energy Redistribution Plan

Where my energy goes with percentages (ie family tasks 25% work 35% husband 10%)
Now (what this currently is): (make long list)
Ideally (what I want it to be): (side by side to the first list, redistribute percentages to ideals)

Example:
Now: Work 65%.   Ideally Work 20%
Now: Chores 20%.   Ideally Chores 0%

Are any of these areas requiring more of me than I want to give? If so, which? Why?

What are some direct steps I can take to redistribute this energy?

Where do I see myself in 1 year?
What do I want to be the same? What do I want to be different?

Action steps:

Where do I see myself in 7 years?
What do I want to be the same? What do I want to be different?

Action steps:

Week Four

CLOSING EXERCISE

Take your pics and measurements – but remember this is not a measure of who you are – just where you are at in the weight loss + detoxification process. It has nothing to do with your worth or abilities!

FEARS

Make a list of *everything* you are afraid of – no matter how seemingly insignificant. Take an honest inventory of whether this fear is founded or unfounded. The only fears worth holding onto are ones that can come true and are imminently likely in the next *instant*. And even those? We take notice for the sole purpose of then creating a new reality. All we have is this moment; the now. Even if you are afraid of someone dying, etc., ask yourself honestly if that is likely to come true immediately or not based on past behaviors and events as predictors. And even if it is? If you can't change it *this instant*, it's not currently any of your concern whatsoever. We don't turn a blind eye to that which needs our attention, but the truth is we are like a home. You only have so much power. If too much is diverted to unnecessary fear and worry, you'll flip your breakers, creating the perfect environment for mental and physical disease. You cannot run a toaster, air conditioner, coffee pot, so forth, off the same exact power source. Unplug what you can. Often this is worry. What has *ever* been resolved by worry?

GUILT + SHAME

List anything you still feel guilty or shameful over – people, things that happened, past actions you took or did not take, the "should haves." Tear this up into the tiniest of pieces. Either throw them out, bury them, or toss them into a body of water (only if highly eco-friendly and biodegradable paper and ink). Anything in this program that is recommended to write; write. That does not mean type. It means write. It changes the nature of the information and moves it around the brain in important ways to handwrite a thing.

CONFRONTATIONS & KARMA SETTLING

Confrontation, when done with the guidance of a therapist or other professional support system, can be very freeing. Who do you still need to have these hard conversations with to free up your energy and clean up your life? If the person is deceased, you can still have the conversation. Begin by writing letters or taking notes of everything you *would* say – whether they are alive or not. Karmic settling is important – some of us have things we need to make right. Make a list of these; anyone you have harmed or to whom you need to repay a debt of any kind. In some instances, it would either hurt that person or yourself more for you to re-enter their life, and the way you make it right going forward will not be directly (ie if you were young and addicted to drugs, and hit someone, reparation for that would not be to contact that person – perhaps you could volunteer at a shelter for people affected by violence, so forth). Definitely do not contact anyone with whom you have healthily and necessarily maintained no contact. Just write the letter, dispose of it as you wish or even save it, and move on. Nobody has a right to you. Toxic abusers will often lay the guilt carpet because they're "family," but if they harmed you or failed to protect you? Nah, bruh. Move right along. Fuck it. Choose your own fam.

LET'S TALK ABOUT SEX

This is it! This is the sex *every single day week*; yes, even with yourself, if single. It is time to work on those relationships and connections, get the good-feeling neurotransmitters flowing, and really dig deep to connect. By now, some of you have realized you need relationship therapy – if so, get it. Schedule it. Today. Live authentically. Speak your truth. Be genuine. And have orgasms. *Communicate* your wants and needs to your partner directly. Or file for divorce, whatever. Get some movement in your relationships, in whatever direction your Soul is urging you to go.

CONTINUED WORK & TRANSITION

After a huge accomplishment such as this challenge, it can be very easy to slip into all or nothing thinking – like "rewarding" oneself with everything you have seen as deprivation – by a huge cheat meal or other destructive behavior. Absolutely begin reframing your self-talk language and releasing guilt. This is a way of life. Make conscious choices about food and move on – do not get mired down in obsession or shame, yo. Also look hard at where you are judging others – whether it be gossip, condemnation, or whatever. The unpleasant things we recognize in others are always what we need to take the closest look at in ourselves. Realize you have made a huge change by even considering this challenge. Do not beat yourself up if you did not do it "all" or "perfectly." That was never the intent, or it would not be a challenge! If it did not come easily to you, that's a good sign.

Change is born by embracing the difficult and giving it your level best effort.

I am so proud of you, spiritual gangsters! We are only just beginning.

Week 4 – HOMEWORK 4

List all fears, regardless their significance, & circle whether founded or unfounded. Fears which are unfounded are those that are unlikely to come true *immediately*. All we have is now, and if a fear probably won't come true in this moment, it is unfounded.

Fear:
Founded/Unfounded
Fear:
Founded/Unfounded
Fear:
Founded/Unfounded
Fear:
Founded/Unfounded
Fear:
Founded/Unfounded
Fear:
Founded/Unfounded

List all areas/people/events for which you still carry guilt or shame:

-*Guilt & shame action plan*: What, if anything, will I *do* to alleviate these feelings?

List all persons & situations which require a confrontation or a karmic settling:

-*Confrontation action plan*: With whom do I need to have confrontational convos?

-*Karmic settling action plan*: To whom do I owe a karmic settling? How to implement.

For the Single Mamas of Tiny Tots

It's like the coolest thing ever to grow a human by yourself. You made an entire freaking *person*. Like, with your body. Stretch marks and wobbly bits aside, that wild animal over there singing wheels on the bus in his underoos while clutching a half-eaten pineapple couldn't exist without you.

You get *all* the snuggles, smiles, and sweetness. You never have to share their love. And you'd be lying if you didn't admit you get a little bit of satisfaction when they won't go to anyone else. And then you remember that they're forty pounds. Of squirming dead weight.

Motivation. How can you give up when you know someone else doesn't eat if you don't make it happen? There's no way to look in that little face and quit. It's like having a coach 100 yards before the finish line.

Because of their frequent exposure to you, you get to see your attitude on their face and in their voice. It's really cute. Until they run their head into the wall because you don't make eggs fast enough. But it gets cute again when they say TANK TOO and smile a scrambled egg mouth full of bliss at you. You can't even be a hater because you know every inch of that sass. They come by it honestly.

You are the one witness to their first haircut, bike, day of school, every single big moment. You, single mama, are holding sacred space as the solitary witness of this human's evolution. Being the solitary onlooker for all of someone's most important moments is a privilege. An honor.

The satisfaction of knowing you're doing the hardest job in the world successfully. There may be peanut butter on the ceiling, clothes piled up at the washer, and a mysterious thing stuck in your hair. But the baby's alive. That counts, right?

They are your biggest fan. We're potty training. Since my son is in my face all. the. time. he is sweet enough to cheer for me when I use the potty. Encouragement never hurts. He also says UH OH when I drop something or stub my toe. Having a mini entourage is kind of fun sometimes.

They can fetch. I cannot stress this enough. New moms – start teaching them to go get and hand stuff to you now. And I *can't wait for chores*! My son has unwittingly signed on to be part of the workforce. Mom for the win. Now go load the dishwasher. *Nevermind.* I am the only one who can do that. I need to put stuff in there a particular way. Unload it. *Nevermind.* I know where everything goes. Just grab me a Diet Coke, will ya?

You are never alone. No really. Never. Ever. Ever. While that foot in the ribs at 3am or the face poking over your shoulder when you're trying to watch Sons of Anarchy may not be all that desirable, a sweet hand on your face or a little who hugs you with all their strength is a joy that cannot be compared.

You're the hero. All the time. Whether it's because you can reach all the things or put the new bike together or get their foot out from under the couch because somehow, it's stuck... You get to be their fixer. The one they run to every time. The one who makes it all ok. And that, my friends, is priceless.

(Caveat: I wrote this when my son was just a baby. I've since met the love of our life, and we are a family now... but all this stuff was still pretty cool, and I wouldn't trade it for anything!)

What All Moms Should Know

Nothing. Absolutely fucking nothing.

And stop reading shit that says you have to do this or need to do that. It's ridiculous.

Motherhood doesn't come with a manual. It doesn't. There are no rules, and I want you to know that. Whether you are an essential oil diffusing, white noise playing, organic cloth buying, baby wearing, breastfeeding Birkenstock mom; or a chicken nugget feeding, time out using, "you eat what we eat or you don't eat," mom – you're doing it right. We are all different. We all have our good and bad days. And nobody, and I mean *nobody* sees the best and worst of us like our children. This is a *good* thing. They'll learn from us that life has ups and downs, and how to navigate those. We are literally their map to adulthood.

If you happen to be in the mood to hear a few tips from someone who is raising a highly spirited four-year-old and also has a few advanced degrees (I've learned more from my kid than I ever did in school, but I digress), here's what I have for you:

1. Build a tribe
This is imperative. If you already have a great family and friend support system, I am so happy for you, truly. But continue to expand. If you don't, find one. This may be in mama groups on social media or in your community, from meetups in real life with other moms, and so many different ways. Don't isolate. Especially if you're a single mom. I tried to do the single mom life with very minimal support for a while and it almost killed me. YOU. MUST. HAVE. A. TRIBE. I remember sobbing as I hired strangers online to watch my infant because I had to go the hospital for cancer treatments when I was living out of state. You can *learn* from other moms, and they can learn from you. You can swap babysitting. You can have someone to call and ask, "Why the fuck is my actual nipple bleeding?" and they will triage that problem faster than an Army nurse. When you have kiddos, it's imperative to build a tribe. They can play with other kids and begin developing social skills. If you are a working mama this is

really hard to do, but it isn't totally impossible.

2. Know when to take a break and figure out how
This is so resource and support dependent. It's really easy to say, "Oh my God, like, just engage in self-care, OK?" Mmmk. Well if there's nobody to watch the baby and you're broke AF at that moment, it's not that simple. *But* there are things you can do from home. You can watch yoga videos and do them together. You can diffuse oil at night to have something pleasant like a spa to fall asleep to when it's been a rough day. Ideally, you have people in your life who you can hand over your beautiful little monsters to and head off for a day at the spa, or surfing, or whatever makes your spidey senses tingle. But if you don't have the help, cash, or time, there are other options. Even if it's right after bedtime and you do a lil Netflix binge or read your fave book or paint your toenails (I am fundamentally incapable of that last one, bee tee dubs)... making time to take care of you in a million ways is so freaking important. You can't help them or anyone else if you keep your tank on empty. I made this mistake for so long it almost killed me.

3. Fight for your rights
It doesn't really matter what this entails. If you are getting divorced, don't give up. If you are attempting to escape a toxic abuser, know that help is out there. If you are battling the school for your special needs child, there are resources. If you qualify for state or federal assistance, *do not be ashamed* to apply for and utilize that to take care of your family. Do what you need to do, mama. Ask for help when you need to ask. Don't suffer silently, and always advocate for your kiddo, in any setting. If you have a gay kid who's getting bullied at school and can't seem to get anyone to do anything about it, trust me when I say there are resources. There are entire groups and companies ready to rally around *any* problem you have as a mama, you just gotta know where to look. Come on over to the page and shoot me a message if you need resources for anything you're going through, and I can try to connect you to the right peeps!

4. Unconditional positive regard
Love. That's basically it. Maslow's hierarchy of needs is important, too, but assuming needs for safety/survival and so forth are met, they just need your *love*. Mom guilt is unavoidable, but if you are loving

them? You are doing this right. And as much time as you can give – that's important too. I hear working moms all the time feel guilty for being gone so much. Stay at home moms feel shame for being so frustrated and tired sometimes. FULL STOP TO THAT BULLSHIT. If you know you are doing the best you can, trust me when I say there isn't one of us who hasn't slid down the outside of the door of our child's room crying thanking God they finally fell asleep after a rough day! *You are not alone and there is nothing wrong with you*. They need to know that you *accept* them, even when you don't accept their behavior. They need to know that you *love* them, and that nothing they can do changes that – on good days, bad days, with a great attitude, during terrible tantrums; nothing changes your love. They need only to know that your love is constant. Attachment forms now. Not trying to freak you out or anything; but, um, every relationship they have for like ever is formed on how they bond with you when they're little.

5. Calming techniques to avoid spanking/yelling

Here's the deal. I don't know a single mom, nope not a single one, who hasn't raised their voice or swatted their child's bottom. Now if you are spanking and yelling daily, you need a play therapist, like yesterday; or perhaps a therapist for you. This doesn't mean anything is wrong with you. But it does mean you need *new tools*. You can turn this train around at any time – and spanking, to be honest, should cease completely. I can't go outside and fix the transmission in my truck, so why would I think I could repair a communication or behavioral issue with any other human being without a little professional guidance? It's kind of like taking a map on a hike through the woods. Why would you try to do that while totally blind? You're going to get lost. Utilize everything you can think of, such as calming corner and sensory techniques; which you can learn about online. It seems crazy but these simple tools have *seriously* relaxed our household. Thank you, Baby Jesus and Tom Cruise.

I cannot stress or emphasize the importance of routine enough, either. If they know everything typically (hopefully) happens at a certain time? They feel safer and more comfortable relaxing into that structure and will typically not press boundaries as hard (ie arguing about bath or bedtime). If it's a certain way every. single. night. they are much more likely to fall into the routine and feel safer knowing it is in place. No reason you can't make it fun. I bribe the hell out of my kid and have no shame in this whatsoever. I taught him to potty with M&Ms. I get him to enjoy baths with washable bath markers and bath bombs and allowing him to take in one toy, among other tricks. Why not make it easier for him? Life was made to be fun, everything doesn't have to be a battle. There are tons of tips and tricks out there. Kids are *searching* wildly and frantically for the boundaries; so, show them where they are. I am a not a fan of "cry it out" sleep techniques. Not. A. Fan. For a variety of reasons backed by research. But this isn't a mama shaming work, so just look into other options if you're considering trying that one because there *are* ones that work in a much less damaging and more effective fashion. Circumcision is also not a good idea, but don't beat yourself up if you have made these choices. I have made mistakes. Lots of them. The most important thing is correcting them. We are molding little humans. It's better for my kiddo to see me lose my shit and hear me apologize and tell him it was wrong than for him to think he has to stuff his emotions deep down, ya dig?

6. Diagnostics

If you suspect that your child might be a-neurotypical, assessments and interventions cannot happen too early. Whether these are private, through a school, or even holistic - it's important to look into ways to help your kiddo if you think they might be on the spectrum or have an attention difference. Some swear by diet changes and vitamin + mineral supplements.

There are tons of great resources online and on streaming services. Some kids need prescription medication. It all just depends. YOU KNOW YOUR CHILD. Start at the very bottom of the least interventional end of things and work your way through what helps and is necessary. Obv, I'm not a doctor, but I don't always fully trust them either. There is a lot that can be done at home with routine and food and so forth that can help kids who are mildly just *different*. Never hesitate in getting any *developmental* delays evaluated immediately by a pediatrician or qualified organization. But sometimes? You might just have a gifted one. And they are weird as hell. And that's ok. Learning how to parent a high-spirited, strong-willed child will be *the* challenge of your life. But remember – these are the kids who change the world. The goal isn't to break their spirit.

It isn't to make them into a mold of who you are. It's to make them safe and confident enough to become who they decide they are. *The goal is to show them that you unconditionally accept who they are becoming*, or you risk losing them for good. Don't be afraid to have your child assessed early on if you suspect a diagnosis like autism or if you even have a question. The sooner they receive help, the more likely it is they can "mainstream." Same thing with things like speech – perhaps they can't hear well; or motor skill coordination – perhaps they can't see well. Easy fixes, but they require you to spot and intervene. I have a whole host of information available to you if you are fighting the school to get help for your kiddos; you have rights you may not even be aware of, even if they are not yet in school!

7. Never underestimate the power of play

I have taken my son all over this world. Luckily most times, I had the resources, health, and financial ability to do so. He's been to Hawai'i. He's been on cruises. And literally on any given day if I'm not trying to get work done, you'll find us at a theme park, museum, zoo, water park, or the like. We go, go, go. It's what works for us both. He came out 100mph and hasn't really slowed down and neither have I. I learn about him when I sit down and play with him too. It's all too easy to fall into the exhausted/I'm trying to make dinner/watch your iPad in your room trap. And that's ok, don't feel guilty about those nights. But sitting down to watch him build blocks, he'll say things to me almost without thinking that he won't say when directly questioned (men, amirite). He'll tell me about things that happened at school or nightmares that bother him or ask me questions that he'd never mention otherwise, because his mind is occupied with us playing. Things just sort of spill out of his mouth, versus when I say, "How was school?" He says "fine." Then over playing blocks I hear all the drama of the day. Don't underestimate the power of playing and going and doing and sunshine and grounding your feet in the earth! My son loves kids' yoga videos, which you can find online. They help him get centered, and it's awesome. There's so much you can do together that's still valuable *and* occupy them with when they're nearby, yet you have tasks to accomplish.

8. Eliminate toxicity

FULL STOP. I know this is not possible for some of us – especially if the toxicity emanates from the current or already ended relationship with the child's other parent. Food too, though. I *do not* feed my son perfectly all the time, but I do aim to keep most processed foods, and those containing flour and sugar, out of his body. I have noticed huge changes in behavior surrounding this, yet I fail at it constantly. And I'm OK with that. What is childhood without cotton candy at the waterpark? We don't aim for perfection, but I do try to make sure the crucial stuff he needs gets in there. I pack smoothies with kale and all kinds of secret stuff then bribe him with treats if he drinks them. Is this right? I don't know – I try not to value judge my parenting and just feel my way through based on his wellness. But it keeps his guts healthy and I know he's getting all the vitamins and minerals he needs. He actually likes the taste of some of them!

The other kind of toxicity may arise from a mind, body, spirit dysregulation. *Literally* go no contact for a while with anyone who brings negativity and pain to your life. If this is someone really important to you, then get into therapy and try to figure out if you need boundaries or how best to limit your exposure. If this isn't feasible, then figure out how to limit their emotional access to you. Check the products you're using too. If you can't afford ones with no harmful chemicals, consider making your own (yes, this is a thing). Try to cut out any and every source of dangerous chemical or toxin, whatever that you can – whether they are of the body wash, human, or environmental variety. None of us can do all of this all the time. That's OK. Just aim in the right direction and do what you can, as often as you are able. Did you guys pull through McD's for some deliciousness today? That's fucking OK too. My kid has literally eaten candy from under a movie seat before I could stop him. He didn't die. You got this.

9. Ignore the filters
OMG. These freaking Kardashians. Like, no hate, for real, but they have billions of dollars amongst them and I have never ever heard one of them say something of substance. I'm not a hater, I swear – actually I admire them just a lil for figuring out a way to live the life they want while being famous for literally nothing. *But remember*, they have entire staff to help them care for their children. My point is, stop comparing your insides to what you see on other people's outsides. If your body doesn't look like that? Cool. It's not supposed to if you just *created a freaking human*. Many of the people we see

and judge ourselves harshly based upon have chefs, personal trainers, plastic surgeons, nannies; you name it. Half the fancy moms I see are popping pills in the bathroom. *You don't really know what happens* behind closed doors, so stop shaming and comparing yourself. If you see all these perfect little families on social media and feel yours just doesn't measure up because you can't afford those brands or you haven't washed your hair in three days and you aren't sure if it's poop or chocolate on your son's hands? You. Are. Still. Doing. This. Right. Good job mama. You kept the baby alive today. That's a good enough day. Go to sleep and get off FB, because he'll be up again in two hours.

10. Trust your instincts. Trust your kid. Trust your intuition. *Always*. That is *it*. Always. I have very strong feelings on the necessity of vaccines, and lots of things; and if you want to know about that or anything else, just ask. For tips on how to protect your kiddos from predators and how to initiate those convos, check out our pages. Believe your children when they tell you something; but teach them the difference between the truth and a lie and how important it is that they always tell you what's up so that no one can convince them to hide what may happen. Trust your *intuition*! I cannot stress this enough. If you get a weird feeling about dropping them with that daycare, pick another one. I mean it. You must trust your kid and trust your gut. *You* know what's best. Don't let family or society pressure you into raising them in such a way that goes against your heart. OK? OK. Glad we got that straightened out. Now get back in the ring with your wild monsters and do your thing, you beautiful mama!

10 Tips to Medically Advocate for Yourself:

What makes things hard for the chronically or terminally ill?

1. Getting a diagnosis, even though they know they are sick.
2. Getting appropriate tests and treatments, even if they have a diagnosis.
3. Getting doctors and the conventional medical system to listen and respond.

MMMK. I am writing this to you from a teaching hospital where I have now been admitted for almost two weeks with no end in sight. This is not a new rodeo for me. For almost 20 years, I have battled everything from multiple bouts of cancer with mets to an extremely rare and progressive fatal autoimmune disease. I have had 18 surgeries, multiple rounds radiation and radioactive iodine, two heavy hitting 8-hour port infusions of biologics, even organ transplant rejection meds as black box experimental trials, and chemo-based drugs as immunosuppressants. I have been medically abused in ways you could not even fathom; the system has epically failed me. Let's skip the whole history; and get to the important part – *you*. I have more advanced degrees than are necessary and have helped thousands on their path to wellness, so let's just skip right on over my earthly qualifications as well and assume I can help you too – the chronically ill, terminal, rare disease, or undiagnosed patient.

1. DEMAND AND KEEP ALL RECORDS (ASK NICELY FIRST)

Do not settle for any sort of horseshit answer that sounds like, "We can only send that to another doctor," or "We can't print that off, you have to go to medical records for that information," or "The doctor will have to finalize their summary before we can release the notes from today's visit."

No. Full stop. Here's why. There have been *so many* times that abnormal labs, path reports, or other information was found on me. Because I did not demand my records, a lot slipped through the cracks over the years that was either misinterpreted or never even told to me, only to be found recently when I started insisting that *everyone everywhere* who ever treated me send my records directly *to me*. I could've healed faster and saved myself a lot of damage had this not occurred. And no, they cannot charge you for your records, although they might try to tell you they can. Well, I guess technically they can, but don't let them.

And it sounds like this, "I am requesting my records for continuity of care. Without them, my current team of physicians cannot effectively treat me. There is tremendous *liability* in me getting sicker because my doctors do not have these records. I prefer electronic transmission (email, fax, whatever) which comes at no cost to you. I would rather maintain my records personally than you having to send them to 10 different specialists." Using words like liability will get them moving if they won't give you your records. If you have been in every damn hospital and doctor's office in America, like I have, try keeping or requesting digital copies – like via CD or thumb drive or whatever. If you aren't getting anywhere with office staff, send a certified letter requesting your records and why, return receipt requested. If that doesn't work, go to their office. Do not leave without your records. If that isn't possible or doesn't work, sign a release form from your primary, get them sent there, and try to get them to give you a copy.

If none of *that* works, begin the negative review process. Ask all family and friends to leave negative reviews across all platforms regarding this physician or hospital not allowing you to have your records so you can get well if they really treated you badly in other ways too. Look, this sounds so harsh but if you haven't been down this road you can't possibly understand. Those labs? That is *your* blood. Those CTs? That is *your* body. If you are sick and don't have answers, then definitely do not accept no as an answer. Those tests are only as good as the techs performing them, the radiologists and docs interpreting them, and may show patterns over time. Seemingly unrelated symptoms may be the key to your mystery diagnosis. You. Must Have. Your. Records.

Make sure if you decide to raise social media hell that your friends @ that doctor or hospital on social media when they advocate for you; you'll get a response from corporate in no time. Save this option for only once literally all else has failed to get help. Hell, look up the administrative team if necessary. If a doctor or facility has truly done you dirty, try the chain of command then email every damn person you can find or stalk them down via Linked In. Main thing is you get help, and if someone incompetent is damaging your health or harming you, they are doing it to others, guaranteed. Find higher ups who will *do something*, by any means necessary, but only employ this nuclear tactic if you absolutely must – and it needs to be over something worse than records refusal. You can even get corporate emails with a little deduction or sleuthing. For instance, find out who the CEO of the hospital is. If your patient advocate is sally.jerkface@hospitals-suck.us, then there's a high likelihood you could plug the CEO's name into that rubric and get in touch with them directly – do this with every member of the corporate team you can find if you've been done really dirty. There are also nursing and physician boards you can file reports/complaints with. I personally haven't had the time to go that route, but if you need to, shoot.

But I digress. Back to the records: *Try* to keep all the incoming records backed up as they start coming in to you in two places so your entire home doesn't end up looking like a file box – so maybe an online drive and an external hard drive. Whatever. Who has time for that? But try. Or at least attempt to keep the paper records together in some sort of semi-coherent organized format. I have shit all over the place and am too busy trying not to die for this one, but try, and if you get an organization system in place from the start, it will keep you going in right direction.

2. DON'T LET OFFICE STAFF PREVENT DOCTOR AWARENESS

Don't be more afraid of pissing someone off than you are of dying or being sick. *Always* start off nice. Always. *Most* people *want* to help you. Literally using the words, "Can you help me?" when they answer will get them in the mind frame of wanting to find a solution to your dilemma. But don't waste your time with whomever is answering the phone if they won't help you and you truly feel your current concern is urgent. Move up the chain of command – especially in a hospital system.

Alrighty then. You've found a good doctor, who seems to know wtf they're doing, and is possibly helping you or at least moving you in the right direction. Yes? Good. But how do you get past the infamous awful medical office staff? Some of the front office peeps with my docs are literally the best in the world. But the ones who suck are awful. This is why it's super important to find a way to communicate directly with your doctor when absolutely necessary; whether that's via cell phone, email, or...

3. SIGN UP FOR PORTALS & INSIST TEAM COMMUNICATES
Always ask if they have an online patient portal. You can see labs and sometimes even other stuff in here. Depending which one it is, outside records sent to your primary might even show up in there (yey). This one is fairly simple, it helps you with all of the above tips – keeping requests in writing, communicating directly with docs (sometimes), keeping track of records, and so forth. But know this – a portal will *never* contain *all* your records, so make sure that not only are your doctors sending pertinent records to one another if necessary but that they actually *talk on the phone* if you have a chronic or terminal condition. This is not too much to ask.

And the job of a Primary Care Physician? To coordinate all that. They should be speaking with or reviewing what each specialist does. So, for instance, if you have cancer? Sometimes an Onco will take over as Primary for a while. If you have an autoimmune disease? Your Rheum will take the lead. But keep a PCP you see regularly. You'll be glad you did, if you find a good one. Hell, a primary can get you in with a badass specialist if they feel you're sick enough by changing a referral to STAT and making a quick phone call – which usually changes your wait time from months to days or sooner.

4. DO YOUR OWN RESEARCH
Not on Google. Or Wikipedia. I get it. Some of us are readers. Researchers. And so forth. If you aren't? Find a friend who is. You *must* be knowledgeable about your condition and symptoms. If you are undiagnosed, make sure to take pics of anything weird – swelling, rashes, high or low temps, and keep a symptom journal if possible, like, "shortness of breath worse at night."

I usually throw in a little ego stroke like, "I know I'm not a doctor, but a physician friend recommended I try this or this test or med," etc. They want to be the boss. Cool. But if they think someone else who knows what they're looking at is watching over your shoulder? They'll be more careful with you. It is a horrific shame that we have to resort to this, but for those with rare or undiagnosed diseases, this is legit how things seem to have to go to get anywhere. Remember, you are a file and a number to them. They don't see you as a mommy. As a daughter. As a friend. If you die tomorrow, your chart will be stored for a few years then destroyed. *Advocate*. When you find a doctor who doesn't treat you that way, like just another insurance claim? Never let them go. *Ever*. I still see my Onco even though I currently am battling an autoimmune disease and cancer is not the immediate issue. Why? Because she's fucking amazing. If you're the academic type, and like studying and reading? Literally put yourself through med school from home; minus the tuition and all the bs they teach docs that make so many of them suck. There's nothing you can't use the internet to learn, so learn it.

Honestly, the best place to start is academic journals – one place you can access these is google scholar search system. Also entering different symptoms and trying to find peer reviewed medical studies is never a bad way to go. I have on occasion found cutting edge research and experimental treatments for my own disease and shown them to my doctors and they simply weren't aware because they were so new. Which brings us to something really important...

5. FIND AND REACH OUT TO THE EXPERTS
IF you have a diagnosis that most of your team is sure of (this took me a couple decades, btw), reach out to the literal best experts in that field *worldwide*. They are doing different things everywhere and some countries are lightyears ahead of us in some disease areas. Find the people teaching at the symposiums, find the ones who have started foundations for your disease, find the doctors researching it at the NIH or just by searching xyz research studies.

There are also specific hospitals for specific diseases. You would be shocked who will answer your emails and/or help you! Find fb forums for your disease – this is how I found the foremost expert *in the world* regarding mine, and she literally calls doctors when I am admitted and explains my disease to them *because by and large they have never even heard of it*. She lets me text her questions and is just an all-around badass (Edit – I used to think she was, but like every doctor I have ever seen in my entire life, she turned out to be a ringing disappointment). Reach out and hunt down people who know about your disease or suspected *type* of disease(s). Email rare disease organizations. Find anyone you can who is an expert and at least get referrals to docs in your area if possible. Many of these peeps know each other from their field.

Also, try to only get referrals to other specialties you need from docs you already trust. For instance, my Rheumatologist is a gangster. He's brilliant. He's the only reason I'm (barely) alive (Edit – Yep. He turned out to be bought and sold by drug companies – also a resounding let down). I went to his eye guy and boom – they found everything from retinal vasculitis (systemic) to optic neuritis to arterial narrowing, all because he used a dye angiogram imaging test. I went blind because two random opthos before him I found on my own couldn't see what was going on with the naked eye so decided not to run further tests. I have literal permanent necrotizing vision loss that wasn't caught in time because I saw the wrong docs. And if I had stopped with them? I would be 100% blind right now. If something doesn't feel right in your gut, just keep going. I know you're tired. I know you're exhausted. But don't stop until you get to doctors who know what the hell they're doing. And the best way to find them is through other doctors who know wtf they're doing. Ya dig? *Build a team*, ask at front desk that each doc send everything to your primary when you are checking out – then follow up to make sure primary received it in the next few days. I know. Full time job.

6. USE SPECIFIC LANGUAGE TO GET THEM MOVING
If you've been doing the above, and have reached out to the experts or read their research, for instance, and they recommend a weird or hard to find/order test, and your doctors scoff at it being necessary... here's what you say, "If I have this test elsewhere, and the results are as I suspect they may be, you have placed yourself in an position of tremendous *liability* (there's that word again) by not allowing me to get well as soon as I could have, and this could even cost me my life." Look, most doctors are some weird breed of human. They just are. They usually don't like to admit if they don't know something, especially if you have a rare disease. They most certainly usually don't like to be told what to do. And they sure as hell would typically rather make the same amount of money off an ear infection as they do by listening to you ramble. So, don't ramble. But don't be afraid to teach 'em about Jesus or hand your doctor their ass either; if necessary.

Similarly, never be afraid to praise, write good reviews, email their higher ups, tell them directly, and so forth if you are receiving exemplary care. Always be as generous with positive reinforcement as you are complaints, if not more so. Let them know timeframes and dates and always take down names and info of anyone you speak with so that they feel some sense of accountability for what happens to you if they do not follow up. Good examples of this include, "What time should I expect a call back from my doctor today regarding this issue?" and "What was your name again and direct phone line; so I know how to follow up?" This will help when you call back for the fifth time and hear some shit like, "We never saw in the system that you called," and you can say, "Actually, I talked to Bianca at 2:47 and she said I would hear from Dr. Amazing before end of business. Would you mind following up with her regarding this?"

7. BE NICE TO NURSES AND ALL SUPPORT PERSONNEL
I'm gonna tell you a secret. A good nurse and a bad nurse can be the difference between life and death for you. They decide to call the doctor if you feel you need it while admitted. They determine who to give pain meds to first as you lay there with a broken leg. They can make your hospital stay paradise or hell on earth. Not to mention they are badass multi-taskers, under-appreciated, bitched at by everyone from docs to patients, and have to catch life threatening mistakes docs sometimes make before they accidentally kill people. *Be nice to your nurses* and they will usually go out of their way to take exemplary care of you. Some nurses are jerks, like any profession. I am not kidding when I say if you are stuck in the hospital, do all you can to make them like you. Literally have pizza delivered to the nurse's station if necessary. Not. Kidding. If a nurse is not taking proper care of you, that's a diff story. *Raise hell* and get a different one, ask for charge nurse to begin this process. But remember – their job is hard. They are overworked and underpaid, and they are like a family or a tribe, so you may piss them all off if you piss one off. Pay attention to shift change. If your nurse sucks but it's a couple hours until he or she is gone, suck it up buttercup. The last thing you want in your charting is that you are crazy or difficult.

Make other allies too. Learn how to work the system in your favor. Do not dismiss the lady who cleans your hospital room or the techs who take your BP; not only because this is a dick move but because they hear and know everything. *They will tell you stuff nobody else will* if you are kind to them. At my teaching hospital, my med team of docs meets in a "war room." I got both direct phone lines to this room from the lady who cleans the floors. And you know what? As someone who is immunocompromised? Her job is just as important, if not more, than the doctors. So, I told her that. And thanked her. Most people treat her like she's invisible. She told me about her grandbaby. Stories about a beautiful little girl that made me smile ear to ear as I was crying in pain before she came in. Thank them. Get to know them. And not just so you can pump them for information; but if the time comes and you need to figure out how to contact a patient advocate or charge nurse or even higher up the food chain? They will know exactly who to go to and why – who can hear your concerns and actually do something about them. And also? Because you want to be a nice human being and recognizing the chronically under-appreciated is just good karma.

8. KEEP EVERYTHING IN WRITING, RECORD CONVOS (?)

Take in your most pertinent medical records from your most credible doctors to any new doctor or hospital, especially if you have a rare or difficult to treat condition. Do not bring in 1,400 FILES. They do not care and will not read them. What I take, for instance, is a one-sheet summary of meds, medical history, surgeries, current docs and their numbers, diagnoses, etc. I also take my most recent progress note (a page or two only) about my most serious conditions from the most prominent members of my team – so that anyone taking a look at me can see I've already been diagnosed. When you tell a new physician you have a disease most of them have never heard of, you will be met with skepticism, so bring along backup if possible (family or friend) and minimal documentation from your most qualified docs which explains what they do know – abnormal labs, treatments tried, imaging that came back with problems, etc.

Write down everything you ask your doctor to do, let them know you want to know the reason for the denial if they do not want to run a test. But know your shit before you go off halfcocked, you have to either have the pertinent actual research to back up your request or have an expert who recommends that testing for your condition. Once it's in writing, they are liable if they don't run it and it gets run later and you got sicker *because* of their negligence or malpractice. I haven't ever pursued these options even though I could have, but you have to prove a lot more than you think and even if you have a good case most lawyers only want the death cases. Don't waste your time suing idiots, spend your time getting well.

Going in there with some crazy list of shit you found on a search engine and demanding $20,000 in tests will get you nowhere. They have to justify everything they do to your insurance and often higher ups. Give them some teeth behind the requests, keep it as minimal as possible, and understand as much as you can when you walk through the door. It is their job to run through a differential – ruling out different things. People who don't fit neatly in the boxes they were taught have a tendency to make them say things that will make you either feel crazy or wrong. Trust your gut. You know if you are sick. Also, sometimes they are scared to order tests they don't understand because then they are responsible for treating those conditions and may not have a clue how to do so (but won't tell you that).

Also: Check reviews. *On multiple sites.* Don't go to doctors who other people think are jerks, duh. If you can't get your doctor to listen to you, record the convo on your phone (if it is legal in your state). I have never had the time nor energy to sue any of my shitty doctors, but you may want to if they end up screwing you up pretty badly, and this is irrefutable evidence. Then get another doctor.

9. GET YOUR ASS TO A TEACHING HOSPITAL, ASAP
More and better equipment. More access to different specialties. On site labs. So forth. In theory. There are new and more awesome facilities popping up every day where you can do in a week what would normally take a year of running around to a million different testing facilities, doctors, appointments, so forth – and have records spread from here to kingdom come between doctors who refuse to communicate anyway. If you can get in one spot with a lot of different minds on the same case, especially in instances of rare diseases, you have a better chance at answers, in theory. At the very least, you will have access to more and better testing options, typically. And once you are plugged into a university type system, you can get your records all in the same portal.

10. FIND AT LEAST ONE DOCTOR TO GO TO BAT FOR YOU

DO NOT, and I repeat, do not go back to a doctor's office where they miss something crucial. Do not trust them with your care again. *Period*. If their front office staff sucks but the doctor themselves is knowledgeable and helpful, keep them. Just make sure you use language like, "My doctor has informed me this is the type of symptom they would want to know about right away," if it's true; otherwise your call and message will sit on a Post-It note on some chick's keyboard while she texts her boyfriend for the next three days and your doc will never know you called. Again, use the portal or go by there if necessary or possible if having a semi-emergency that doesn't require 911 yet can't wait and front office staff don't seem to care. I have most of my doctor's cell phone numbers because my disease is rare and acute and luckily (Unluckily?) they seem to be fascinated with it. I can walk into any doctor I see and be seen right away. It took years for me to cultivate this, but they know I don't do it unless absolutely necessary. *Never, ever* abuse this extension of trust if they offer their cell or same day standing appointments with no notice. Literally only text them if absolutely necessary. If you need an immediate appointment, insist they ask the doctor specifically if they are trying to set you out for months and you know it can't wait.

Also, don't judge a physician by their bedside manner. Some of them are just weirdos, and that's ok. They slice open people's bodies – that takes a certain type personality sometimes, just like cops or teachers or politicians – some doctors are weird AF. Doesn't matter if they are smart and into your case and will work hard on your behalf. You can have an excellent doctor who is a dick and you can have a terrible doctor who is friendly. The first one is ok, the second one is not. Find at least one doctor, preferably connected to a hospital type system so most of your records go to and remain in one spot. I have one front office staff member who prints records other doctors send to her on my behalf – they aren't supposed to do that. Cultivate relationships. I'm not saying manipulate them. I'm saying get to know them. Be kind to them. Become more than a file and a number to them. Make them *want* to help you. And try not to be a dick.

I have one doctor on my team who I can message through the portal. She trusts me. She has seen me for years. She knows I know my body. She will call in things like antibiotics and other meds if I request them, without forcing me to come to an appointment every single time. She will also send me to any specialist or order any test I request. This is invaluable, but honestly can do more harm than good if you aren't informed about what you're needing or what may be wrong with you.

More on all this later. My whole team of docs just showed up in my hospital room. Do you know why? Because I insisted on testing that they didn't think was necessary, and it revealed that not only do I need 24/7 oxygen, but that I am in the middle of a cardiac crisis. So, I wrote this for you as I waited for them.

If you can't advocate for yourself, stop hesitating to ask yourself for help; and let someone, anyone, do it for you. A family member. A friend. A Facebook tribe. It doesn't matter who it is – get someone on the phone, sending emails, whatever. It is *exhausting* to be sick and manage all the appointments, tests, and other bs that comes along with being chronically or terminally ill. It's even worse when you can't get appropriate care. And *even worse than that*, if you know something is wrong and are made to feel crazy. You. Are. Not. Crazy. Don't wait until you're dying like I did to learn this stuff. Use it now. Use it aggressively. And get well! I guarantee you if you utilize some of these tips, you will begin to get answers and treatment in a totally different way than before. Remember, they work for you; or ideally, they work with you – you are a team. They do not have all the answers. Help them realize you understand your own body and disease process and insist on getting help.

I, personally, am starting to lean towards a holistic approach and away from western traditional medicine, but that's another story for another day. This is *not* a doctor hating rant. There are some wonderful and amazing ones out there, and some purposes for which they are absolutely necessary. And I hope you find them when and if you need them.

How to Actually Help a Sick Friend

So... "Let me know if there is anything I can do to help," is literally awesome. And useless. You may have the best of intentions, but nothing will usually come of it.

Because most of us will tell you, "Nothing, I'm good," or "OK." Many of us don't know how to ask for help or who to ask or pride gets in the way. Especially when dealing with the chronically ill or someone facing a terminal or even new diagnosis, there is *a lot* more you can do than you think. I am making this list from things people who love me have already done for me, unprompted and unrequested by me, and I can tell you it has been the most gratitude inducing, humbling experience ever. These tips can apply to those who have children with special needs, someone who is hospitalized, anyone you know who has recently experienced a death in the family or has a new baby; the list is infinite.

If someone is struggling or going through a major change and you aren't sure what to do, try some of these amazing things I have been so blessed to have wonderful people in my life do for me. If you have a person who clearly needs help but says no, I would recommend you do *some* of the things anyway, minus the ones that require showing up unannounced. So many of us are incapable, literally, of reaching out.

Stuff that costs a bit of cash:
1. Meal train – make a plan with other friends to take meals to that family for a set period. This is particularly helpful if someone just had a baby or is perhaps recovering from a surgery. If you aren't in touch with this person's network, take a meal to them yourself.

2. You can even have a meal or treat delivered. Someone from out of state just sent doughnuts to my hospital room via a food delivery service and let me tell you *wow*. Made. My. Whole. Freaking. Day. Who can have a bad day when it starts that way? *Food*, just any kind of food. Or even groceries – you can have these delivered via the internet or so many other methods if you aren't close or even send a gift card for them to get food when they get the chance. There's a

reason that humans find food comforting, and that's because it just is. Another friend sent a whole personalized basket of healthy stuff – like celery and cream cheese, one of my faves – and it was the thoughtfulness of the gesture that meant more than the amazing snacks ever could.

3. Shop for items you know they need but can't get to right now – like if it's 2am and your homegirl is crying because their baby *just won't sleep*, show up on that doorstep in the morning with Gripe Water. *For real though*, I swear to Christ that people kept me sane when I had a newborn, when I had (have) a terminal illness, and so forth, just by being there in so many ways. Get them comfy. Know they need sweats and socks and so forth? Grab a bag at Target and head on over – with whatever it is. Then take their kids to the park for a few hours.

4. Help them experience what they may be missing out on. For instance, during Easter I was heartbroken that I was too weak to take my son to hunt eggs. Some amazing friends drove quite a few hours and had a wonderful Easter egg hunt and water gun fight with my son in the yard they had freshly mowed as I sat there in tears. Some of these gestures are lifelong ones that are never ever forgotten. Ever. They have a tremendous impact on healing.

5. Offer to cover a copay. Or a small bill. Or literally anything. Most people with tremendous medical problems are drowning in debt, have wrecked the hell out of their credit, and can barely keep their head above water. If it's a close friend or a family member, do what you can. Every little bit helps, literally, whether you think it does or not. Even things like donating air miles to get to out of state treatment or time off work to a coworker who's out of paid time can be life changing. Did you know it can even ruin your spouse's credit, if you are on their policy, and they are totally healthy?

Stuff that's free:
1. *Keep in contact*, even if they don't reply. Texts and messages to let that person know you love and are thinking of them are *never* a bad thing. Ever. Don't take it personally if they don't respond. They may be suffering from serious depression over their situation, they may not know what to say, they may be vomiting all over the house.

Reaching out from time to time to let them know they aren't forgotten is so meaningful.

2. If you can tell there is a financial need, start them a fundraising page and share to social media! Or have a raffle of items and sell tickets for medical and related expenses. Both of these were done for us as I underwent treatments and it literally kept us on our feet. I don't even know where you begin to thank someone for these types of actions that are so selfless, but they're mind blowing.

3. Visit them! Always make sure it's a good time to come by but sometimes human contact is literally all that's needed for those of us who prefer to be strong and isolate. Nobody wants to feel invisible. And when you're sick, it's easy to feel alone even in a crowded room. While you happen to be visiting, advocate for them! Some patients don't speak up and receive substandard care that could literally kill them. Fight for them. Question their care teams and find out what's up and argue on their behalf if anything doesn't seem right.

4. Flowers, balloons, edible arrangements, etc. will make any person stuck inpatient long-term in the hospital smile from ear to ear. The end. These can even be hand-picked and stuck in a bucket and brought by in person.

5. Care packages! Stuff like lotion, lip balm, face wipes, just whatever. Comfort items. This can change based on what the friend is going through. A new baby care package looks way different than a cancer patient care package. But receiving one of these is just so, so sweet. People have sent me hats, jewelry, and all sorts of sweet things along the way as well – and you know what? In those moments, knowing someone believed in me and I was on their mind made all the difference in the world!

6. If they have kids, use actionable item phrases like, "Can I come get Melody and take her to the park for a few hours so you can grab a nap?" Sometimes literally parents who are suffering with illness or traumatic events can't even heal because they don't have enough of a support system in place to get a break.

7. The house! Good God the house. It is so hard to keep your shit together when you are terminally ill or have a new baby or someone dies, etc. Do laundry. Or dishes. Or mow the yard. Whatever. They will be embarrassed and ask you not to and feel so guilty that they need so much help, but once you've done it? They will be super thankful.

8. Volunteer secretary or research time! Managing appointments, doctors, insurance, and so forth is freaking exhausting and sometimes nearly impossible, especially in diseases where there is a neurological or concentration component. See if there are benefit or assistance programs they qualify and help them apply. Help them figure out the best doctors via reviews, make phone calls for appointments, or even research cutting edge tests they may need. If you need help medically advocating for someone, holler at us. We love connecting people to resources wherever able.

9. Get them *out*. Do they like paddle boarding? Strap them to your board and give them a tow. Do they enjoy camping? You can take a wheelchair into the woods. Are the stuck in a hospital bed? Advocate hard for "privileges" and just get them out of what begins to feel like a cell after a while if you can.

10. Tell other people! If you love someone who tends to hide when they are sick and literally stop speaking to everyone for weeks, months (Years?) at a time, and y'all are connected, let other friends and family know an intervention is in order.

Stuff that's not free but is low cost and means a lot:
1. An actual card sent in the mail. It brings tears to your eyes to realize someone took the time and effort. It can even be handmade!

2. Any other handmade items; a drawing, a painting, a crochet scarf, a head wrap for chemo patients losing hair, literally anything you can make or create with stuff you already have is so kind.

3. Take them to appointments! Life doesn't stop when illness or tragedy strikes. If they need to see doctors or plan a funeral or take a brand-new baby to a wellness check, an extra set of hands NEVER hurts. Just gonna cost you a little gas. Many times, spouses and

family members are working and constantly being alone during tests and procedures and doctor appointments is very daunting and wears dramatically on the spirit.

4. Have them make an online shopping wish list of the things they actually need and share it! This can be anything from multivitamins to baby wipes.

5. Help them get organized – downloading apps, cleaning house, making sure all those little life details are in order can be invaluable! There are even apps to help budget, track spending and when bills are due, organize calendars that can be shared, so forth. Get them set up as best you can to manage things once you are gone; and if you want you can get them a gift card to purchase these items and even other stuff like books and so forth on their phone.

Don't take no for an answer. Reach out to that friend you know has been struggling. Like right now. I'm good, I've been overwhelmed with love and kindness. This portion of the book is more about how you can help people or if you need help *how you can show people what you need* – post to your timeline if you're struggling and say, I AM STRUGGLING, please read this.

If you're anything like me, you will feel guilty and weird and awkward accepting help and you need to just get right the fuck on over it. Don't deprive people who feel helpless watching you suffer of the opportunity to love you, and don't let them push you away, even if they try, and most of them will.

What Your Sick Friends Won't Say but Wish You Knew

1. Their spouse is not a saint. Even if they are. For instance, my wife has gone through a ton to keep up with everything – keeping me on her insurance, picking up the slack by doing some chores, and so forth. I have also carried more than my share during times in our relationship. I have been our sole earner while she took off for months; like right now. That's marriage. Yes, this is hard on her. But it's not a favor or a gift for someone to stay with you when you're sick. My worth isn't suddenly diminished because I am disabled. I bring more light and love to her life than she ever had and we feel the benefit of being together is mutual. Don't add to the burden of guilt someone who's dying feels by making comments such as, "Poor so and so," or "I can't imagine how hard this must be for her," or "Lucky you that she's standing beside you." If I'd known I'd be this sick, I wouldn't have tried dating or marriage. But if she'd known, she wouldn't have changed a thing. I bring more to her half dead than a healthy chick would at full strength. We drive each other insane and the love is strong. I refuse to feel as though I'm some ball and chain around her neck because I'm sick. I'm still sexy. I still pack her a hot homemade lunch. I still hold her when she's sad. Never underestimate the power of a good partner's love just because their body is failing. This isn't to diminish the effects of terminal illness on the people who love that person – it's devastating and by all accounts it IS harder to be a caretaker than the person who's sick. And they need support. And they are, by and large, saints. But the last thing someone who's dying needs is to be made to feel by other people like their spouse stays out of pity. I have a more grateful heart and positive attitude than anyone else she could ever meet in the best of health. And dat ass doe. Don't feel sorry for my wife. She's a lucky dog and she knows it. So am I.

2. Your prayers matter. Your beliefs matter. But I, for instance, don't believe there's a magical man in the sky who decides if little kids should get cancer and whether they live or not. Saying that God will cure me, to me, is almost an insult. I have a god of my own understanding that flows along lines of power and connection of love through people in the universe. I do not feel God picks and chooses

who to heal and who not to or that there's anything even remotely resembling that on this planet. Because why me and not someone else? And if I die, then what? God reviewed my file and decided I wasn't worth it? No. I appreciate your prayers. I welcome them. But don't shove it down my throat. Should you comment your prayers on my posts? Absolutely. I appreciate the time and energy of you exercising your faith on my behalf. But don't put a cross on my head and douse me with water. I'm not here for it. I believe in God. To believe we are hurtling through space on this rock with no purpose would be insane. But my god may not look like yours. Mine also loves the gays.

3. Be careful with limiting language and toxic positivity. Telling someone, "Keep smiling," or "You've got this," aren't as useful as saying, "It's OK to cry, I'm coming over at 2pm with ice cream," or "When it's too overwhelming, call me and I'll take your kiddo to the park so you can nap." People don't know what to say. I get that. You feel helpless. I understand. Saying anything, even this stuff, is better than saying nothing. But implying that if someone just "fights" hard enough they'll "win" isn't really how terminal or incurable diseases work. You remaining in denial doesn't help me. I feel that all diseases can be healed, unless our time is up here – but even then – it requires us to cease fighting, not struggle even more. Don't cover your eyes. Don't tell me to cover mine. Show up and hold my hand. Even when I tell you not to come.

4. It's great that you want to relate. It is. But telling me about your uncle's cousin's friend who had cancer once has nothing to do with me and my disease. Telling me about your awful bout with the flu is tone deaf. Stop. I fight every day to lift my head. To walk. To see. To breathe. My body is literally rotting from the inside out before my eyes. I've had countless surgeries and rounds of radiation and I am the happiest person in the morning I've ever known. It's a choice I make. Hearing stories that I can't connect with does not help me. Again, show up. Physically be there. Even when you're pushed away. We don't know how to respond to, "Let me know if you need anything." We need everything. And we appreciate you. There is a lot that can be done from afar, so, "I wish I wasn't so far away," does not cut it. Don't get upset when we cancel plans or can't respond for

days or even weeks. I might be leaving a trail of blood from one room to the other and not able to tell you that. Love us anyway.

5. Unsolicited advice. Full stop. Don't do it. I don't need the Internet MD. I have multiple advanced degrees. I'm always open to new ideas – but if you fly my way with "just drink juice" or "maybe take B12" level advice and a few articles, rest assured my doctoral candidate ass has already read thousands of pages on any possibilities. Also? If you aren't actively making yourself a part of my life, don't ask questions that extend beyond the details I've given. This isn't a spectator sport. I'm not a reality show. What I share is what I share.

I appreciate anything you've ever said to me, even if it's in the categories above. But when we know better, we do better. I'm more or less unflappable, but if this advice helps down the road with how you speak to those who are dying, good.

If you're wondering if you've ever offended me after reading this, you haven't. I'm very direct. Dying removes the need for space between words.

I understand this may not apply to everyone. But I've done a lot of work with those who are dying and have even held them in my arms as they took their last breath on this earth. These are widely held sentiments for many. We can all learn.

I'm afraid to say these things. I want your approval. It's the human condition. But boundaries mean it's my job to teach you how to talk to me. I'm afraid this will shut down you even trying. So, don't stop trying. The cool thing about friends with firm boundaries is you always know exactly how we feel – there's no mystery.

Anytime you're dealing with a marginalized population, and make no mistake, the terminally ill are some traumatized folks – it's your job to listen.

Please don't think we aren't grateful for *all* you've said and done to and for us. We are. Immeasurably.

The Importance of Telling Your *Whole* Story

1. Authenticity, vulnerability, and genuineness. These are virtues. We have been taught to hold it all in, all the time. This is not healthy. It's not healing. Boundaries are great. You don't have to share everything with everyone. But shutting out the world when you are having (any kind of) a hard time will not heal you. Pulling your wings in and being alone is restorative. Human contact is too. Find balance. So very many of us have been taught it's not OK to cry or be sad or show "weakness." Exposing vulnerability is true strength. Cry. Scream. Tear the cabinet doors off if you need to; then call a therapist. There is no shame, *no* shame, *no shame* in needing help in any way or expressing sadness and pain.

2. When you reveal your challenges and struggle to others, you give them permission they may not have known they hadn't given themselves to be vulnerable too. You don't need to look or feel or act perfectly all the time. It's OK to not be OK. You may not be as alone as you think. And if you are? Borrow my tribe. I've got a good one. I have received literally thousands of messages from abuse survivors, all because I told my story – many of whom had never previously told theirs. You have no idea who your voice may create wings for until you allow yourself to speak.

3. All situations are transient. Each of us will die. Everything is temporary. When you have reached your low point, of any kind, sometimes the most surprising things can give you just a little more gas to power your engine. If nobody knows your struggle, nobody can love you through it. Love heals. One of the most toxic things in today's society is the literally filtered view through which we see one another. Don't try to keep up with the best version of people, which is usually all they show. Just try to be the best you there is. You are like a house. You can only power so many things without throwing a breaker; so unplug that which does not serve you so you have more flow for that which matters.

4. In a few generations, nobody will remember most of us. Or our children. Or theirs. Have you already read this a few times in here? Good. Some of y'all are hardheaded and won't hear it the first time or

even three. What people think of you and how you dress or who you love or the way you live won't have mattered. Don't waste this life chasing what you think is ideal because of something you saw on a magazine cover. What's ideal is what's inside. How have you served others? Did you make a difference? Did you give up on a goal or a dream? Can you take one small step today towards walking back that direction? Can you take *one single action* today to revive the dreams you set aside so long ago?

5. What you think matters usually doesn't matter. I'm sorry, but it doesn't. What matters is the impact you have on others. What matters is following your true and sacred heart – santay ishtah (I can't seem to find the correct spelling of this anywhere, but that is a phrase and that's it's phonetic spelling). What matters is authenticity, vulnerability, and genuineness. I'm repeating that because it's important. Share your truth. Live out from that truth. Don't waste a single moment trying to be what anyone else told you that you were. The human condition is to want to seem our best all the time. I'm not my best today. And I want you to also be OK with not being your best all the time. Do what actually matters today. Do not be afraid to start that book. Get on that plane. Submit that application. Text that girl. Quit that job. Make that move. There are also ripple waves of energy that radiate out through anyone you help, in any way. Selfless acts of altruism change the entire cosmic universe. Do something for someone else today. And don't tell anyone you did it. You might inadvertently change the course of history.

You only think you have time.

You don't.

What will you make of yours?

Section Seven:
Afterthoughts from Between Worlds

*I went to the woods because I wished to live deliberately,
to front only the essential facts of life,
and see if I could not learn what it had to teach,
and not, when I came to die,
discover that I had not lived.*
-Henry David Thoreau

Archangel Convos

While much of the material herein is channeled, and those of you familiar with me can probably tell the difference regarding what is of and from me and what is of and from them by now; the following was directly related during my initial conversations.

We thought you might find the humor we saw in our early attempts to speak with them. As many of you know, I do not use my conventional human senses for this – there is no physical or audiovisual apparition. It's more like I get into a space between worlds and then try my best to translate what they input to my software into the human language of English. I actually translate from deep within my own limbic system, and strangely – the closer one is to death the thinner the barrier to travel. Even our own cells do not function the way we were taught. Common knowledge used to be that cells were powered by DNA, but even without this, they stay alive for 90 days or longer. It is the membrane through which things must enter and exit that is crucial for health – which begins, is maintained, and ends at the cellular level.

1st **Question & Answer Session**

<u>Molly asking Metatron</u>

Why do innocents experience pain and suffering at the hands of others?
Moulding (not molding) character
None pre-ordained nor planned; sanctioned nor allowed
Evil exists as the counter to creation of this *timespacereality*.
Perfect good (love) is deeper felt by those who have *painexisted*.

<u>Wife asking Metatron, answered by Molly</u>

Is something seriously wrong with my body?
Nothing you can't fix.
Molly really tried to resist answering this.
She wanted to tell you she couldn't.
But you need to know this
You can fix it
Now
In the before
But not if you wait until the after

When should I quit my job?
Really?
I am all that is, was, and ever will be.
The alpha and the omega.
And you trouble me with this?

Is Molly going to completely heal?
God, the father, the son. The tides. The earth's core. The milky way.
It is me.
I am here.
She is me.

<u>Molly asking Metatron</u>

Does evil exist?
Yes

Wife asking Metatron, answered by Molly

Are me and Molly going to be ok?
Questions FOR THE SAKE OF HUMANITY, GOOD GOD

Molly asking Metatron

Is there anything on planet earth other than fully human people?
Yes

Are there other planet earths?
Yes

How do you know if you should stay married?
It doesn't matter.
It is literally the least important question ever asked.

Wife asking Metatron, answered by Molly

Why are people evil?
Just as some parts and equipment wear out on your human planet, souls tire.
When they wear down after going downwards rather than upwards on the scale of all that is, they rot if you will. They rot into new things until they dissolve into the black nothing. The more they rot, the worse they behave – the more humans can smell them if you will. These are the rapists, torturers, child molesters, so forth. Killing more of a passion crime.

(Metatron addressing me, rather than Wife:)

Too complicated.
Sorry.
New to communicate with you.

(Me: Nice to have met you.)

You too.
But I've known you forever. You saw me when you burned.

Molly asking Metatron

Do some people not have souls?
Goes back to the above. Their souls get less dense, if you will, the more they rot when going downward, not upward.

Is everyone given a chance to know of the choice to go downward or upward?
Absolutely. It is born into their knowers.

Why are some children born incredibly disabled and harmed?
Same as all other answers.
There is no predicting what will happen.
Your chemicals poisoned the earth.
This wasn't written into the original design of the veil/matrix/vortex
The game has warped (melted?) as evil has progressed

Metatron (Michael) randomly begins discussing other matters

Restructuring, move energy around to clear blocks
Flow flow flow flow flow
Practice of outflow good
Way of life = all that is asked

Molly asking Metatron

What about Abraham?
Real. New. Younger.

How do you overcome trauma?

(Abraham answers randomly)

Re: convo about lunch chomo

[this is referencing something Molly recently watched by Esther Hicks where Abraham is channeled and explains we have to get to a place where we give trauma as little thought as what we had for lunch a few weeks ago]

Wife asking Metatron, answered by Molly

What's the key to happiness?
My little darling,
You do not believe.
You indulge your crazy wife.
I see you.

(Abraham answers randomly)

Must break free, to do so must see

Metatron

(Me: LOLOLOLOLOLOL)
It's not funny.

…

Random channeled notes from Metatron to Molly

Can only trust self.
Nothing else exists – re: plug into matrix

Goal is to level up
To rise
To ascend each trip
Some two steps forward, one back forever – grouchy old people
As they get near the veil, they realize they have to do this again and again ad infinitum

Life becomes progressively easier as we come back again and again
We do not travel to other universes in this current soul iteration
Infinite possibilities exist
Many can be accessed by some
Some can be accessed by few

Good/Evil warfare
Spiritual plane and here simultaneously

Visualize earth tiny spots of bad/pain to the millions of good/happy
Evil only absence of good; Darkness only absence of light

Disease caused by shifting tectonic plates
Key to happiness is not picking up key to not happiness – run other direction

Speak it all everywhere.

Information Block Delivered December 2019

Microwaves will make you sick.
Celery can heal your bone marrow.
Much disease is caused by shifting tectonic plates.
Pineapple cures coughing, unless it is from your spine.
Cranberry for kidneys. Liver for liver.
Most things may be healed with their Same.
Ginger and tumeric for inflammation, root included.
Raw aloe vera for gut inflammation.
Seeds for sleeping. Marijuana oil extracted for painless sleeping.
Do coconut pulling of the mouth.
Draw out poison as string from the mouth, up the throat.
Do not sever ties, unhook completely or anchors remain.
Never use tampons – that material does not belong in your body – inflammatory.
The red light can heal.
A vascular hemangioma on top of the head denotes God status earth living.
Tighten your Oikos Circle.
Lemon water for everyone.
Turn off your WiFi router as much as possible.
Stop using screens.
Put the feet of your children to the earth for vibration.
Sunglasses are harmful.
So is sunscreen.
All vaping causes cancer.
So does trauma.
12 rays are real. Meridian healing works.
Press your spleen into alignment to relax Anxiety.
Arthritis is the body's inflammatory response to foods, often wheat.
Sugar has no purpose.
Red dye causes mood and memory disorders.
Artificial sweeteners will kill you.
Do not bleach hair that touches skin. Do not bleach hair at all, ideally.
The sliph. The bodach. Real.
Stand naked each day. Wrap not Yourself in blood stained clothing.
Wrap not Yourself in Fabric of Another Nation. Only take what is Yours.

Smoke no chemical tobacco.
Use a metronome or grandfather clock to restore balance to limbic system; this is where your inner God lives.
Healing frequency for autoimmune disease is Tibetan bowls.
Ravens and crows have scrambled faces. Do not look directly at them.
A newborn with a cord wrapped around neck is able to Prophecy.
No cow dairy.
An egg placed under the bed will draw out disease.
A spoonful of salt per day plus arrow poison will repair dysautonomia; which is a spiritual malady.
The iron cannot be absorbed without magnesium.
Fiber from husks.
Stop using so much gas and creating waste or the planet will poison you in return; this is demanded by balance engineering of the universe. Use less.
Only one drop of Blood necessary to tie to your People.
Throw out all Keurig and like devices.
There is no pharmaceutical for which a better remedy does not exist in nature. Check Zimbabwe. Nigeria. Check with the Sioux. Lakota. Cherokee. Ask humbly of the Mayans. The Aztecas. The Meztizos. The Guatemalan Mountain People. They will help you. Help them in return or do not ask of their Ritual. India. Asia. The Middle East.
Spin in same direction earth core moving to boost signal.
Comb your body. Send unwanted colors under your door or into earth.
Chemotherapy has never healed. It has accidentally had placebo affects but is only poison.
Much disease caused by new and undetected viral herpes strains.
Deodorant and toothpaste also poison. Fix with charcoal.
The eyes can only heal by unseeing what was not meant to be seen.
Reverse engineering memory through replaying time backward to unravel.
Do not let Flies into the Top of Your Head.
Eat mold so it cannot eat you. Kombucha.
There is medicine in trees.
Sacred water flows from springs.
Almost all other water poisoned on American continent.
Move your body to Haka for battle if you need Spiritual War Powers.
Spend time on a volcano.

Spend time in the ocean, one which is not facing land on its other side. Face the open water to give thanks.
Move between worlds but do not get trapped.
Do not play dangerous games with things you don't understand.
Salt the perimeter of your home while playing Spiritual sounds from your Higher Culture. Wear a talisman necklace. What is not Of and For you will break it to leave. Let it remain on the Land where it is broken.
Learn to breathe correctly or nothing can flow. Tai Chi.
Greta is a more than person.
The magic children have come to turn the tide.
Never strike someone smaller or more vulnerable than yourself. If you have done such, make it right from a soul level with a deeply bowed acknowledgment.
I am 100% sober. If this message makes no sense to you, then it is not for you.
Cell phones a thousand years ago certainly would have sounded like an odd concept.
As surely would airplanes.
When an idea is before your time, that does not mean it is crazy or not real.
No one asked if the lightbulb was possible. Or the wheel. They were just Made. You were Made and permission was not asked First. These are Truths.
If it sounds like I am in left field, you are not centered, and it means you are too young to lead the charge towards progress. What is coming is a big deal. Prepare now or do not weep when you find yourself unready. The Old Guard will Die and the New Shall Rule by their Olds.
I go blind so I can see. Heal anything you like, but not my eyes. I must lose my Sight to keep my Vision.

I have begun working with indigenous tribal leaders and healers from multiple nations and continents. They do not like those words – indigenous, tribal. You do not have the right to name them. They do not reveal their true names because you have not earned their knowing. The land belongs to them and their blood is in the soil, the soil in their veins. Indigenous is a White Word. Until they allow you to know their Names, you may call them The Originals. I have held the Wakinyan lightning and Heyoka laughter in my arteries and watched liquid fire rain down around me as I spoke conduit for them all in languages I do not know. They performed a fire dance for their healer with the meteor landing. I say that with reverence, not to brag.

I hold this honor into my heart higher than if the President sought my help; for him We could not Answer. He is Faceless. He is falsely seated on a Throne of Wrong Creation over a Stolen Land.

This is how they found me. I spoke their Secrets.

I know not what most of this means either.

Many of the Colorless need Nordic, Viking, or Celtic Ritual, not Indian; for healing.

Have I Gone Crazy or have I Come Home? And which are you?

Channeling Question and Answer Session
December 2019
questions asked by humans who wish to know their answers, received by Souls, and rendered here

Q: If we are brought back here to learn more, what happens to those souls who are aborted?

A: Hello. It is really good to be here today. You are not brought back here to learn more, firstly. The purpose of human life is not learning; it is not lessons; it is not hardship. Over time, you have often been made to believe that the struggles that you face are necessary for the survival of your species but you are not brought to learn anything; and if you are, most of you are failing, because you are neither studying nor completing the assignments that you have been given. You were brought here to add to the collective Vibration of All, and learning implies a power dynamic, a differential, such that there is a teacher (above) and a student below.

The purpose of your human earthly life is not to learn. You wanted to come here. You wanted to do this. You asked for this. You sought this. You looked for this earthly experience; and when you were offered the chance to live in a pain-free, trauma-free, griefless world that is also gray and devoid of joy, and all the Opposites of those, you refused that option. You did not come here to learn.

You came here to *evolve*. Your Soul remains behind in the Other. Your spirit comes forth into your human skin form and you begin your life on earth as a perfect pure positive being as an infant. You come here knowing that you will experience the agony and ecstasy that is this particular reality, because there are infinite ones from which you could choose and you chose this one, just like you chose the family that you were born to and the personification that you would take on during this lifetime. So rather than to take away; which is to learn, from something greater than you or above you; you are instead here to add to and to create equally with others.

No human life is valued above any other human life. And so, there's no possibility for learning during your earthly lifetime because you are all equal. You are meant to get as close to your Soul's purpose as your Spirit here in this current dimension *timespacereality* in human earth can be. You are meant to journey deep within yourself.

Even in your religions, your teachers talk about this. Jesus said, the kingdom of heaven is inside you. He said I am the way, the truth, and the life. He said you may only come to the father through me. (And) he said all that as a human being. Then why would that not be true of all of us – that the way to Divinity, the path to the Ethereal, the route by which your Soul's evolution takes places as your lifetimes progress, that route is only by journeying deep within. You are not meant to be taught or come here to sort of learn these exterior lessons from what the difficulties of life thrust upon you. You are here to add to a collective stream of which you are a part, that you can then, in equal amounts, draw from – like a bank account or a gas tank. As you add to and elevate Humanity, you can bring forth from Humanity unto yourself.

What happens to Souls who get aborted, you ask? It's an interesting way you phrased that question because it doesn't ask about miscarriages or, um, anything else; so, there's an inherently political and religious bent to that question, which is not something that We answer.

But I can tell you that all Souls who send forth Spirits into earth have a purpose, and in the case of a very, very early death like abortion or miscarriage or in infancy, that purpose can sometimes be that that Soul needed its wholeness, its entirety, back to complete another mission, another imperative mission.

All times are occurring now. You just have no way to understand this. All worlds are here and now. The space between words is where you can hear. The moments between seconds is where you can feel time. Who is to say that a life lived for a moment, for an instant, for a hundred years; has any more or less value?

The ripple effect, the butterfly effect, is real because of the interconnectedness of all things. So, every time a woman has a menstrual cycle, is that a Soul? This gets into the argument amongst yourselves, amongst human beings, that is often held of; when life begins? And life begins at viability. Life begins when, even with your extreme medical interventions, life begins when a Soul (a Spirit, because your Soul stays behind, it's just your Spirit that comes – it's like a video game, is the way Molly explains it, you don't want to take your whole self into the game because if that player gets killed, you can't come back, so your Soul always remains There, which is also Here – all of the Theres and the Heres are now)… and so your Spirit comes into these babies and something that seems relatively small can have an infinitesimal, there's a word that we are trying to say that Molly doesn't know, can have a deep and profound effect on everything and everyone. What happens to the Souls of the, in human years, as you quantify it, young, is the same thing that happens to all Spirits. They return, they reunite with their larger Soul and they go on about their other work.

If you're asking about why this sometimes happens, it's literally like they got dispatched to another call. They have another mission. They might have had to lead a war in 1400 France. All times and all realities and so many more potentialities than you can possibly fathom exist now, here, now, here, now, now, now. You could do and be anything right now. And so when you ask what happens to the Soul of the very young, the Spirits is the correct term, of the very young when they are reunited with Soul – is what happens to all of you when you are reunited in that way – which is perfect peace and ease, then moving onward into your next iteration. Thank you.

Q: Are souls genderless? Is the body dysphoria and the transgender explosion we see today; is it a result of past lives bleeding into this present one? Do our spirits change physical body forms in the past and present renditions of ourselves?

A: Hello. Are souls genderless? Yes. To address the second part of your question we would need to kind of re-engineer it. So rather than "the trans explosion we're seeing today," I would ask that you conceptualize it like this: Although still dangerous, it is now safer; and although still not accepting, it is now a more tolerant world in which to come out. Trans people have existed since the beginning of time and they always will.

The Native Americans called them the two-spirited and revered them in some tribes. So, all human embryos in this realm begin as female and some become male. A lot of disease and problems on your planet are caused by shifting tectonic plates. Transgendered individuals are a special kind of magic trapped in a certain type of Hell. To be in a body that does not match your mind is torturous. As far as; is that your past lives bleeding into today? No, it isn't. But your past lives can traitmanifest such that if you were a warrior and you burned cities to the ground; you may have quite the temper during this iteration of yourself even if you are now a soccer mom.

So, no, transgender people are not a result of being a different gender in a past life. Although you fluidly change genders throughout your lifetimes. Souls have no gender. You come back in many different iterations. Something happens in utero; but make no mistake, they are perfectly made and the embodiment often of the human virtue of courage. It takes bravery to walk against the wind towards your true face. That's it, thank you.

Q: Hey Molly! What's the purpose of why we are here?

A: Hello. This is such a delightful question. This is an easy one and an exciting one. I am so happy to answer it. The purpose of why we are here is hard to describe without you being able to see the visual. I don't typically receive this information in any sort of auditory or visual way, like an apparition. It's just more like big globs of information. So, the way it looks if I could explain it, is like a love field where everyone is connected to every other one and all things are interconnected by red strings. If you were to visualize it from a wider and deeper perspective, the Earth from a distance, and see all the pain as red dots; and all the moments of goodness, kindness, love, joy, ecstasy, beauty, selflessness, acts of service as white dots or blue dots; the whole world would be lit up and very few red dots could be seen at any given time. Although horrifying and deeply tragic things do occur here, it is the balance that is demanded by the way that this Earth construct *timespacereality* is set up.

So, for each thing, there must exist an equal and opposite thing for the balance of this particular iteration of the Earth to work. And so the purpose of why we are here is to teach one another, but not to learn;

it is to give, to enjoy; to bask in the deliciousness of a hot doughnut, or a deep, earth shattering orgasm, or a sunset that brings tears to the eyes, or a vision of mountains, snow-capped in the distance in the reverence of the majesty and power of that. It is to know, deeply, the fact that the entire blueprint and design for all of creation is within you. You are god and god is you.

Or are you just poor, pathetic, ignorant humans being cast about by the waves of life; beating up against the rocks and the shore of it; are you not in fact the creators of reality? Would it exist were you not here to perceive it? The purpose of life is death – because it is the one thing that you all do.

You are marching towards it right now – sand out of an hourglass. Every single moment needs to count for something, even if they're restful moments in which nothing is done.

The purpose of life is to spend less time enduring, tolerating, settling; and more time celebrating, cherishing, questing. It is to arrive bent out of shape and dirty, half broken, hair flying behind you in a frazzle, back on the other side, and say, "What a ride."

We all add to all that ever Was, Is, and Will Be, which is contained inside of each human mind. All of that empty space is atoms, cells in constant motion. Millions of particles of you are in constant motion and yet you appear to be perfectly still. There is science that claims that we only use a tiny, tiny portion of our brains. What is happening in the rest of it? That is where God, by all the names they are called, lives. You are God. God is you. The purpose of life is to enter these human bodies and experience those moments of depth and weight and take that back; and in so doing you evolve your Soul. I wish you could see it like I can. I feel I've failed to adequately describe it, but it's incredible. Thank you.

Q: My question is: Is there truly a God and where did they originate from? And then also; if there is a God or multiple Gods, how do they feel about how some people have perverted their worship to further their own beliefs and agendas?

A: Hi! Is there a God? Well... everything is God and God is everything. God is a grain of sand. God is giving birth, running a marathon. God is waking up from surgery. God is attending a funeral. It is a flower petal. God is rain.

That's complicated. God is the cosmos and every inch of you. You are magnificently made. Where does God come from? Molly uses the term God for lack of a better word, but Source is a better word that We're going to give to her.

Something cannot come from nothing and motion does not arise from stillness; sound not from silence. The Source of all that ever Was, Is, and Will Be is the only exception. It has never not existed because time is a construct which is not real.

You ask, if so, how do God or Gods feel about how they're worshipped? OK. For the second part of your question, a lot of what makes up Source energy and larger consciousness is the Souls that remain on the other side and they do not experience human emotion the way that we do so they would not be capable of feeling horror, for instance, about the religious wars that have been fought.

So, God has been misapplied; has been used as a weapon who has been turned inward against so many people; has been brandished like a dart, Bible in hand, Quran in hand, enter any word – in hand. The misapplication of the spiritual idea of the notion of Source of creation has caused more heartache than if the notion had never been noticed. People on this planet and in this reality often say, "God is love."

And that's not untrue – but the words are inadequate. God is the actual, physical, energetic, vibratory frequency running and flowing between all beings and all things at all times that feels like love. Love has been perverted as a human construct. When I say, "I love you," it means, "I want you." I want you around me, or whatever, versus its original intent – which meant, "I grateful you. I thankful you. I appreciation you."

So, God is that basking in the essence of all that is good and of the light and of the unselfish and unconditional appreciative, rather than possessory, kind of love. If and because Source is; it cannot judge good, evil, or in between. Value judgments can't be made on human beings because the very nature of that act would be anti-God, like humans taking inventory, taking stock of one another. A very wise prophet says that if we could only view one another as trees, we would all get along. You don't look at a tree and say, "Oh, that one's too tall," or, "That one's too wide," or, "That one has knobs on it," or, "That one's got a broken limb."

So, no, God doesn't feel any type of way about what's been done in God's name, because God is a disembodied force like an electrical current; not a human in the clouds with personification. Thank you.

Q: It seems like suddenly I am seeing big numbers of pedophiles outed and arrested. It's like discovering cancer so it can be healed, but on a Soul level. I know that trauma can be healed, like Molly has, but the ones that don't survive – do these Souls reincarnate to a better life more quickly because of self-sacrifice or do they have longer healing on the other side? Thank you.

A: Hello. The big numbers lately of pedophiles and others being caught, if you will, do not indicate that the frequency of these acts has changed. If anything, it's actually diminished because it's become less accepted by society. The proliferation of suddenly seeing more of it is due to a higher consciousness that is changing as the old few die off and the new magical children come to rule the Earth. So anytime you're out in front of a great idea that is later widely accepted as fact, you sound crazy. But it only sounds crazy because you're among the first to know it. And so, I posit that larger numbers of these specific type people are being brought to justice because consciousness is shifting and being raised to a different level and will continue to do so. As that occurs, more of the darkness will be rooted out by necessity, like expanding a garden – you pull the weeds so new may grow.

For the second part of your question, you asked if this is happening for Soul healing. Yes, but we would say it as soul evolution or even (r)evolution. So, do Souls have a better life more quickly or longer healing on the other side, you ask? At the moment of death, there's perfect peace and ease. A thousand years on the other side feels like an instant here, and vice versa; there's no construct of time. Time is a necessary measurement unit for things like when you should go to work and how long a line takes and whether traffic will be backed up in such a way that you will be delayed.

So, no Souls require any healing but the injured and damaged Spirits returning to the Souls, at the exact moment they fully cross over, are at perfect and ease. There are only certain types of dead. There are those who do not know they are dead, and so remain. There are those who do know they are dead, yet choose to remain. There are those who are in transit and who have a message to deliver, prior to fully crossing. There are those who are fully crossed immediately, and are relaxing, if you will, in the waiting room of the other side. There are those who are fully crossed immediately, and go onto other business in their realm, back to this world in this time, or other worlds and times.

Of those who are in transit, some are essentially in a holding pattern and some are actively active. So, if you are asking if the young or those who suffer trauma in one lifetime are gifted, if you will, with a better lifetime? No. Yes. No in the sense that there's not some sort of point counting, token earning system for good and bad behavior with a scribe keeping track to determine your next incarnation. Yes in the sense that we evolve our greater Soul at large with each Spirit's journey into Earth over and over and into elsewhere and into other places and times. As we add to the collective consciousness, as we add to the Source energy running to and through us and all things.

We can sometimes select a life that is easier but when we are over there picking our families, and we do pick our families, and choosing our life path, we do not have the same value judgments as Souls as you do in human form containing Spirit. So, we do not experience pain, trauma, sadness, difficulties, challenges, or heartache the way it is experienced here. Life paths are selected prior to arrival for what is needed to evolve consciousness as a whole when you are the larger Soul sending the smaller Spirit portion of yourself into your body.

I think that's it, thank you.

Q: What is the key to happiness?

A: The key to happiness is not picking up the key to not happiness. It's mindfulness, directionality, and acceleration. That's it, thank you.

What is Maverick Academy?

Purpose:
To become able to create any reality you seek, to become aware of the soul purpose of all that is, to become aligned to design an existence that is to be celebrated rather than tolerated, and to become awakened to the full potential of your spirit and experience + create the most good on a universal spiritual level.

Goal:
The end game is a profitable non-profit brick and mortar school which encompasses leading edge thinkers, doers, and life lovers of all ages teaching one another. In the meantime; online group courses, seminars, cruises, guest appearances, and one on one sessions will help lead you to a total and permanent soul (r)evolution, which comes about from a journey within. Adults and children alike will be able to learn freely in this unconventional co-creative space for world- and un-schooling.

Method:
Our cutting edge 7 step process can get you to your heart's deepest desires and help you fulfill every dream you ever had – health, wealth, and love. All can afford what we offer, and in the end, connection with one another will carry on this work infinitely as it is already taking place in the form of a consciousness shift across our entire human earth. Our apothecary features handcrafted, nature-made products, spiritual items, and artists from around the world.

heymaverick.com
www.Facebook.com/HeyMaverickAcademy
www.YouYube.com/C/MaverickAcademy
mollyllama.com
Facebook.com/heymollyllama
Twitter.com/heymollyllama
Instagram.com/heymollyllama

I Wrote

I wrote through tear and snot stained shirts.

I wrote through sweat soaked sheets, nightmares I won't remember.

Shaking awake.

I wrote.

I wrote as blood poured from my nose and mouth, lips and tongue split open, the inside of my face disintegrating. Didn't miss a keystroke. Blood splatter. Just one more sentence. A crime scene made of history.

I wrote with a kid on my lap. And a dog. And sometimes a wife. Often, all three.

Because I am lucky. And they wrap themselves around me like a blanket.

So I wrote.

I wrote.

I wrote even as my fingers turned dark, necrotic.

I wrote when my eyes failed, add steroids.

I wrote when I should have slept.

I wrote in my sleep.

I wrote while you were dreaming.

I wrote as I was deleted. Screamed at. Hated.

Erased by flesh and blood.

I wrote.

Parts of me died for this.

But I wrote. And I wrote. And I wrote.

Through radiation. Through biologics. Through surgeries.

The words were so hard to read my eyelashes ran away from my face.

I wrote as new parts of me were born for this.

I shook myself, much as parts of a tree, branches violently harangued until the fruit of them fell to your hand.

My words.
The book you hold.
The book I wrote.
I wrote.
And now it is written.
It will live long after I do.
It is born; outside of my body now.
And so, I give it to you.
Take good care.